Sing Peace, Sing Gift of Peace

Sing Peace, Sing Gift of Peace

The Comprehensive Hymnary of

Jaroslav J. Vajda

Concordia Publishing House • Saint Louis

ISBN 0-7586-0275-8

3558 S. Jefferson, St. Louis, MO 63118
Manufactured in the United States of America

2 3 4 5 6 7 8 9 10 12 11 10 09 08 07 06 05 04

To my wife Louise—
still my constant companion,
supporter and inspiration
in our struggles with worship
on the journey of faith

ACKNOWLEDGEMENTS

Most of the 225 texts in this complete collection would not have been written had they not been commissioned, requested or inspired by congregations and individuals. To all of them I express my thanks.

Certain individuals deserve special mention, beginning with Carl Schalk, composer of the music for *Now the Silence* and many other tunes since 1967; Rodney Schrank and Ruth Lewis, publishers of *Now the Joyful Celebration* and *So Much to Sing About*; Ruth Ann Johnson, who was responsible for my acquiring ownership of my texts; and Tom Leeseberg-Lange, who tirelessly promoted my work and produced the first and most of the subsequent hymn festivals for the past twelve years.

To the many composers of tunes and choral settings, without whom the texts would have remained poems.

To my ever-inspiring and supporting wife, Louise, and primarily and continually to the inspiration of the Holy Spirit.

CONTENTS

FOREWORD

The publication of ***Sing Peace, Sing Gift of Peace*** marks an important milestone in the story of hymnody in America. This volume, for the first time, presents all the original hymn texts as well as the translations of Slovak and German hymns and carols of a man who has made a singular contribution to the hymnody of the latter half of the 20th century. In the midst of what has been called the "hymn explosion" of recent decades, this writer stands out for his remarkable talent and extraordinary gift.

It was in 1969—the year of his fiftieth birthday—that Jaroslav John Vajda (1919–) first came to public attention as a translator and writer of hymns. That year saw the publication of ***Worship Supplement***, a product of the Commission on Worship of The Lutheran Church—Missouri Synod, containing four of Vajda's texts. Two were translation of texts from Vajda's Slovak heritage ("Greet, Man, the Swiftly Changing Year" and "God, My Lord, My Strength, My Place of Hiding"); two were original texts which first appeared in that volume ("Thank the Lord, for He Is Good" and "Now the Silence").

These four texts were emblematic of the future course of Vajda's work: 1) a continuing interest in translating texts, especially from the great repertoire of Slovak hymns, and 2) the gradual development of a creativity which expressed itself in a flood of significant, newly-written hymn texts which would find wide acceptance in the coming years. These two translations from the Slovak, together with other subsequent translations, continue to find a place in Lutheran hymnals. Of the original hymns, *Now the Silence* quickly won the attention of a wide audience. Pronounced a ***tour de force*** by Erik Routley, a leading British hymnologist of the day, and as an "example of the new talent for poetry that Lutherans are fostering in America," this unusual and impressionistic "Entrance Hymn for Holy Communion" soon found a place in almost every new hymnal produced in the latter half of the 20th century. Its unique literary style—it contains no punctuation and no finite verbs—contributed, in part, to its broad acceptance and placed the name and work of Jaroslav Vajda at center stage, a writer of hymn texts to be reckoned with. The promise of those early translations and original hymns was to come to fruition in the years ahead in a way that neither the church nor the writer himself could possibly envision.

The groundwork for Vajda's interest in poetry and hymnody had been a long time in preparation. The grandson of immigrants from Slovakia, he grew up in a home where the old traditions and language were valued, honored, and preserved. Names such as Tranovsky and Kucharick and hymn collections such as the ***Cithara Sanctorum*** (the "Tranoscius") and the ***Duchovna Cithara*** were familiar companions in the Vajda home. The son of a Lutheran pastor, Vajda grew up in what is now East Chicago, Indiana, playing the violin at the age of 12, and by the age of 16 was translating Slovak short stories into English. During his college and seminary years, he received an education which placed heavy emphasis on the study of classical languages. This background, together with a fluent grasp of the Slovak language first learned as a child, provided a solid basis for the development of the skills necessary to begin translating some of the literature and hymnody of Vajda's own Slovak heritage. It was a task he soon began with dedication and enthusiasm.

Jaroslav Vajda seriously began to write poetry at the age of eighteen, and three years later made a translation of the monumental 32-sonnet sequence "A Song of Blood" written by Slovakia's greatest poet Hviezdoslav. Clearly evident in all his work of translation is an attitude which reflects a loving and careful use of language, a trait that would be of inestimable worth as he later set out to fashion original texts for congregational singing. His vocation as pastor and preacher in parishes in Indiana and Pennsylvania, and later as editor and book developer at Concordia Publishing House, helped hone the crucial skills necessary to both the translator's and hymn writer's art: clarity of imagery and the ability to convey that imagery with economy and power.

His work includes translations of a wide variety of Slovak hymns, Slovak carols (***Slovak Christmas***, 1950), German hymns and carols, and several Hungarian hymns, as well as original hymn texts which constitute the greater part of his writing. Vajda's translations and especially his original texts are found in virtually every major hymnal and hymn supplement published since ***Worship Supplement*** in 1969. Many of his texts have been translated into a variety of languages.

Several aspects of Vajda's approach to writing deserve special comment. First, for Vajda the creation and shaping of texts reflects his Lutheran understanding of vocation: that a poet must first of all be knowledgeable and competent in one's "secular" literary art before it can be transformed into a Christian calling. Just as a Christian cobbler first of all makes good shoes, not inferior shoes with crosses on them, a Christian poet is first of all, a good poet. For Vajda, piety, however well meant, can never replace competence and skill in one's craft. It is to that end that Vajda's study and careful workmanship is directed; out of that understanding flows all other aspects of his vocation as Christian poet.

Second is Vajda's ability to fashion a new and striking image, to reshape an older image, or to recast it in such a way as to bring fresh insight and understanding to a text. To mention such lines from his Christmas carol text "Before the Marvel of This Night" as "then tear the sky apart with light" or

"Give earth a glimpse of heavenly bliss / A teasing taste of what they miss" is simply to begin to touch the surface of writing consistently marked by fresh, sparkling turns of phrases, and vibrant, provocative imagery which catch the imagination of the reader. His "God of the Sparrow God of the Whale"—a text with an unusual first line, again without punctuation—clearly carries the Gospel proclamation with familiar images, yet ones which unwrap new understandings of the relation between God and his created and redeemed children.

A third important aspect of Vajda's writing is his affinity for less usual textual forms and meters, less usual at least in the context of traditional hymnody. The large number of texts employing a wide variety of meters, in addition to many texts set to irregular meters, reflect this inclination. It is interesting to observe that among his most popular and successful texts are those written in unusual metrical patterns. "Amid the World's Bleak Wilderness" (in the classic form of the ***terza rima***), "Christ Goes Before" and "Now the Silence" (both Irregular or Peculiar Meter), "God of the Sparrow God of the Whale" (5.4.6.7.7) and "You are King" (written in sonnet form), are a few examples among many which employ textual forms and meters not ordinarily associated with traditional hymnody. This aspect of Vajda's style obviously presents a challenge to musicians who would attempt to set these texts to music for congregational singing. That many of these texts have indeed been successfully set for singing by ordinary congregations is a tribute, first of all, to the stimulation and generative force of textual forms requiring new and different musical solutions. A fourth aspect of Vajda's writing is the strong theological thrust of his texts which are always biblically grounded and theologically informed. The notes to each of the texts in this volume reflect that concern, and a study of them will be amply repaid with insights into the workings of a mind not only linguistically fertile, but rooted in a strong confessional and sacramental understanding of the faith. Trinitarian language, for example, not only informs much of Vajda's writing, it frequently determines poetic structure as well. Vajda seems to like to write in "threes." One need only look to texts like "Christ Goes Before" with its parallels drawn between the Kingdom, the Power, and the Glory, love, peace, and joy, and Christ who is the Way, the Truth, and the Life, to see the poet at work. His "Catch the Vision! Share the Glory!", firmly rooted in a sacramental theology, and with its "show" and "tell" missionary thrust, exemplifies Vajda at his best.

Special mention must be made of the significant number of texts written for particular liturgical purposes. Hymns for Baptism, Holy Communion, and dismissal, fresh Psalm paraphrases, Entrance, Kyrie, and Credo hymns, as well as hymns for the various times of the church year form a substantial part of Vajda's writing.

Amid the current flood of hymnody—so much of it bland and insipid, on the one hand, or dense, obtuse, or overly clever, on the other—the work of Jaroslav Vajda stands as a unique testimony to clarity of expression, careful craftsmanship, and theological integrity. His writing is in the mainstream, as its reception in countless congregations has amply demonstrated. It is accessible and popular in the best sense of both words. At the same time, Vajda is careful to avoid trendiness in style, language, and subject matter—so ***de rigueur*** in the 60s and 70s, as well as the political correctness so characteristic of much contemporary religious language. Vajda's hymnody is, to be sure, both the result and the expression of one man's lifelong spiritual journey, yet it is a journey which we all—in one way or another—share.

This collection will have three immediate uses. The first two are obvious and rather utilitarian: as a source book for future hymnal editors as they seek out the best writing of the latter half of the 20th century for future hymnals and worship books, and as a resource for church musicians and hymn tune writers looking for substantial and carefully crafted texts. The third, and certainly not to be overlooked, is for those who read to revel in the sheer delightfulness of language, who take pleasure in a new and freshly revealing image, who savor an unexpected turn of phrase. Yet behind all the concern which Vajda demonstrates for words is a concern for the Word, the good Word of the Gospel which, in one way or another, is at the root of all his texts. In a beautiful passage from his writing ***On the Last Words of David***, Martin Luther [with parenthetical additions by this writer] wrote:

> St. Ambrose [and Jaroslav Vajda] composed many hymns of the church. They are called church hymns because the church accepted them and sings them just as though the church had written them and as though they were the church's song. Therefore it is not customary to say "Thus sings Ambrose, Gregory, Prudentius, Sedulius, [and Vajda]" but "Thus sings the Christian Church." For these are now the songs of the church, which Ambrose, Sedulius, [and Vajda] etc., sing with the church and the church with them. When they die, the church survives them and keeps on singing their songs.

Ultimately, the hymns, carols, and translations of Jaroslav Vajda are a sign to God's people, a sign of hopefulness, expectation and promise. They are a sign that the Holy Spirit has not forsaken his church. They are a sign that we are still given new songs to sing—songs which the church will surely continue to sing until the time when all our singing will be joined to that last and greatest song of the Lamb in eternity. For such a sign in the work of Jaroslav Vajda the church is eternally grateful.

Carl Schalk

THE MAKING OF A HYMN

Just as there was a time when nothing existed but the Creator, so there was a time when the first of the thousands of hymns in existence today came into being. And each one thereafter was written and composed by someone.

Let me state at the outset that this is one person's description of how a hymn comes into being. Any other of the growing number of hymn writers would agree with some details of this essay, while legitimately reporting a different understanding and method of composing hymns for corporate worship.

So then, why do I write hymns and how do I come up with what approximates my ideal hymn? I write hymns for two reasons: because I'm inspired to write this type of sacred verse, and because I am asked to provide a text for a certain occasion or to fill a gap in worship resources.

Before I elaborate on the reasons and methods for my hymn writing, I must state my amazement at the route by which I came to write original hymn texts at the age of forty-nine. I believe everyone who writes creatively can trace elements and experiences that led up to the production of that first hymn text.

Until the age of forty-eight I never dreamed of writing original hymns, and was never driven to seek a reputation as a hymn writer. The most I thought of doing was translating hymns, carols, and religious treasures from foreign languages. But then, out of nowhere, came—

The Watershed Hymn

The catalyst that produced the first published original hymn came in 1968 when I was editing <u>This Day</u> magazine and had to fill a blank page in an issue that was to go to the printer in three days. While shaving on the first of those mornings, I was haunted by a question that had been troubling me for most of my lifetime as a worshiper and worship leader. Why did David say, "I was glad when they said to me, 'Let us go to the house of the Lord'"? Reviewing the features of a liturgical service, I composed a free verse, "Now the Silence" and entitled it "An Entrance Hymn." It all came together within half an hour, in an unusual poetic form without rhyme or punctuation.

Now the Silence

Now the silence
Now the peace
Now the empty hands uplifted

Now the kneeling
Now the plea
Now the Father's arms in welcome

Now the hearing
Now the power
Now the vessel brimmed for pouring

Now the Body
Now the Blood
Now the joyful celebration

Now the wedding
Now the songs
Now the heart forgiven leaping

Now the Spirit's visitation
Now the Son's epiphany
Now the Father's blessing

Now Now Now

When the "hymn" appeared in print, church musician Carl Schalk asked to try to set it to music. His melody provided the essential dimension of music to the words, and that hymn became the watershed for more than 200 original and translated hymns since then, most of them in the first ten years of my retirement at the age of sixty-seven.

The inspiration for this hymn exposed and revealed to me my lifelong *struggle with worship*. Confessing this struggle in most of my hymns, in hymn festivals, and in hymn writing workshops has uncovered a similar personal spiritual experience in practically every worshiper!

The Struggle with Worship

This struggle engages only Christians. The unconverted have no such Pauline inner conflict expressed in the confession: "The good that I will to do, I do not do, but the evil I will not to do, that I practice." The conscientious child of God wrestles with the problem daily, even when it comes to worship. Even pastors and worship planners struggle with the dilemma. I know!

I wonder how much this struggle accounts for the revival of revivals, contemporary "alternate" services, the rapidly changing styles of sacred music, the appeal of spectacle and theatricality, the casualness and superficiality of some worship services in the attempt to make people "glad to go to the house of the Lord."

In fifty years of full-time and part-time ministry, I wonder how often I was (unintentionally) responsible for turning off the person in the pew with my style of preaching, the focus of my message, my selection of hymns, the conduct of the liturgy—or with some personality quirk or annoying mannerism.

Since my retirement, I have discovered that I am not attracted to certain churches because I do not agree with their theology, or because the services border on cultism, or I can see through the preacher's theatrics, or the predominate music is too shallow to waste another Sunday of my life missing the depth and awesomeness of a substantive hymnody that has nourished millions of worshipers for centuries, or because the Eucharist Christ prescribed is missing, or a fitting reverence is destroyed by the attitudes and irreverent behavior of the churchgoers, or because a particular church is exclusive or racist. Many of these reasons for not going to church echoed ones I heard from members and nonmembers during my ministry.

Also to be considered: a person may be "glad" to go to the church for the wrong reason, like the Pharisee who kept the Sabbath faithfully and contributed generously—and still went home unjustified. Or worshipers who are "glad," but bring leftover sacrifices shamed by the widow's mite, or are carried away by the music and sing "Lord, Lord," but their hearts are far from the God in whose presence they stand.

The hymn writer must be aware of this universal struggle with worship while taking into consideration the essential elements of worship, the theological content of the hymns, the language of the times, and the culture the Gospel is trying to reach and transform.

Most of the experiences and struggles of hymn writers influence their hymn writing in some way. In preparing a hymn text, I have tried to reflect and honestly express universal faith experiences common to all saints and sinners, thus making it suitable for corporate worship. Anything less would be artificial or contrived, not grounded in sincerity or truth.

Now the Songs

In writing a hymn for today's worshipers, one has to analyze the makeup of the typical congregation in a certain denomination. That audience will generally reflect the culture of the age and the region. In some churches, the worshipers are very much alike in background, theology, and taste. Someone with a different background and taste will feel out of place and will probably not even attempt to sing along, and if they do, it will be out of politeness. I can imagine Pentecostals feeling out of place in a Roman Catholic mass, or a person of northern European background unable to participate in an African American service as more than a spectator.

In more and more congregations of mainline denominations, there is a mixture of genres of hymns and songs, not all of them reflecting or satisfying the tastes of everyone in the church. A poll would reveal how many prefer country music, rock and roll, folk songs, praise songs, or classical. Personally I would get the most out of a service composed exclusively of the music I like, but I find myself increasingly in a distinct minority of worshipers, many of whom would not even open the hymnal to sing or learn my favorites. So, in preparing a worship service, I find myself trying to please the majority's repertory with hymns that come closest to matching the theme of the day.

Which leaves me with the dilemma: what kind of liturgy and hymnody should the church be offering? Will it attract or detract? Is the popular, crowd-pleasing style of preaching and music uplifting, expanding, deepening—or dumbing down? Should we discard the nearly two-millenia-old liturgy, or keep its valuable content and dress up the music in contemporary clothes? How much of the service should "contemporary" songs occupy? And if a majestic chorale best reflects and applies the message of the day, should it be foisted on a congregation that does not care for it and will silently suffer through it, waiting to get back on familiar ground?

No matter the culture, the background, the tastes, worship should begin with *reverence*. This requirement troubles me probably more than anything else about my own worship. Do I realize what I am about to do in worshiping the one eternal divine Being? Am I conscious of my creatureliness, my indebtedness to God, my need for communication with my Creator, Redeemer, and Sanctifier, that would exceed my anticipation of meeting a celebrity or powerful official, or someone I admire among my fellow creatures? How serious or casual should I be when I hear God speaking to me in the Bible, or join in prayers, or partake of the Body and the Blood of the world's Redeemer? What kind of body language would be most appropriate for such a meeting? How would Jesus have conversed with his Father in the temple and synagogue? How can hymns prepare us for reverence, self-examination, absolution, thanks, and praise?

Despite the differences in backgrounds, culture, and tastes of today's American population, there are common universal needs that worship should address. All are mortal, all are the targets of Satan, all sin and come short of the glory of God. All are in need of God's love, grace, and forgiveness. By the death and resurrection of Christ, eternal life is available to all.

The Pastoral Plus

An examination of the sources of most hymns reveals that the authors were either clergy or lay theologians, with a scattering of unordained, nonprofessional hymn text writers. Of all the qualifications for writing hymns for *corporate* worship, the most important is the hymn writer's biblical and Christ-centered *theology*. This is not just a vague, pious, sentimental cliché. As it is, the faith of most worshipers is often confined to, and expressed in, the person's repertory of familiar sacred songs.

In practice, true hymns derived from Scripture constitute a confession of faith in harmony with the ecumenical creeds. In a recent service, the preacher's very good sermon was almost completely obliterated by a defective sound system. The loss of that part of the service was compensated for by seven solid hymns—condensed sermons that applied the theme of the day—plus the liturgy, the assigned lections for the day, and the observance of Holy Communion. The experience convinced me again of the need for worship hymns of theological substance.

The revelation of God by the written and incarnate Word is so vast, profound, and practical that worship is impoverished when worshipers are not permitted or challenged to launch out into the deep to harvest the riches that fill more than 1,200 pages of small print in the Bible. Rather than repeating a handful of familiar hymns over and over, let's use some of those precious minutes of that brief one-hour service to sing sermons on many other ramifications of God's attributes and marvelous works.

What Shall I Write About?

Every hymn deals with one or more subjects. The liturgical and topical index of any hymnal will list more than the 114 subjects in the 239-hymn supplement I consulted. Most of those hymns cover more than one topic. Even so, if the average congregation's repertory is only 100 different hymns sung at least once in two years, many of them will not be learned or used if the most popular are repeated even once a month.

Facing this fact, the hymn writer is inclined to wonder why another hymn should be added to the mounting number already filling 900-page hymnals to overflowing. Just having a hymn chosen for a new hymnal does not ensure that the hymn is going to be used. Checking the latest list of published choral settings of some 50 of my hymns, I found their occasional use ranges from five to 5,000.

It is at this point that the hymn writer must ask: why am I writing this hymn? Isn't this subject matter already treated adequately and effectively in classic hymns with wedded and popular melodies? Am I secretly looking for recognition to flatter my ego? Or, is the hymn being requested by some individual or congregation to mark a certain occasion? Or, am I truly inspired by an event or experience or Scripture verse or insight that struck me with a special impact, which I just had to express in hymnic form whether anyone ever uses the hymn of not?

In responding to a request for a hymn, I may find that the subject is one that has been treated so well in a well-known hymn that another text would be a weak imitation of the classic. But I can address myself to a familiar subject through my particular style and insights and create a fresh statement in today's language and culture. What I will be doing, as a once full-time pastor, is drawing upon the experience of preparing some 1,200 sermons on a wide variety of texts, which were expounded and applied to the faith-life of average American Christians. The result would be a sermon condensed into three, four, or five stanzas (watch that attention span!), composed on several levels, so that it would be exhausted in one singing.

What Language Shall I Borrow?

The American hymn writer of this new millennium is challenged by the devaluation and the trivialization of words attributed to God exclusively. Over the years and most recently in the United States, words and concepts have been crippled by ravenous consumerism, by the advertising and entertainment industries and the culture. Many superlatives and absolutes no longer carry the force of their original literal meanings. Words originally reserved for the deity are misappropriated for their power value. One day's scanning of the newspaper and viewing television provides a long list of exaggerations flung about for momentary shock or appeal.

Here are just a few. "The Greatest Sale on Earth." "The Almighty Dollar." "Wonder" (bread). "Miracle Gro" (plant food). "Infiniti" (a car). "Everybody buys their vans at…" "Everybody's doing it…talking about…going to be there." "You always say…do..." "You never listen…do…" "You'll never find a more faithful companion" (a pager). Etc., etc.

If these colloquialisms cannot be taken literally, how literally can a person take the promise of God: "I will never leave you nor forsake you," or Christ's assurance: "I am with you always"?

Beginning with love: How does the average person define "love"? There is little or no differentiation made between *philia* (friendship, preference), *eros* (romantic, sexual attraction), and *agape* (the Scriptural, divine concept of love: undeserved total concern). The Bible, and Jesus specifically, defines love as total concern for the other, expressing itself most fully in the life and death of Christ, who was willing to sacrifice himself for sinners, including his enemies! God's love is never merely an emotion, but an action.

This generation and culture, like many others, increasingly uses the word *love* as a synonym for affection, preference, attraction, or lust. Making love, or loving games, songs, clothes, or whatnot is not the meaning of the biblical use of the word in the revelation that "God is love," or in the Gospel in a nutshell: "God so loved the world…" "Love one another." "Husbands, love your wives as Christ loved the Church, and gave himself for it." Such love for one's neighbor or spouse is willing to sacrifice even one's life for the loved one, much less donate an organ for transplant, or forgive an offense. In writing hymns, does that divine concept have to be surrendered, abandoned, or replaced by a stronger, more accurately defined word?

Consider the devaluation of the holy name of GOD in widespread profanity and cursing. We are told that blessing and cursing should not be uttered by the same lips. In the Decalogue, the commandment forbidding the taking of God's name in vain is just as serious and binding as the commandments forbidding murder, adultery, theft, covetousness, and idolatry. Yet audiences made up of the 90 percent of the American population that believes there is a God, applaud actors in TV programs every time they exclaim "Oh, my God!" in the most frivolous situations. If that exclamation erupts continually in conversations that have nothing to do with God, what kind of cry is available at the news of a terrible tragedy, one's loved ones wiped out in an accident, the diagnosis of cancer or AIDS, a natural catastrophe, or the judgment of a holy God? If the sight of a schoolmate's nerdy outfit elicits a scream of "Oh, my God!" how strongly will I be moved by the cry of God's

Son suffering the punishment for the sins of the world: "My God, my God, why have you forsaken me?" There must have been a reason why the Hebrews could not bring themselves even to utter YAHWEH or to spell it out in the Old Testament for fear of blaspheming that holy name. In our references to God in today's society and culture, how seriously can God's divine promises and commandments be taken? Can the average churchgoer make the transition from street usage to worship to get the full force and meaning of God's chosen words?

Another serious concern in hymn writing today is the use of inclusive language. I have personally been conscious of the need for inclusive terminology in reference to persons. But I draw the line when the demand is made to ascribe feminine names (not metaphors) to God, contrary to the practice and example of the one who was one with God from eternity, and gives him the name of Father. Jesus refers to him by that name throughout the New Testament and, as one of the most precious gifts, gave us the Prayer of prayers. This question centers on the very theology of our faith.

My stance is similar with regard to the movement to eliminate or reduce the title "Lord" as being indicative of male domination. To me it is the most appropriate designation for the highest being who is in control of the universe for the sake of his beloved creation and creatures, who alone is able to contend with the forces of evil, and overcome death itself. I can't find a more fitting title in the thesaurus for this comforting name God ascribes to himself.

Making Melody in Your Heart

At this point in the process the hymn writer follows the advice of St. Paul, a prisoner in chains awaiting his execution: "Be filled with the Spirit. Speak to one another with psalms, hymns, and spiritual songs. Sing and make music in your hearts to the Lord, always giving thanks to God the Father for everything, in the name of our Lord Jesus Christ" (Eph. 5:16b–20 RSV).

This prescription implies the combination of words and music to convey a Spirit-engendered message whose content would edify, strengthen, and fill with hope pilgrims on their way to the Eternal City. Obviously, a hymn is therefore not words alone, but words wedded to music. Without the musical dimension, a hymn is just poetry, sublime as it may be.

There's a reason why music exists only in human beings. Although this gift is appropriated for lesser purposes, such as ditties, folk songs and love songs, its loftiest expression is as an offering of thanksgiving to its Creator.

What gems and masterpieces of sacred music have been Spirit-inspired since David and Asaph composed the Psalms, one of which our Lord sang with his disciples the night he was betrayed, until the present age of the worshiping community of Christ! Thousands of worship books, cantatas, anthems, arias, that no one's lifetime can exhaust or even sample!

How does each generation sing a new song? I can only speak of my own procedure. I can write a text for an extant tune, or I can write one for which a new tune is written. Rarely does one person compose both text and tune, although a small number of hymn writers are capable of doing both.

Obviously, if a poem is to inspire a melody, it must possess certain poetic qualities. It must be metrical, and in most cases, strophic, that is, divided into stanzas. The text need not be rhymed; e.g., "Oh, Come, All Ye Faithful." Or it may have a refrain at the beginning or end of each stanza. It may conform to any number of meters and lines, or it may have an irregular form, as in my first collection, where 108 hymns are set to 69 different meters while an additional 20 are classified as irregular. This variety of poetic forms challenges and sometimes inspires the composer of the original melody.

The subject of the text also suggests the mood of the tune, which should not conflict with the expression of the words, or come out of the same musical sausage machine, restricted to one style, when the most appropriate one may suggest a reach beyond the trite and commonplace. In any case, the new tune should be memorable, accessible to the average churchgoer in a particular culture, and within an average singing range.

The writing of a hymn presupposes a poetic skill and a knowledge of music. Composers should not be expected to rewrite the words to conform to a melody. The melody composed for a particular hymn can make or break a hymn. There are plenty of instances of good, even outstanding sacred poems that are demolished by a bad tune; and vice versa, a good tune can perpetuate a poor text. I won't quote the all-too-painful examples.

In any case, the music should not override the words, drown out or crowd out the words, or draw attention to itself to the loss of the message of the text. Nor should the music prevent the singers from contemplating the words because of its tempo or inappropriate bombast. Better to understate than to exaggerate. Otherwise forget the words and just keep on repeating alleluias.

But what a treasure is occasionally (alas, too rarely) created when the new song is truly a *new* song that comforts, inspires, edifies, and raises the spirit of the singers, and is remembered beyond the worship gathering in the sound of its first line!

Original Hymns, Carols, and Songs

A Comet Blazed Across the Skies

A comet blazed across the skies
above a sleeping, dying sphere,
just as a lost and hopeless race
saw its last lamplights disappear.

"Repent!" the angel-star proclaimed,
"Cling to the Savior God has sent;
this is the one true light of grace,
believe this Gospel and repent!"

Before that cry the idols crashed,
old chains were shattered, darkness cleft,
faith kindled, hope revived, and Christ
alone upon his throne was left.

For that bold angel we give thanks,
and for the Gospel he confessed,
his burning faith and legacy,
and for the freedom long suppressed.

In these last days of sore distress,
give us Your Star to see and heed,
that like the Magi we may find
the Savior we most crave and need.

Meter	LM (8.8.8.8.)
Based on	Revelation 14:6, 7
Theme	Commemoration of Martin Luther's birth
Written	1 July 1982
Suggested tune	ERHALT UNS, HERR

In view of the approaching 400th anniversary observance of Martin Luther's birth in 1983, I wrote this commemorative hymn without an assignment. It was meant to illustrate Rev. 14:6, 7, traditionally held by Lutherans to be a prophecy of the Reformer. To connect the text subliminally with Luther and his hymn, "Erhalt uns, Herr, bei deinem Wort," it was written with that tune in mind. Line 5:1 is taken word for word from Catherine Winkworth's translation of line 2:1 of Nikolaus Selnecker's hymn on the preservation of the Word and the Church, "Ach bleib bei uns, Herr Jesu Christ" *(The Lutheran Hymnal*, 292). Selnecker was one of the great champions of Lutheran orthodoxy and one of the framers of the unifying *Formula of Concord,* 1577. To my knowledge this hymn was not used in the commemoration, though it may be appropriate for commemorating the Reformer's birth on or near November 10.

A Life Begins, a Child Is Born

A life begins, a child is born
And placed into our care.
How shall we mold this special life,
How train God's precious heir?
Where is the model and the plan
To build the life that God began?

Christ Jesus, Teacher sent from God,
Through whom all blessings flow,
You are the wisdom that we seek,
To whom else shall we go?
You have the word that sets us free
To be what we were meant to be.

You want the whole world to be saved
And come to know the truth;
Your Spirit draws us to your love
Beginning in our youth.
Like pupils sitting at your feet,
We learn what makes our joy complete.

See what a harvest we still reap
From seeds sown long ago;
So will the wisdom we pass on
Bless more than we can know!
Lord, keep on teaching us your ways,
Your wisdom guide us all our days!

Meter	8.6.8.6.8.8.
Based on	John 3:2; 8:31,32; 15:11; Deut. 6:6,7; Psalm 86:11 and parallels
Theme	Teaching/Training/Christian education
Written	5 November 1995
Suggested tune	GRACE CHURCH NEW by Carl Schalk

To commemorate the 100th anniversary of its Christian day school, Grace Lutheran Church of River Forest, Illinois requested a hymn to be sung by children of all ages to express their appreciation for their spiritual training. The focus of the hymn is placed on Christ, the Teacher sent from God, to instruct the human race in the life-giving, peace-producing Gospel.

A Woman and a Coin

A woman and a coin—the coin is lost!
How much it means to her, what time and toil,
what part it was to play in her bright dreams!
Am I that treasured coin worth searching for?
I'm found, and You rejoice! What love! What love!

A shepherd and a sheep—the sheep is lost!
Far from the flock, the one in hundred cries,
then—risking life—the shepherd's voice and staff!
Am I that treasured sheep worth dying for?
I live, and You rejoice! What love! What love!

A parent and a child—the child is lost!
The parent feeds on memories and hope,
the prodigal on husks and one last chance.
Am I that treasured child worth waiting for?
I'm home, and You rejoice! What love! What love!

Dear God, You sought us when the world was lost,
You gave Your only Son at what a cost;
Your Spirit welcomes home the tempest-tossed:
Now we can be all You were dreaming of.
We're safe, and You rejoice! What love! What love!

Meter	10.10.10.10.10.
Based on	Luke 15
Theme	Divine Mercy/Restoration
Written	25 March 1990
Suggested tune	NYGREN by Carl Schalk

The impetus of the text was a request from the First Presbyterian Church of Champaign, Illinois, to mark the retirement in September, 1990 of Dr. Malcolm Nygren after 38 years as senior pastor. Luke 15 is our Lord's picture of our relationship to God, the revelation of God's heart and will toward human beings. Inexhaustible, the three parables spark individual identification and interpretation. Each person can find a place in all the stories, filling in experiences and lessons learned from life and from the sayings of the Good Shepherd. The central point is the joy of God (and of the angels) over one penitent sinner. The repentance (turning and restoration) comes with the finding of the lost coin, sheep, and child. This finding is the reason for rejoicing in the sinner's life. It is the culmination of God's love and grace and of the Good Shepherd's sacrifice. Hence it is a universal theme, applicable to all human beings of all times and places.

The metric pattern, though rarely found in hymns, with its two-line refrain seems to be appropriate for this theme. The three stanzas are unrhymed to suggest the search, whereas the last, in its trinitarian pattern is rhymed to suggest the reunion of the seeker and the sought in a closely-knit unity.

Add One More Song

Add one more song to that unending one
that rose up from the cosmos newly spun
by one almighty Word: orbs, stars, and sun—
add our notes to that music then begun:
Sing Gloria, sing Gloria, sing Gloria!

Add one more song of sorrow and regret
much like the one the watching angels wept
when our first parents sinned and faced God's threat—
"Have mercy, Lord! We are your children yet!"
Cry Kyrie, cry Kyrie, cry Kyrie!

Add one more song that only we can sing
who recognize and worship you as king;
embraced, adorned with royal robe and ring,
ourselves the best of offerings we bring:
Hosannas raise, Hosannas raise, Hosannas raise!

Add one more song of faith and victory,
of captives saved and set forever free,
of peace and good, of love and harmony,
of unity with you, great One-in-Three!
Sing thanks and praise, sing thanks and praise, sing thanks and praise!

Add one more song of Paradise restored,
join with the saints in one exultant chord
before the Lamb enthroned, by all adored,
the one creating, recreating Word:
Alleluia, Alleluia, Amen, Amen!

Meter	10.10.10.10.4.4.4.
Based on	Job 38 (7); Psalms 32, 51; Luke 15:20–24; Revelation 7:9–17
Theme	Worship/Praise
Written	26 November 1992
Suggested tune	PARK RIDGE by Carl Schalk

Park Ridge Community Church, celebrating its 150th anniversary February 7, 1993 in Park Ridge, Illinois, requested a festive hymn of praise and celebration as its gift to the church-at-large. Since the church's praise is a response to the wonderful works of God centered in God's love for and redemption of humanity, culminating in the everlasting song of the saints around the throne of the Lamb, this theme pervades the composed text. The hymn is therefore appropriate for any celebration of God's people reviewing their relationship with the Creator, Redeemer, and generating and regenerating Spirit.

All Bless the God of Israel

All bless the God of Israel
for promising Immanuel:
from Abraham, a man like us,
from God, divine and glorious:
someone to share our every woe,
someone to conquer every foe.

All praise the God of Israel
for sending us Immanuel,
to do what God had sworn He would,
what only the Messiah could:
live, die, and rise, and clear the path
to life from certain, endless wrath.

All thank the God of Israel
for being our Immanuel,
whose Spirit opens eyes to see
the Word, the Truth, that makes us free
to live unfettered by our fears,
to serve our Savior all our years.

All bless the Lord, the God of all,
for Christ, our great Immanuel!
Come, welcome David's greater Son
with Zechariah and with John,
and, living, prove our gratitude
to be the Israel of God.

Meter	8.8.8.8.8.8.
Based on	Luke 1:67–79
Theme	The Benedictus of Zechariah
Written	3 July 1989
Suggested tune	by Gerhard M. Cartford

In the preparation of a supplement to *Laudamus* for the next conference of the Lutheran World Federation, Gerhard Cartford requested a versified paraphrase of the Benedictus of Zechariah as an alternate to the plainchant canticle.

In determining a meter for the new text, which I established with the opening two-line refrain, the similarity between that couplet and the closing couplet of *VENI, IMMANUEL* suggested the 8.8.8.8.8.8. form.

As the text developed from the Song of Zechariah, a kinship of themes with "Oh, Come, Oh, Come, Emmanuel" appeared, suggesting an Advent use for the versified "Benedictus." To indicate the universality and timelessness of Zechariah's Song, each stanza directs "all" to bless, praise, and thank the God of Israel, not just the physical decendants of Abraham and Jacob. The last stanza underlines the universal deliverance of the Messiah by the phrase "the Israel of God," referring to the spiritual descendants of Abraham and Jacob (Romans 11, esp. vv. 25–32).

Gerhard Cartford prepared a tune for the new text for the LWF hymnal supplement.

All Things Are Yours

All things are Yours, my God,
Creator of all that exists,
all wisdom, all beauty, and might.
You made me, You own me,
Your glory surrounds me;
I live by your mercy and love.
All things are Yours, and so am I.

All things are Yours, my Lord,
Redeemer of all who have sinned,
new Master of all who repent.
You sought me, You found me,
You call me, You lead me;
now have me live only for You.
All things are Yours, and so am I.

All things are Yours, my Guide,
Renewer and Giver of life,
Transformer of hearts and of minds.
Renew me, transform me,
inspire me, refine me,
and give me the spirit of Christ.
All things are Yours, and so am I.

"All things are yours, My child,
so live like the heir that you are,
entrusted with all that you have.
Be faithful, be prudent,
be daring, be caring,
as giving as I am toward you.
All things are yours, and you are Mine."

Meter	6.8.8.6.6.8.8.
Based on	1 Corinthians 3:21—4:2; Matthew 25:14–30; and parallels
Theme	Stewardship
Written	5 May 1989
Suggested tune	DALLAS by Carl Schalk

An invitation by the Worship Committee of the Texas District Pastor-Educator Conference, Lutheran Church—Missouri Synod for a hymn on the subject of Christian stewardship provided the impetus for a composition dealing with a subject that had obsessed me as long as my struggle with worship. It was that struggle that inspired "Now the Silence" and numerous other texts that tried to show the response of the creature to God's creation and his mercy revealed in Christ. The response is gratitude expressing itself in worship and service, including the management of all that passes through our hands and lives.

Again I used the trinitarian pattern, for all three persons are involved in the lavish bestowal of gifts. The first three stanzas are directed by the steward to the triune God, whose heirs we have become by Baptism. The last stanza tries to express the theme of the divine revelation: "I am your God, and you are My people." The divine pronouns are capitalized in this stanza to clearly indicate the Speaker of these endearing and reassuring words.

Carl Schalk, commissioned to prepare a melody for the text, says this about the music: "The tune attempts to reflect what I catch as the mood of quiet, firm confidence and hope…This is what led me to set the anthem setting for just choir and organ, rather than attempting to include brass and timpani…The melody climaxes on the last syllable of the second-last line of each stanza (on) what seems to me a crucial word." The tune is named *DALLAS* for the location of its first presentation.

Amid the World's Bleak Wilderness

Amid the world's bleak wilderness
A vineyard grows with promise green,
The planting of the Lord Himself.

His love selected this terrain,
His vine with love He planted here
To bear the choicest fruit for Him.

We are His branches, chosen, dear,
And though we feel the Dresser's knife,
We are the objects of His care.

From Him we draw the juice of life,
For Him supply His winery
With fruit from which true joys derive.

Vine, keep what I was meant to be:
Your branch with Your rich life in me.

Meter	Irregular
Based on	John 15:1–8
Theme	Faith/Witness/Union with Christ
Written	19 December 1975
Tune	GRANTON by Richard Hillert

This hymn was written at the suggestion of the sainted E. Theo DeLaney, who indicated a need for a hymn on the subject of the Vine and the Branches as a hymn of the day for the Fifth Sunday of Easter in the *Lutheran Book of Worship* then being prepared.

In studying the various Scriptural references to this subject, I thought of having the verse form of the hymn resemble a grape vine. It occurred to me that the classic form of the *terza rima*, which Dante used in the *Divine Comedy,* by its definition depicts the interwoven nature of a vine; "a verse form consisting of tercets usually in iambic pentameter with an interlaced rhyme scheme (as aba, bcb, cdc, etc.) in English poetry." I took the liberty of rendering the verses in quadrameter along the lines of such familiar three-line stanza hymns as *O FILII ET FILIAE.* I hoped that the composer of the melody for the text would try to reflect the interwoven nature of the text by using a rhythm similar to that of *O FILII ET FILIAE,* in a major key and allowing for the repetition of lines one and two as the tune for the last stanza, which is a sort of refrain. Visually and melodically, the hymn was to resemble a vine and its branches. Richard W. Hillert's tune *GRANTON* succeded in expressing this intention.

Around the World the Shout Resounds

Cantor: (chants) Christ is risen!
Congregation: (chants) He is risen indeed!

Around the world the shout resounds:
"Christ lives again, and life abounds!"
The Serpent's head is crushed,
the grasp of death is broken;
atonement has been sealed,
the empty grave its token.
What happier news on earth than this:
Christ's life is ours, and we are His!

Women: (chant) Christ is risen!
Men : (chant) He is risen indeed!

God bless the cloud of witnesses
who share the faith that we confess:
The women at the tomb,
and Martha in her grieving,
the thief upon the cross,
and Stephen killed believing.
With Job we know the life God gives:
"We know that our Redeemer lives!"

Men: (chant) Christ is risen!
Women: (chant) He is risen indeed!

The wonder grows, remembering,
considering and marveling,
not with fast-fading cheers,
but with a steady knowing,
a growing certainty, a peaceful, joyful glowing,
that sings convinced and unafraid:
"This is the day the Lord has made!"

Cantor: (chants) Christ is risen!
Congregation: (chants) He is risen indeed!

Meter	8.8.6.7.6.7.8.8. and Chants
Based on	Easter Sunday Pericopes
Theme	Easter/The Resurrection of Christ
Written	1 March 1994
Tune	SIOUX FALLS by Carl Schalk

This text was inspired by the implications of the accomplishment of the Messiah's mission: the fulfillment of the first and all subsequent prophecies of the victory of the Woman's Seed over Satan and death. The three stanzas respond to the shout of victory with which most Easter services begin and end.

The hymn was dedicated by Our Savior's Lutheran Church, Sioux Falls, South Dakota, to its Director of Music, Don Levsen, upon his retirement in May 1999, in recognition and appreciation of his decades of service in the congregation's worship.

As Once in Eden Music Filled the Air

As once in Eden music filled the air,
when our first parents knew no fear or care,
so God still longs to hear it everywhere: Alleluia!

At last! at last! the lost and lonely cried
when Christ, their last and only hope, arrived,
and welcomed all whom others brushed aside: Alleluia!

In our despondent wasteland far from home,
you answered when we prayed, "Your kingdom come!"
In Christ you showed us how your will is done: Alleluia!

How shall we praise you for this glorious place
where you transform us by your word of grace,
where we find rest in your sincere embrace: Alleluia!

Give us a zeal like yours that will not rest
while someone you can free is still oppressed.
We cast our nets again at your behest: Alleluia!

Amazed, we see your wonders year on year,
within our loving reach new lives appear,
among us Eden's song re-echoes, hear! Alleluia!

From Kyrios to kirk to church you grow,
from laity to liturgy we go
and thrill to see the fruit of seed you sow: Alleluia!

Meter	10. 10. 10. 4.
Based on	Colossians 1; Luke 5:5 and parallels
Theme	The Church in Mission/Anniversary/Rededication
Written	29 September 1988
Suggested tune	ENGELBERG

Second Presbyterian Church, located in the Central West End of St. Louis, reached its 150th year of existence in 1988, and now occupies its third location since its founding as a pioneer congregation. In the 1950's the congregation decided to stay in its present neighborhood and to continue to serve a diverse and scattered membership. Over the years, Second Presbyterian helped to establish many Presbyterian churches in greater St. Louis. The hymn text is meant to commemorate the faithfulness and blessings of the congregation as it carried out its mission of gathering the people of God around the Gospel. The occasion also afforded an opportunity for rededication to Christ and the Great Commission.

ENGELBERG was suggested as the tune for the text. The hymn was first used on October 9, 1988 at the opening of the anniversary year.

An optional last stanza was meant to have particular significance for the celebrating congregation. The Church begins with the *Kyrios*, the Greek word for "Lord." The *Kyrios* gathers his flock into local flocks, into "kirks" as the Scotch Presbyterian communities were known, and these join other Christians in the Church Universal. "Kirk" and "church" are derived from the word *Kyrios*. "Laity" are the people of God, and "liturgy" (literally from *leiturgia,* the work of God's people) a life of worship.

Astonished by Your Empty Tomb

Astonished by Your empty tomb,
the news still ringing in our ears,
our doubting hearts begin to burn
as gently You dispel our fears,
and with Your promised Spirit's light
the pieces all begin to fit:
You are the Christ, the only One
like us, yet pure and infinite.

No one but You has sought us out,
who else has loved us as You have?
No one but You could take our place,
who else but You has life to give?
No one but You keeps every vow,
who else but You has earned our trust?
To miss You is to forfeit all,
without You all must turn to dust.

Now knowing You and God through You,
You are the reason why we live;
now having found Your peace and joy,
You are the reason we forgive.
Who would not follow such a Lord?
With You in us and us in You,
the loving heart knows what to say,
the thankful heart knows what to do.

Meter	8.8.8.8.8.8.8.8. or LMD
Based on	Philippians 3:8–15; 2 Corinthians 1:17b–22
Theme	Commitment/Following Christ
Written	26 August 1988
Suggested tune	KEMPER by Carl Schalk

On the occasion of the 50th anniversary of the Southeastern District of The Lutheran Church—Missouri Synod, a new hymn was commissioned for use by the church in its recruitment of ministerial students and for continued use on related themes beyond the anniversary year and by the church at large. Carl Schalk was asked to provide an original melody for the text.

The hymn begins at the starting point and basis of the Christian faith: the Resurrection of our Lord. Out of that new life comes our new life and the message to which the first and all succeeding apostles have committed their ministry. All candidates for the holy ministry can do no better than to adopt St. Paul's motto: preaching Christ crucified and risen.

Before the Marvel of This Night

Before the marvel of this night,
Adoring, fold your wings and bow,
Then tear the sky apart with light,
And with your news the world endow.
Proclaim the birth of Christ and peace,
That fear and death and sorrow cease:
Sing peace, sing peace, sing Gift of Peace,
Sing peace, sing Gift of Peace!

Awake the sleeping world with song,
This is the day the Lord has made.
Assemble here, celestial throng,
In royal splendor come arrayed.
Give earth a glimpse of heavenly bliss,
A teasing taste of what they miss.
Sing bliss, sing bliss, sing endless bliss,
Sing bliss, sing endless bliss!

The love that we have always known,
Our constant joy and endless light,
Now to the loveless world be shown,
Now break upon its deathly night.
Into one song compress the love
That rules our universe above:
Sing love, sing love, sing God is love,
Sing love, sing God is love!

Meter	8.8.8.8.8.8.8.6.
Based on	Luke 2:13, 14
Theme	Christmas/The angels' song
Written	1 January 1979
Suggested tune	MARVEL by Carl Schalk

In response to a request for a Christmas or Epiphany song from the editors of *CHRISTMAS:* An American Annual of Christmas Literature and Art, for their 1981 edition, this was one of five Christmas songs chosen for publication. One of the suggested themes was the angels' song. But what could one possibly say in music that had not already been covered in the hundreds of extant Christmas carols and songs? I decided to conjecture how the angel hosts may have prepared and rehearsed that first Christmas song with a handful of shepherds as their audience. Projecting my experience in choir singing and conducting to that divine chorus, I wrote the text for which Carl Schalk composed a new melody, since it was not intended for any existing meter. Subsequently this song has enjoyed wide popularity and usage in Schalk's choir arrangement published by Augsburg Fortress Publishing.

Before Your Awesome Majesty

Before Your awesome majesty,
We humbly bow, we bend the knee
As to no merely earthly king,
Creator, Lord of everything.

Almighty, holy, unborn One,
Whose glory far outshines the sun:
Who can approach You and yet live,
Who dares to sin, and You forgive?

The oceans roar at Your command,
You tame them when You raise Your hand;
Into that sea You cast our sins,
With water our new life begins.

No God is there besides You, Lord,
No life is there without Your Word;
Yet neither might nor glory move
Us to adore You as Your love.

Beginning and the End are You,
To You all praise and thanks are due;
What stars and saints and angels see,
Grant us to share eternally.

Meter	LM (8.8.8.8.)
Based on	Psalm 93
Theme	Adoration/Praise
Written	12 October 1985
Suggested tune	DER HERR IST KÖNIG HERRLICH SCHÖN

Alphabetically listed, this is the first of eight Becker Psalter texts prepared for the 15th Annual Bach Cantata Series presented at Grace Lutheran Church, River Forest, Illinois, 1985–86. The Cantata Series committee selected eight versified Psalms (23, 30, 46, 93,103, 104, 111, and 130) from the Cornelius Becker Psalter of 1602 in their Heinrich Schuetz (1628) choral settings and asked for a new set of psalm paraphrases to fit the particular chorales.

The following texts were prepared for the series in contemporary language and imagery and to give them a New Testament application by unfolding the fulfillment concealed in their Old Testament version. The meter and rhyme schemes were suggested by the German texts for which the Heinrich Schuetz settings were made, though the English texts, while based on the Biblical Psalms, are not translations of the German texts, but are original paraphrases/hymns.

This background commentary applies to all eight "Becker Psalter" texts:

Before your awesome majesty (Psalm 93)
Count your blessings, O my soul (Psalm 104)
Give glory, all creation (Psalm 103)
I praise you, Lord, in every hour (Psalm 30)
In hopelessness and near despair (Psalm 130)
Lord, I must praise you (Psalm 111)
Though mountains quake and oceans roar (Psalm 46)
You, Jesus, are my shepherd true (Psalm 23)

Begin the Song of Glory Now

Begin the song of glory now:
the Son has risen from His grave!
The night of mourning long is past;
life has a purpose, after all.
Our Samson smashed the gates of hell,
and we are free at last, at last!
Begin the song of glory now:
the Son has risen from our grave!

Prepare the song of glory now:
the Son has risen from His grave!
Composers, players, find new sounds
for every instrument and voice:
a note, a chord, an aria,
a Kyrie, a Gloria.
Prepare the song of glory now:
the Son has risen from our grave!

Repeat the song of glory now:
the Son has risen from His grave!
Complete the Easter overture,
and join the Alleluia choir
"In Jesus' name" the song begin,
and end: "All praise to God alone!"
Repeat the song of glory now:
the Son has risen from our grave!

Meter	LMD (8.8.8.8.8.8.8.8)
Based on	1 Corinthians 15
Theme	Easter/Resurrection/Music/Praise
Written	21 April 1985
Suggested tune	KLAMATH by David Deffner O GROSSER GOTT

Prompted by a search by the Hymn Society of America for hymns on the theme of music, this Easter hymn attempts to tie the ultimate reason for singing to the key event in history and our faith-life: the Resurrection. "If Christ is not risen, your faith is futile; you are still in your sins" and hence without any reason for singing. "But now Christ is risen from the dead," and we indeed have reason to revel in his victory with shouts of triumph, with music and praise, like the "Resurrexit" in Bach's *B-minor Mass.* Another clue from Bach's dedication of his music is referred to in 3: 5, 6, his superscription "INJ" and his postscript "SDG." The composition of this hymn was inspired also by the tercentennary celebration of Bach's birth in 1985.

Be Happy, Saints

Be happy, saints!
Of all who pass this way
You are the blest who live as in the day.
Who more than you has so much love to give,
Who has a richer legacy to leave?

Be happy, saints!
The lost Christ came to seek
He found; made you the merciful and meek,
The pure in heart, the patient and the true,
The righteous sufferers, the faithful few.

Be happy, saints!
So many wait for you
Who know the risen Savior as you do.
So many have a pain or peace to share,
So many need your prayers and selfless care.

Be happy, saints!
Go singing to your task,
Christ promises to give you all you ask.
Who better knows the joy of coming home,
Delights with God to see the kingdom come?

Be happy, saints!
While what is seen erodes,
From strength to strength the inner person grows,
The glory brighter as the goal appears,
The song of angels welling in your ears.

Meter	10.10.10.10. or 4.6.10.10.10.
Based on	2 Corinthians 4:7–18 and the Beatitudes
Theme	Service/Aging Christians
Written	24 June 1991
Suggested tune	ARLINGTON HEIGHTS by Carl Schalk

Searching for a theme for the 100th anniversary of the Lutheran Home for the Aged, Arlington Heights, Illinois, the Cycle B second reading for Pentecost 2 and 3 of the Three-Year Lectionary struck me as being ideal: the picture of the outward person wasting away while the inner person is being renewed for continued reflection of Christ to the world. Paul is describing the living out of the Beatitudes. Some translations render the word "blessed" as "happy," and a review of the many Old and New Testament passages depicting the happiness of the believer revealed a harmony with the Beatitudes. There was an opportunity also to incorporate one of my long-time observations: that a person becomes an ancestor from the moment of birth. Other inferences are drawn from the rich Second Corinthians passage addressed to Christians living in a world very similar to our own.

Blessed Chosen Generation

Blessed chosen generation,
saints and heirs and priests and kings,
now the Savior's blood relation,
wearing royal robes and rings:

Refrain
We have a gift to give,
a legacy of life to leave,
good news for all who want to live,
a living hope for all who grieve.

Join that heaven-bound procession
where the aim of love is life,
children of that new creation
where the aim of life is love.
Refrain

Grasp this momentary impulse,
act upon the Spirit's prod,
like the ancestors who called us,
brought us to our gracious God.
Refrain

View the world with Christ's compassion,
feed its hunger, hear its cries;
partners in our Lord's commission,
thankful, joyful, share the prize!
Refrain

Meter	8.7.8.7.and refrain: 6.8.8.8.
Based on	1 Peter 1:1, 3–10; 2:9; Psalm 145:4; Matthew 28:19, 20
Theme	Evangelism/Missions
Written	21 February 1992
Suggested tune	HAMPTON by Carl Schalk

The Lutheran Laymen's League, headquartered in St. Louis, celebrating its 75th anniversary in 1992, chose as its anniversary theme, "Tell a New Generation." For the commemoration a hymn expanding on that theme was commissioned.

The word "generation" led to the two related passages, Psalm 145:4 and I Peter 2:9 and to the place every believer has in one of the successive generations, each playing an ancestral role in passing on the Gospel promise. The hymn text echoes other passages relating to membership in the Kingdom, its characteristics, mission, and goal. It is hoped that each resinging of the hymn will uncover another reference to the way we receive and pass on the gift of grace and faith.

The poetic structure of the hymn deliberately changes from stanza to refrain, prompting the composer to indicate that transition by a change of rhythmic accent from trochaic to iambic. The dactyl in the first line of the refrain serves to bridge the transition, since it can be scanned as trochee and iamb.

Blessed Jesus, Living Bread
Pericopal Hymns on John 6

(Opening)
Blessed Jesus, living Bread,
by your self our souls are fed:
give us all the eyes to see
all that you were sent to be.

(Insert appropriate stanzas for Pentecost 10–14.)

(Closing)
We are in that crowd you fed
with your blest, abundant Bread.
Moved by every human care,
bless the Bread we eat and share.

Stanzas 2 & 3 for John 6:1–15 (Pentecost 10)

"What is it" old Israel cried,
ate it and were satisfied.
Now the same prolific hand
feeds them in a barren land.

"Who is it?" who gives himself
bread-like from a baker's shelf?
Never-ending food supply:
those who eat it never die.

Stanzas 2 & 3 for John 6:24–35 (Pentecost 11)

To the House of Bread you came,
there received your saving Name;
from that lowly manger bed
all the dying world is fed.

Not by this world's bread alone
can our life become full-grown,
but by every word that goes
from the mouth of God—one grows.

Stanzas 2 & 3 for John 6:41–51 (Pentecost 12)

Word of God by which we live:
what we hunger for you give—
for the body and the soul,
life with God, life new and whole.

All we ever need and more,
flowing from your boundless store;
at your table every guest
sees your mercy manifest.

Stanzas 2 & 3 for John 6:51–58 (Pentecost 13)

No more perfect food is there
than the food you came to share,
not to be admired alone,
lest one spurn it for a stone.

On that table made of wood
lies our sacramental food:
"Take and eat and live" you call,
"here is life for each and all!"

Stanzas 2 & 3 for John 6:60–67 (Pentecost 14)

Ah, what welcome words you speak:
comfort to revive the weak,
God's own wisdom, hope, and cheer
starving souls are blest to hear

Word incarnate, Word divine
Word that comes in bread and wine:
Love that we have come to know:
Lord, to whom else shall we go?

Meter	7.7.7.7.
Based on	John 6:1–15, 24–35, 41–51, 51–58, and 60–67
Theme	Christ, the Bread of Life
Written	23 August 1990
Suggested tunes	SONG 13 or other appropriate 7.7.7.7. tunes

At the initiation of the Concordia Publishing House Music Department, a series of five hymn texts was requested for Pentecost Sundays 10–14, Series B of the Three-Year Lectionary, to be used in the *Worship Resource* for 1991. Since the five texts based on John chapter 6 all revolve around the theme of Christ the Bread of Life from heaven, I decided to use a bracketed format consisting of an opening and closing stanza for all five Sundays with two inner stanzas for each of the Sundays focused on some distinctive feature of the particular pericope.

A liturgy was to be prepared to harmonize with the accents for each Sunday of the series.

By a Lake We Come to Know You

By a lake we come to know You,
Son of God, for what You are.
There You called Your first disciples,
there they followed You in faith.
So You look for us and find us,
so You call us one by one.

When Your friends returned from fishing
all night long without a catch,
doing what You said convinced them
that You know where blessings wait.
So You redirect our efforts,
so You fill our empty lives.

When You saw the crowd that gathered
on a hillside by the shore,
You were moved to teach and feed them
with an everlasting feast.
Like those thousands, hungry millions
still feed on that bread today.

With a word You calmed the tempest,
saving, soothing those You love;
they could even walk on water
when they fixed their faith on You.
So You rescue and sustain us
in the lifeboat of Your Church.

Risen, proven true Redeemer,
You await Your feeble friends;
You prepare for them a dinner
on the shore where You first met.
So, too, pardon our denials,
re-enlist us in Your plan.

Jesus, let a lake remind us
what You said and what You did,
how You sought us, how You called us,
how You gave our life a goal.
Now we know why we are living;
we can share the joy You give.

Meter	8.7.8.7.8.7.
Based on	Matthew 4:18–22; 8:23–27; 13:1,2; 14:22–32; Luke 5:1–11; John 21, and parallels
Theme	Vocation/Discipleship
Written	24 February 1997
Suggested tune	ARCADIA by Carl Schalk

Camp Arcadia, on the eastern shore of Lake Michigan, marked its 75th anniversary as a Lutheran family vacation and retreat center in 1997. Over the years, the camp's programs have left significant impressions on thousands of campers and conference participants. The hymn requested for the commemoration reviews the various lake and lakeside events in the ministry of Jesus Christ. At least six events suggest parallel experiences in the lives of Christ's followers in the two millenia since those holy feet walked the Galilean shores and waters, and where his call transformed fishermen into "fishers of souls."

Carl Schalk, like myself an alumnus of Camp Arcadia, was asked to compose a musical setting for these transmillenial recollections and comparisons for today's disciples.

Catch the Vision! Share the Glory!

Blessed children, saints, elect of God,
Globe-encircling cloud of witnesses:
We have heard the Christmas angels,
We have seen the Easter sunrise,
Cried with joy when Christ began his reign.
　　Catch the vision! Share the glory!
　　Show the captives, tell them: Christ is here!

Universal Body of the Lord,
Chosen, called, made just, and glorified:
Ours the faith, and ours the triumph,
Ours the peace the world is seeking;
Who on earth as privileged as we?
　　Catch the vision! Share the glory!
　　Show the captives, tell them: Christ is here!

Heirs together of the grace of life,
All baptized into the death of Christ:
Born again, in love maturing,
From the altar free and cheerful,
Caring, winsome family of God.
　　Catch the vision! Share the glory!
　　Show the captives, tell them: Christ is here!

For this time and place have we been born,
Gifted by the Spirit, trained, and sent:
With the eyes of Jesus seeing,
With the hands of Jesus helping,
With the words of Jesus bringing life,
　　Catch the vision! Share the glory!
　　Show the captives, tell them: Christ is here!

Meter	9.9.8.8.9.8.9.
Based on	Matthew 28:18–20; Acts 1:8
Theme	Church/Mission/Evangelism/Witness
Written	26 February 1986
Suggested tune	VISION by Carl Schalk

The American Lutheran Church, for its "Vision for Mission" program, 1986–87, requested a theme hymn for the church-wide, year-long evangelism effort, coupling the spiritual and social concerns of the church. The hymn emphasizes the proving of the church's confession of faith by agape and acts of charity, concern for the whole person with Christ the motivator. The refrain suggests captivating the unconverted by a display of Christ-like concern and then defining that love by the proclamation of the Gospel. The risen Christ lives in his Body, the Church.

The hymn can be used apart from its original purpose as a mission and witness hymn to illustrate various parallel Biblical texts.

Christ, Around Your Word Assembled

Christ, around your word assembled,
see Your students, chosen, called,
eager to proclaim and practice
truth and justice, faith and hope.
What a vast array of talents!
What commitment to ideals!

Take us to the mount of glory
there to hear Your course endorsed;
guide us through the Sacred Record,
there to find You at its core;
meet us at the cross and garden,
sealing all You say and are.

Where is all this searching leading,
what is all this training for?
Who will serve a world still bleeding,
feed the hungry, clothe the poor;
bring the Gospel's hope and healing
and the thrill of knowing You?

Word eternal, word of splendor,
word of judgment, word of grace,
word of wisdom, word of power,
word of love and joy and peace,
word of mercy, word of pardon:
sing through us Your words of life!

Meter	8.7.8.7.8.7.
Based on	Matthew 7:29; Luke 9:35; 24:25–27, 44–48; John 3:2; 14:25,26
Theme	Seminary Training/Ministry
Written	25 September 1990
Suggested tune	SWEENEY by Gayle Sarber

This hymn was written at the invitation of Christian Theological Seminary, Indianapolis, Indiana, on the subject of seminary training, for a lecture, workshop, and hymn festival for seminarians, pastors and musicians in October 1990.

I like to imagine seminary students gathered, as were the disciples, around their Lord, forming an inner circle of disciples during their three-year instruction and preparation for their world-changing, life-changing ministry. This tutoring by the Word made flesh was endorsed at Christ's baptism and transfiguration, and sealed at the cross and empty garden tomb.

The connection with Christ, the Word brings the disciple into the closest relationship between divine Teacher and human student, a connection that theological students enjoy millenia later, when the Holy Spirit carries on the teaching ministry of the risen and ascended Lord of the Church.

Christ Goes Before

Christ goes before, and we are called to follow,
and all who follow find the Way, the Truth, the Life.

Where is that Way we near despaired of finding:
the way that comes from God and leads to God,
the realm where God is love and love is King,
a whole new order for a world astray?
Who wants to live where there's no love like this?
Is this the Kingdom we are ready for
and desperate to find?

Christ goes before, and we are called to follow,
and all who follow find the Way, the Truth, the Life.

Where is that Truth we near despaired of knowing:
the truth that comes from God and leads to God,
the power to set us free, the power to change,
that faces Pilate and the cross and wins?
Who wants to live where there's no peace like this?
Is this the Power we are ready for
and desperate to know?

Christ goes before, and we are called to follow,
and all who follow know the Way, the Truth, the Life.

Where is that Life we near despaired of having:
the life that comes from God and leads to God,
the hope of glory only Christ can give,
that shatters death and grief with Easter joy?
Who wants to live where there's no joy like this?
Is this the Glory we are ready for
and desperate to have?

Christ goes before, and we are called to follow,
and all who follow have the Way, the Truth, the Life.

Meter	Irregular
Based on	John 14:6; Matthew 6:13
Theme	Christ/Discipleship
Written	18 January 1987
Suggested tune	RIVERSIDE by Carl Schalk

For some time I had been pondering the implications of the conclusion of the Lord's Prayer, when I wondered if there was not a parallel between the Kingdom, the Power, and the Glory and the Way, the Truth, and the Life. As I explored this possible connection, I thought of the third parallel trio: love, peace, and joy—all promised by him who is the Way, the Truth, and the Life. A request from Ascension Lutheran Church, Riverside, IL, for a text inspired by their 50th anniversary provided me with an opportunity to offer this text. The hymn is meant to begin with a refrain in the manner of "Lift high the cross."

Come at the Summit of This Day

Come at the summit of this day and hour
to God the Word, the source of love and power;
with offerings of self and bread and wine
approach the One who waits, the Host divine.

In solemn joy come join that global throng
who raise their hearts and lives in thankful song,
each one a treasured guest, each called by name,
here by this feast the death of Christ proclaim.

Meter	10.10.10.10.
Based on	Luke 22:8,15; 1 Corinthians 11:26
Theme	Communion Offertory
Written	6 May 1992
Suggested tune	by Paul Manz

To commemorate their 100th anniversary, Christ Lutheran Church of Washington, D.C. requested an offertory hymn to be used during the offertory procession. No Eucharistic offertory hymn can possibly contain the many thoughts that come, or should come, into the minds of the communicants. This one attempts to prompt a chain of references that bring the coming communion into focus, to be further expanded by the hymns and canticles surrounding this "summit experience" of the day.

Come, Lord Jesus, to This Place

Come, Lord Jesus, to this place,
Cheer it, fill it, with your grace;
Guest and friend, none more desired,
Bless the vows by you inspired.

Witness of this moment rare,
Free from sorrow, free from care;
For the years that lie ahead:
Promised joy and promised bread.

Seal the love that makes them one,
Love, their never-setting sun,
Love enough to face all fears,
Love enough to dry all tears.

As you love the Church, your Bride,
In such love may they abide;
As your Bride is bound to you,
Keep them faithful, Lord, and true.

Meter	7.7.7.7.
Based on	John 2:1–11; Ephesians 5:22–32
Theme	Wedding
Written	27 June 1968
Suggested tune	SONG 13 by Orlando Gibbons

This text was prompted by the forthcoming marriage of our first child, Susan, to Henry Raedeke, Jr. on August 11, 1968, in St. Louis. It was sung by the congregation at St. Lucas Lutheran Church to *SONG 13* by Gibbons. It was later set to a new tune by Donald Busarow and published as a vocal solo.

See notes on marriage at "This Love, O Christ," most of which apply to this text as well.

Come, Rest a While

Come, rest a while,
the journey's hard,
take time to pause and pray.
Stay close to Me,
converse with Me,
together end the day.

Come, follow Me,
I know the way,
I've walked this road before.
Tomorrow rise,
refreshed, inspired,
to feed the crowds onshore.

Remember Me
and Who I am,
the words of life I said,
My empty tomb,
our walk, our talk,
My breaking of the bread.

Count on the rest
that never ends,
as sure as I'm alive;
Our Father's gift
is yours to claim—
we'll hug when you arrive!

Meter	4.4.6.4.4.6.
Based on	Mark 6:30ff; Matthew 11:28–30; Luke 24:13–35
	Hebrews 4:9,10
Themes	Discipleship/Worship/Rest
Written	31 August 1998

Propmted by Shirley Lightner Paxton's favorite biblical stories and her deep-awareness of the awe, mystery, and beauty of corporate worship, this tribute to her on the occasion of her 65th birthday. This text focuses on the implications of the commandment to keep the Sabbath Day holy and the application to the observance of Sunday as a weekly remebrance of Easter. The hymn deals with the subject of rest in the life and future of God's children as experienced by the followers of Jesus before and after His atonement, resurrection, and ascension.

Count Your Blessings, O My Soul

Count your blessings, O my soul,
For each one God's name extol,
See them all with Adam's eyes,
Every one a fresh surprise;
Splendors, glories everywhere,
Majesty beyond compare,
One and all his might declare.

Praise him, sky and sea and land,
Creatures exquisite and grand,
Who but God has power to spare,
Power to feed and love to care?
Everything he makes he keeps,
What he sows, he duly reaps,
What he watches, safely sleeps.

Time-bound creatures, praise the One
From whose hand the sun was spun;
Marvel that the Lord of earth
Chose to have a human birth,
In our time to live and die,
Thus our time to glorify,
Timeless now enthroned on high.

Wait no longer, heart and tongue,
Let the grateful song be sung;
Break into spontaneous praise
With the glee of holidays;
Start with nature's overture,
Add a chorus mightier,
Let the cosmic anthem soar!

Meter	7.7.7.7.7.7.7.7.
Based on	Psalm 104
Theme	Praise/Thanksgiving
Written	29 April 1986
Suggested tune	HERR, DICH LOB´ DIE SEELE MEIN

This is another of the Becker Psalter texts, a paraphrase based on Psalm 104 and presented for the first time at Grace Lutheran Church, River Forest, Illinois, on May 18, 1986. Additional notes on the series may be found at “Before Your Awesome Majesty.”

Creator, God, Eternal Source of All

Creator, God, eternal Source of all:
what all-consuming vision made You say,
"Let there be light!" And everything began,
        and it was good!

Then by a Word a dwelling place was made,
a fertile planet, pulsing, full of life,
crowned by two perfect beings, living souls,
        and it was good!

Your heart was broken when the world You loved
did not return Your love, but chose to die
apart from You—the vision lost to pride—
        But You were good.

You made the vision possible again,
You planned a new creation by that Word,
a second Adam, starting a new race
        forever good.

That vision saves us at the brink of death;
where Christ alive prepares a glorious home
for all who heed the Spirit's call to live
        where all is good.

Keep that bright vision daily in our lives
to draw Your loved creation to that place
where all can walk with you in Paradise,
        and all is good.

Meter	10. 10. 10. 4.
Based on	Genesis 1:3; 3:15; Isaiah 53, 54, 55; Proverbs 29:18; John 3:14–16; 2 Peter 3:4–13; Revelation 21:1; etc.
Theme	Promise/Vision/Purpose
Written	14 February 1997
Suggested tune	STARS by Carl Schalk

Redeemer Lutheran Church in Austin, Texas, embarking on a major building expansion program under the theme "Expand the Vision, Building Hope," requested a hymn expressing the theme. The vision prompting the resulting hymn is that which motivated the creation of the world and the human race, rejected by Adam and Eve, but retrieved and reinstated with the promise of the Messiah immediately after the Fall. That vision comprises the message of the prophets and apostles, and became the message of hope Christ commissioned His Church to proclaim. This Good News is meant to gather the lost sheep into the fold of the Good Shepherd, the Second Adam's offspring, whom Christ makes the emissaries of the vision of a new heaven and a new earth of peace, love, and joy without end, where the relationship between the Creator and the creature is never broken. Without this vision, the world will perish. But God wants no one to perish, but to enjoy the heaven and earth for which we have been created and redeemed.

Creator, Keeper, Caring Lord

Creator, Keeper, caring Lord
Of all You deign to make,
Direct us toward Your goal for us
With every breath we take:
In You we live, in You we move—
The ones You chose to love.

To faith and hope and love, dear God,
Add one more gift of grace:
Sound health of body, soul, and mind—
Your Spirit's dwelling place;
And should You let the body fail,
Keep mind and spirit well.

In wisdom let us guard the gift
Of wholeness You supply.
In mercy turn our ears and hands,
Like You, toward all who cry
We know who heals our hurts and ills,
We know Your gracious will.

Though far from perfect, we revere
Your earthly masterpiece:
The body Jesus shared and gave
To banish all disease,
That all who rise with Him from death
May know the bliss of health.

Meter	8.6.8.6.8.6.
Based on	Matthew 4:23; 25:31 ff.; Luke 9:1, 2 and parallels
Theme	Wholeness/Health and Healing/Concern/Care
Written	2 August 1986
Suggested tune	BROTHER JAMES' AIR

To fill a need for a hymn for health and healing to be sung by congregations, institutions of care, care-takers and care-givers, this hymn was commissioned by the Missouri District Pastors and Teachers' Conference of The Lutheran Church—Missouri Synod held in October 1986. It holds up Christ as the example, motivator, and enabler of the healing ministry of the church as it embraces the whole person and offers the gift of wholeness and the promise of total and perfect wholeness in the life to come.

Because of its familiarity and associations, *BROTHER JAMES' AIR* was selected for the introduction of the hymn. The allusions to the Good Shepherd echoed in the tune support the image of the caring Lord to whom this text is addressed.

Eternal Word, Your Church's Heart and Head

Eternal Word, Your Church's Heart and Head,
Creative Word, by whom all things were made,
True Word, by which our lives are led and fed:
Alleluia!

What love that reaches out to make us friends!
In You we find the love that never ends,
And learn to care like Good Samaritans:
Alleluia!

Like Mary lauding You there in her womb,
And Mary running from Your empty tomb,
We claim You came to end sin's curse and doom:
Alleluia!

Hold all Your precious children close to You,
That every test of faith may find us true,
Your little "Christs" in all we say and do:
Alleluia!

We know the peace You died and rose to bring;
Forgiven to forgive, to You we cling,
Together now to live in peace and sing:
Alleluia!

Meter	10.10.10.4.
Based on	John 1:1–4,14; 8:31; Colossians 3:12–17 and parallels
Theme	Church/Mission
Written	20 April 1995
Suggested tune:	ENGELBERG

A hymn was requested for the 1995 Convention of The Lutheran Church—Missouri Synod in St. Louis, Missouri, on the Convention theme, "Sent Forth by God's Blessing," and reflecting the Fivefold Vision Statement based on Dr. Al Barry's five points on the witness of the Church: "Be in the Word," "Care for One Another," "Tell the Good News," "Remain Faithful" and "Live in Peace." The hymn attempts to express how the Church responds to God's love in Jesus Christ through the gift and power of God's Holy Spirit.

The tune *ENGELBERG* by Charles Villiers Stanford (1852–1924) was chosen as a melody expressing the mood and pace of the words. The stately melody has been gaining recognition and popularity in recent decades, also in Lutheran hymnals in texts other than "For All the Saints," for which it was originally composed in 1904 in *Hymns Ancient and Modern.*

Ever Since the Savior Came

Ever since the Savior came
nothing is the same.
One day of all the days of earth,
one solitary promised Birth,
one Name, and gloom is turned to mirth:
nothing is the same.

Ever since the Savior came
nothing is the same.
For shepherds callused, tired, and bored,
whose spirits with the angels' soared,
who ran to worship Christ the Lord,
nothing was the same.

Ever since the Savior came
nothing is the same.
For learned sages, worldly-wise,
who searched for meaning in the skies,
and saw the Morning Star arise,
nothing was the same.

Ever since the Savior came
nothing is the same.
God's just demands are satisfied,
and death destroyed by One who died,
and Christmas ends in Eastertide:
nothing is the same.

Ever since we followed You
everything is new:
a love we never knew before,
a joy we never felt before,
a peace we never found before,
everything is new!
everything is new!

Meter	Refrain and 8.8.8.5.
Based on	Prayer of the Day for Christmas, 2 Corinthians 5:16–17
Theme	Christmas Day/Christ the Light /Epiphany
Written	28 September 1991
Tune	PILGRIM GEORGE by Paul Manz

The Lutheran School of Theology at Chicago requested a hymn based on the Prayer of the Day for Christmas, focusing on Christ the Light of the world and the light by which we walk our pilgrim path. The hymn was to be sung for the first time at the Advent/Christmas Vespers, on December 8, 1991.

Faced with the same question facing the writer of contemporary Christmas hymns or songs, namely, "What can be written that has not been treated in countless songs and poems on the Nativity of our Lord?" I was moved by the thought that the Advent of Christ constitutes the center of history and the turning point of human destiny. Nothing in human experience can ever be the same once Christ enters the picture and becomes a part of life's equation. St. Paul's statement in 2 Corinthians 5:17, that the person who is in Christ is a new creation, for whom all things are thereafter new. Everything is seen in a new light when viewed under the light Christ brings into the world. John implies the same radical change in history and in people when Christ comes into the heart of those who accept him as the Word of life (John 1:4,9,12) The hymn is about the change that takes place in people and in the world when their lives reflect the light of Christ. God, however, does not change. His love, grace, and mercy are unchanging. The Light does not change, but it changes forever those in whom it shines.

Far From the Time When We Were Few

Far from the time when we were few
And left our homes abroad,
We stand today in blessing new
And rich before our God.

The seas were crossed, a home was found
Beside bright freedom's streams;
Your Word was planted, blessed, and crowned
Beyond our fathers' dreams.

Great miracles of service fill
Our memory so brief:
The wondrous working of a will
That conquers disbelief.

We stand before the world a proof
Of what God's grace can do
With children selfish and aloof
On whom the Spirit blew.

How much of this have we deserved?
How did we grasp the Truth?
How is the Good News still preserved
For us and for our youth?

New songs be made and work be done
In penitence and praise
For our amazing God, whose Son
Keeps smiling on our days.

Meter	8.6.8.6.
Based on	Deuteronomy 32:7 and parallels
Theme	Commemoration/Church Anniversary
Written	23 March 1972
Suggested tune	PLYMOUTH ROCK by William Rowan

In 1972, The Lutheran Church—Missouri Synod was celebrating its 125th anniversary. This text was requested and used in the commemoration of that event.

Gather Your Children, Dear Savior, in Peace

Gather your children, dear Savior, in peace.
And draw us to you with your passionate pleas;
Still seek us and call us to come and be blessed,
To find in your arms, Lord, safety, comfort, and rest.

Knowing you, loving you, naming you Lord,
We cluster around you and grow by your Word,
One day to remember these moments so rare,
Of caring and closeness, just because you are there.

Love be our banner, forgiveness our theme,
Compassion our nature, your vision our dream;
Who knows what the Spirit of God yet can do,
What joy may be tasted, or what promise come true?

Host at our table in our house and yours,
Here bind us together with love that endures;
Like parents, like children, let this be our fame:
That, blest, we bless many, to the praise of your name.

Meter	10.11.11.12.
Based on	Ephesians 6:1–3
Theme	Family/Mother's Day/Father's Day
Written	23 March 1985
Suggested tune	SLANE

Apart from a commission from the First Congregational Church, Webster Groves, Missouri, for a hymn for Mother's Day, I have long felt the need for a more comprehensive hymn for Christian families that would be useful not only for Mother's Day but for other occasions as well. The importance of the family is being acknowledged more in the church and in society as it is fractured and weakened to the loss of future generations. Here was an opportunity to draw a parallel between the family of God and Christian families. *SLANE* was chosen for its familiarity and appropriateness and for its tenderness. In using this tune, the meter of this version should be noted, as other versions shorten one or more lines.

Gaze in Amazement

Gaze in amazement how God's hand
Pours blessings on this place!
From small beginnings until now,
What glory and what grace!
In Word and Water, Bread and Wine
We share a heritage divine:
Make known such wondrous works!

Hear in amazement God's own voice
Of welcome, love, and care,
He runs to greet us coming home
With tears, "My child! My heir!"
The love that did not spare His Son
Provides the bond that makes us one:
Make known that wondrous name!

Hold in amazement all the gifts
That from the Spirit flowed:
Forgiveness, freedom, peace, and life,
Here promised, here bestowed.
All that we have is ours to share
With saints and sinners everywhere:
Make known those glorious deeds!

Sing in amazement: God is here!
Join heart and voice in praise!
Cheer up a dying, crying world
With hope for all its days!
What David once rejoiced to do,
What David's greater Son did, too —
Make known our gracious God!

Meter	8.6.8.6.8.8.6.
Based on	1 Chronicles 16:8, 9 (7–36), and parallels
Theme	Mission/Commemoration/Anniversary
Written	2 February 1995
Suggested tune	by Charles Ore

To commemorate the 110th anniversary of Trinity Lutheran Church, Cedar Rapids, Iowa, this text was inspired by the Psalm of David celebrating the return of the Ark of the Covenant, a festive song echoed in Psalms 96, 105, 106, and others. The theme is identical to the commission and mission of the New Testament Church.

The hymn was introduced to a tune to be composed by Charles Ore at a hymn festival on April 30, 1995 in Cedar Rapids, Iowa.

Gift of Joy

Gift of Joy—for a people steeped in restless gloom,
Gift of God—would it ever come?
Suddenly, in the night, bursting through the skies,
See the promised Dawn arise!

Gift of Peace—for a people paralyzed with fear,
Gift of God—how would it appear?
Suddenly, in the night, bursting through the skies,
See the promised Dawn arise!

Gift of Love, Gift of Grace, Gift of Hope and Life
For a people tired of strife.
Suddenly, in the night, bursting through the skies,
See the promised Dawn arise!

Meter	Irregular
Based on	Luke 1:78, 79
Theme	Advent/Christmas
Written	15 July 1977
Suggested tune	Anthem by Albert Rykken Johnson

This Advent/Christmas text was composed to fit an anthem by Albert Rykken Johnson, of Brainerd, Minnesota, set to a text originally entitled, "In a far lonely manger," which determined the special meter of this alternate text.

Give Glory, All Creation

Give glory, all creation,
Great seas and stars and blazing sun,
All join in adoration
Before the only holy One!
The God eternal name Him,
The One who rules alone;
The King of kings acclaim Him
Upon a heavenly throne!
No light exists without Him,
No life but by his Word,
So gather, all, about Him,
And own Him our God, our Lord!
And own Him our God, our Lord!

No realm is there so spacious,
No rule demanding greater might;
No one is there so gracious,
Yet just and holy, good and right;
Beyond all comprehension,
Beyond the last surprise,
Comes Love's divine invention:
This God for creatures dies!
No wonder angels praise Him
And live in constant awe,
Should not all creatures raise Him
An endless Alleluia!
An endless Alleluia!

Meter	7.8.7.8.7.6.7.6.7.6.7.7.7.
Based on	Psalm 103
Theme	Adoration/Praise
Written	25 August 1985
Suggested tune	NUN LOB, MEIN SEEL, DEN HERREN

This paraphrase of Psalm 103 was requested for the Becker Psalter series and was presented for the first time at Grace Lutheran Church, River Forest, Illinois, September 29, 1985. For additional commentary on the series, see note on "Before Your Awesome Majesty."

Giver of Every Perfect Gift

Giver of every perfect gift,
You shape my life from womb to grave.
Reveal Your good and gracious will
that plants me in this time and place.
Display the gifts
assigned to me,
make them a witness to Your name.

You planned and know the gifts I have;
Creator, God, from You they come,
unique and special, from Your heart,
intended for a chosen role.
Thrill me to find
and recognize
the talents only You can give.

Revealing Word, sent Son of God,
Proclaimer of the Kingdom's dawn,
it is for You, because of You,
that every talent is bestowed.
You have a plan
for me to fill,
a purpose for this life of mine.

Enabling Spirit, Gift of gifts,
empower me, stir up my faith,
make me an instrument of grace,
of mercy, blessing, peace, and joy.
Let me not miss
another day
in seeing what Your gifts can do.

Meter	8.8.8.8.4.4.8.
Based on	Matthew 25:14–23,29; 28:19,20; Mark 13:10; 1 Corinthians 12:4ff; 1 Timothy 4:14; 2 Timothy 1:6
Theme	Stewardship of Talents/The Kingdom of God
Written	1 November 1997
Suggested tune	Anthem by K. Lee Scott

Prompted by the forthcoming installation of Barry Bobb as Vice-President of Concordia Publishing House, the Parable of the Talents and their application to the Great Commission seemed an appropriate theme for an installation hymn which dealt with the subject of stewardship of God's gifts in the service of the Kingdom.

Knowing many Christians, both laymen and church workers, the use of whose God given talents have advanced the Kingdom of God, I am convinced that many influences are untapped in most followers of Christ. Therefore, a hymn of this kind, in the first person, can be sung honestly by any worshipper commissioned to proclaim the Gospel to the whole world.

Glorious Jerusalem

Glorious Jerusalem
and Zion her gem,
Home of beauty, joy, and peace,
and heavenly grace:
Beacon beckoning to all,
mindful child and prodigal,
pilgrims on a holiday,
chanting psalms along the way:
Alleluia! Alleluia!
Praise the Lord, Jerusalem,
Praise your God, O Zion!

Glorious Jerusalem
and Zion her gem,
Home of beauty, joy, and peace,
and heavenly grace:
There the Savior long foretold,
there the Savior twelve years old,
there the Savior crucified,
there the Savior glorified:
Alleluia! Alleluia!
Praise the Lord, Jerusalem,
Praise your God, O Zion!

Glorious Jerusalem
and Zion her gem,
Home of beauty, joy, and peace,
and heavenly grace:
That same glory fills this place
with our God's astounding grace,
lives and hopes and peace restored
by the sacraments and Word:
Alleluia! Alleluia!
Praise the Lord, Jerusalem,
Praise your God, O Zion!

Glorious Jerusalem
and Zion her gem,
Home of beauty, joy, and love,
come down from above:
There at last the perfect place,
there one great harmonious race,
like her Bridegroom glorified,
sings the Church, His glowing Bride:
Alleluia! Alleluia!
Praise the Lord, Jerusalem,
Praise your God, O Zion!

Meter	12(7.5).12(7.5).7.7.7.7.8.7.6.
Based on	Psalm 147:13–20; Revelation 21:2,10, et al.
Theme	The Church/Worship/Praise
Written	12 June 1989

Jerusalem Evangelical Lutheran Church, Schwenksville, Pennsylvania, marked its 150th anniversary in 1985, grateful for a blessed and sustained history. A hymn was requested for a "Celebration of the Church" on Reformation Sunday, October 29, 1989, when the congregation would be celebrating the 15th anniversary of their pipe organ. The refrain of the hymn text is Psalm 147:12. The unusual name of the church inspired the content of the hymn.

The biblical references to Jerusalem are rich in meaning and symbolism. The holy city continues to be central in the memory of Jews and Christians to the present day. Physically, the city, and especially its crowning jewel, the Temple, glowed in the sun and excited the hearts of those who made the pilgrimage to Jerusalem, and who sang the Psalms of Ascent on the way up to Mount Zion. Jerusalem figured importantly in the life of our Lord from his birth to his ascension. The images climax in the prophecy of the New Jerusalem, the city built by God, coming down from the heavens like a Bride adorned for her Bridegroom.

The poetic form chosen for this text suggests metrically the beginning of each person's pilgrimage on a broad lower elevation, then proceeding in a steady ascent until the refrain in its shortening lines depicts one's arrival at the summit—the Temple.

Go, My Children, with My Blessing

Go, my children, with my blessing, never alone;
Waking, sleeping, I am with you, you are my own;
In my love's baptismal river
I have made you mine forever,
Go, my children, with my blessing, you are my own.

Go my children sins forgiven, at peace and pure,
Here you learned how much I love you, what I can cure;
Here you heard my dear Son's story,
Here you touched him, saw his glory,
Go, my children, sins forgiven, at peace and pure.

Go, my children, fed and mourished, closer to me;
Grow in love and love by serving, joyful and free.
Here my Spirit's power filled you,
Here his tender comfort stilled you;
Go, my children, fed and nourished, joyful and free.

I the Lord will bless and keep you, and give you peace,
I the Lord will smile upon you, and give you peace;
I the Lord will be your Father,
Savior, Comforter, and Brother:
Go, my children, I will keep you, and give you peace.

Meter	8.4.8.4.8.8.8.4.
Based on	Numbers 6:22–27
Theme	Dismissal/Close of Worship/Benediction/Baptism/Peace
Written	26 July 1983
Suggested tune	AR HYD Y NOS

Concordia Publishing House was looking for a text that would make the charming and popular Welsh tune, *AR HYD Y NOS,* available for daytime use, broadening its usage beyond its traditional association with an evening text. To me the soft and contemplative melody suggested a setting of the benediction as a hymn of dismissal. To set it apart from other versifications of the benediction, I placed the words of the hymn into the mouth of the blessing triune God dismissing the congregation after worship while drawing together a review of the events that transpired during the service. Quite unconsciously, this hymn became the counterpart of "Now the silence," which previews what is about to take place in the worship service. This hymn, either in its entirety or by the selection of certain stanzas, is suitable for close of worship, post-baptism and post-communion, benediction, and other occasions.

Concordia published this text as an alternative to "God who made the earth and heaven."

Go, My Children, with My Blessing
(Wedding Stanza)

In this union I have joined you husband and wife,
Now, my children, live together as heirs of life:
Each the other's gladness sharing,
Each the other's burdens bearing,
Now, my children, live together as heirs of life.

Meter	8.4.8.4.8.8.8.4.
Based on	1 Peter 3:7
Theme	Marriage
Written	29 December 1989
Suggested tune	AR HYD Y NOS

Pastor Harold M. Rau, then of Dexter, Missouri, suggested a stanza appropriate for weddings that could be inserted into the hymn or substituted for one of the stanzas in the hymn. The "wedding stanza" here published was composed with the suggestion that it could be substituted for stanza two.

God Beyond All Worlds and Time

God beyond all worlds and time,
God no human mind can grasp:
Who You are and Your intentions
Your Incarnate Word revealed.
What our founders found, they deeded
Their prized Gift to us.
Please, please,
With Your fullness fill our lives,
God beyond all worlds and time!

God of perfect, boundless love,
Unexpected, undeserved,
Freely offering to sinners
What was earned upon a Cross.
Lacking love all life is empty,
Selfish, fruitless, vain.
Please, please,
With Your fullness fill our lives,
God of perfect, boundless love!

God of perfect, lasting joy,
Joy announced in Bethlehem,
Joy fulfilled for all adopted,
Happy in the Shepherd's arms.
Lacking joy all life is tragic,
Dreary, dismal, bleak.
Please, please,
With Your fullness fill our lives,
God of perfect, lasting joy!

God of perfect, endless peace,
Give what only You can give:
Peace, the kind that rules in heaven,
From the Spirit sent by Christ.
Lacking peace all life is futile,
Troubled, hopeless, doomed.
Please, please,
With Your fullness fill our lives,
God of perfect, endless peace!

Meter	7.7.8.7.8.5.2.7.7.
Based on	John 1:16; 15:11; 16:24; Galatians 5:22; Ephesians 1:23; 3:19; 1 Thessalonians 5:23,24; and parallels
Theme	Fullness of love, joy, and peace/Church Anniversary
Written	29 June 1998
Tune	GLORIA DEI by Carl Schalk

This hymn was requested by Andrew P. Tecson, a member of Gloria Dei Lutheran Church, Downers Grove, Illinois, for its 50th anniversary in 1998. The suggested theme was spiritual fullness and wholeness, which God wants His children to have, to enjoy, and to employ in the spreading of the Gospel of Christ.

In examining numerous passages of Scripture revealing God's desire to have a rich measure of grace and faith fill the lives of His children, the first three fruits of the Spirit mentioned in Galatians 5:22—love, joy, and peace—seemed to summarize the essential gifts of grace and faith: the love of God who is Love, who gives the world His only Son out of love for doomed humanity, whose birth brings joy to the world, and whose atonement bestows the peace that passes all understanding. There seems to be a parallel between these three fruits of the Spirit and the first three petitions of the Lord's Prayer.

God First Made a Fruitful Garden

God first made a fruitful garden,
sowed with life a barren field,
knew what peace and joy and beauty
that blest living seed would yield.
Oh, if only every soul would be such soil.

That same God prepared another
Seed with power to sprout and grow,
Seed of Abraham and Mary,
Seed from which all blessings flow,
freely scattered
over all this desert globe.

Jesus came, the Word from heaven,
growing from that special Seed,
Bread of life to feed the hungry,
satisfying every need.
Christ the promised
Seed we see and Word we hear

Word eternal, word of splendor,
word of judgment word of grace,
word of wisdom, word of power,
word of love and joy and peace,
word of mercy, (word of pardon),
sow through us your words of life.

Meter	8.7.8.7.7.7.
Based on	Matthew 13:3–43 and parallels, Genesis 3:15, Galatians 3:16; John 6:51
Theme	Ministry/The Word
Written	1 February 1991
Suggested tunes	GUIDE ME CWM RHONDDA

To commemorate the retirement from the ministry of their pastor, Walter M. Schoedel, Concordia Lutheran Church, Kirkwood, Missouri, commissioned a hymn on the subject of the ministry of the word, befitting their pastor's dedication to proclaiming the Gospel throughout his forty-one year pastoral service, a large portion of it spent at Concordia.

The hymn expands upon and applies our Lord's Parable of the Seed and the Sower, with references to the prophecies of the Seed which Christ identifies with the Word, Himself and the saving Gospel.

The hymn is written to fit either *GUIDE ME* or *CWM RHONDDA*, both of which are used for one of Pastor Schoedel's favorite hymns, "Guide Me, O Thou Great Jehovah." If the latter tune is used, the last two lines should be repeated.

This text contains the first instance of the appropriation of a stanza written for another hymn, the fourth (last) stanza of "Christ, around your word assembled," a hymn with a closely related theme.

God Has a Plan for All

God has a plan for all
born children of the night,
and calls the victims of the Fall
to live in light,
where love and grace
their fears replace
and fill their hearts with pure delight.

God has a plan for us
new children of the light,
delivered from our ominous
and hopeless plight,
to know the peace
of Christ's release,
and how His death sets all things right.

God has a plan for each
to play an honored role,
with Christ to teach us how to reach
God's lofty goal.
Reborn, and one
with God's own Son,
we grow in heart and mind and soul.

Ascended Lord, we ask
and wonder at the grace
that calls us to this noble task,
this time, this place?!
What love You show,
what gifts bestow
on those You seek and find and bless!

Meter	6.6.8.4.8.8. or 6.6.8.4.4.4.8.
Based on	Ephesians 4:12 (7–16), 1 Peter 2:9
Theme	Talents/Mission/Service
Written	22 February 1991
Suggested tunes	DARWALL'S 148th
	LOVE UNKNOWN

In its 15th year of ministry to the church and community, the Lutheran High School of Indianapolis, Indiana dedicated its new building on April 28, 1991. The theme for the occasion, "Equipping Saints for Service" draws on numerous passages referring to our participation in the proclamation of Christ's Kingdom and the growth of his people toward the stature of the Church's Head. One is reminded of the high calling to be a partner with God, Creator, Redeemer and Sanctifier, in the fulfilling of the Trinity's universal plan.

The meter for the text was chosen to fit one of my favorite tunes, *LOVE UNKNOWN*. The mood of the text would suggest an equal preference for *DARWALL'S 148th* .

God of the Sparrow

God of the sparrow
God of the whale
God of the swirling stars
How does the creature say Awe
How does the creature say Praise

God of the earthquake
God of the storm
God of the trumpet blast
How does the creature cry Woe
How does the creature cry Save

God of the rainbow
God of the cross
God of the empty grave
How does the creature say Grace
How does the creature say Thanks

God of the hungry
God of the sick
God of the prodigal (wayward child)
How does the creature say Care
How does the creature say Life

God of the neighbor
God of the foe
God of the pruning hook (olive branch)
How does the creature say Love
How does the creature say Peace

God of the ages
God near at hand
God of the loving heart
How do your children say Joy
How do your children say Home

Meter	5.4.6.7.7.
Based on	1 John 4:7–12; 1 Thessalonians 5:18; Psalm 136
Theme	Gratitude/Service/Christian life
Written	27 October 1983
Suggested tunes	ROEDER by Carl Schalk

Having been fascinated for more than 40 years in the ministry by the proper and effective motivation for Christian service, a request from Concordia Lutheran Church of Kirkwood, Missouri, provided an opportunity to compose a hymn text that would provoke answers from the users of the hymn as to why and how God's creatures (and children) are to serve him. The Law of God demands perfect love from every creature; the love of God and the Gospel coax a willing response of love as an expression of gratitude. "We love because he first loved us." God's adopted family responds both as creatures and as children, thus fulfilling the expectations of the Law with the fruits of the Spirit, and in doing so "saying" with actions something of significance to God and the world.

Concordia congregation introduced this hymn during its celebration of its 110th anniversary with a tune composed by organist and choir director David Christian. Another setting has been made by Carl Schalk, also fitting the mood of the text. Alternate readings are provided in the fourth and fifth stanzas to accommodate the musical accents, with my personal preference for the original wording.

God the Father of Us All

God the Father of us all,
caring, strong, and merciful,
pure, unselfish, patient, good,
model for all personhood:
make all fathers more like you
in all they do.

Christ, the Church's loving mate,
spouse for all to imitate,
like the bridegroom who would give
his life that his wife might live:
so, too, keep all husbands true
in all they do.

Holy Spirit, you can bless
all our homes with happiness,
when our fathers join their wives,
to one aim devote their lives,
and in all regard God's Son
their paragon.

Someone's children we must be,
we, your noblest progeny,
every reborn child an heir
of the kingdom you prepare.
Until then may all we do
reflect on you.

Meter	7.7.7.7.7.4.
Based on	2 Corinthians 6:18; Isaiah 63:16; Matthew 5:14a,16; Ephesians 5:25
Theme	Fathers/Husbands/Fatherhood of God
Written	1 July 1992

The subject chosen for this hymn is one of growing concern in American society in recent years: the absence or abdication of male role models in the home and community. Fatherhood especially has gained a bad reputation, to the extent that the poor image of many fathers has diminished the image of God the Father. Likewise, unfaithful and abusive husbands (men) have corrupted the image of a model spouse in Christ's relationship to his Bride, the Church. In studying the subject of God's Fatherhood in the Scriptures, one is overwhelmed by the pervasiveness of this name, image, and relationship. It is the most convincing way God has (and has deliberately chosen) to describe the unique relationship between the Creator and the human progeny of that Creator established in our baptismal adoption. God as Father in the Trinity must be retained and accorded the name He has chosen to reveal to His creatures, and the specific place of the Son in the Trinity is the best validation of our atonement. Furthermore, the only One who has been from eternity gave us the model Prayer, in which we address God as Father and count on that relationship to open the door to the throne of God.

My conviction is that we ought rather teach and encourage human fathers to model their lives and behavior on God the Father, rather than try to remake God in the image of his fallen creatures. That kind of fatherhood is embodied in the command: "Be merciful, as your Father in heaven is merciful."

God, Who Built This Wondrous Planet

God, who built this wondrous planet
And all worlds beyond these bounds,
Crown your work and ours with blessing,
Meet us here on hallowed ground.
With your glory fill this temple,
Here be sought and here be found.

Christ, you build a holy structure
That, like you, outlasts the earth;
Chosen, like yourself, you make us
Living stones of priceless worth;
Home, where prodigals returning,
Celebrate with holy mirth.

Spirit, make your church a beacon
Beaming hope where hoping wanes,
Daily in these stones creating
Life where death no longer reigns,
And in grateful hearts forgiven
Spark the love the world but feigns.

Living Father, living children,
Living servants, living Lord;
Living Savior, living Body,
Living members, living Word;
Living Spirit, living temple:
We adoring, you adored!

Meter	8.7.8.7.8.7.
Based on	1 Peter 2:4–10
Theme	The Church/Sanctuary/Worship/Dedication of a Church
Written	1 March 1986
Suggested tunes	REAVIS BARRACKS by Thomas Leeseberg-Lange
	ASCENDED TRIUMPH by Henry V. Gerike

Peter compares the building of the Body of Christ, the Church, to the structure of a temple. Christ and St. Paul also use the same metaphor. For the dedication of its new church building, Holy Trinity Church, located at Reavis Barracks Road in suburban St. Louis, commissioned a hymn for the occasion to be based on the 1 Peter text. Other related allusions to the church were incorporated into the text.

To be sure that the congregation could sing the hymn without difficulty, it was written with the tune *ASCENDED TRIUMPH* by Henry V. Gerike in mind, hence the same meter and rhyme scheme as in "Up through endless ranks of angels." However, when the text was completed, the organist, Thomas Leeseberg-Lange prepared an original tune for the hymn, *REAVIS BARRACKS.* The melody was picked up enthusiastically by the celebrating congregation at its dedication service May 18, 1986.

God, You Made This World a Garden

God, you made this world a garden,
every harvest bearing seed.
Loving God, today as ever
You anticipate our need;
You are ready with Your answer
long before we plead.

Take us through that other garden,
tragic, dark Gethsemane,
where our Savior faced our future,
set to win our amnesty:
Seed of woman, Seed of promise
from a barren tree.

Now a universal garden,
seeded with your living Word,
grows with peace and love and beauty,
songs of freedom there are heard;
by Your mercy, by Your Spirit,
thankful hearts are stirred.

In this corner of Your garden
planted by a faithful few,
we have thrived by their endeavor;
as You blessed them, bless us too.
Find us, as you walk among us,
bearing fruit for You.

Meter	8.7.8.7.8.5.
Based on	Genesis 1:29–31; Matthew 16:36ff.; 1 Peter 2:24, etc.
Theme	The Church
Written	6 September 1989
Suggested tune	HAMPTON AVENUE by Kim Kolander

Gethsemane Lutheran Church (ELCA) of St. Louis, Missouri, celebrating its 95th anniversary in 1989, commissioned a hymn text to mark the ongoing grace and blessing of God as members of the Communion of Saints in the Chippewa-Hampton area of St. Louis. The congregation was established by Swedish Lutheran immigrants in the late 19th century. The theme was inspired by the name of the church—Gethsemane—which suggested the picture of a garden, and that in turn reminded me of the Garden of Eden. The expulsion of our first parents from that perfect garden necessitated the Garden of Gethsemane. The cosmic struggle that took place there led to the creation of the Garden of the Church, the Kingdom of God. The seed-bearing plants reflect the providential nature of God's creation, always providing seed for the next generation from the past generation's harvest. Similarly, with the Seed of the Word (written and incarnate), our spiritual life is generated and regenerated, and each harvest of souls bears seed for the next one.

Numerous other allusions recall the promise of the Seed of a Woman, a promise made in Eden in anticipation of our need of a Savior. Three images occur: in Eden, on Calvary, and in the last chapter of Revelation. Other images will occur to the worshipper as the hymn is sung repeatedly by the heirs and ancestors of faith in the local congregation's corner of God's holy Garden.

Good Shepherd, God's Beloved Son

Good Shepherd, God's beloved Son,
From heaven's realms You came;
Like sheep You saw us scattered here,
You called us all by name;
And then, to prove Your boundless love,
Would die for one lost lamb!

We find ourselves among the flock
You loved and sought and called.
Delivered from the stalking beast,
From fear and death's strong hold,
Your ewes and rams and tender lambs
Rest safely in Your fold.

Now give us shepherds like Yourself
Whom we can trust as true,
Who know our weakness, share our joy,
Who lead and feed us, too,
Unselfishly, devotedly,
Who speak —and we hear You.

Meter	8.6.8.6.8.6.
Based on	John 10:11–29; Matthew 9:36–38; 17:5 and parallels
Theme	Ministry
Written	24 February 1995
Suggested tune	BROTHER JAMES' AIR

A hymn recognizing the retirement of the first bishop of the Florida/ Bahama Synod of the ELCA, Lavern G. Franzen, in May 1995, was to appreciate his dedicated ministry of the Gospel according to the model set forth by St. Paul in Ephesians 3:14–21. Since the mark of a true pastor (shepherd) is faithfulness to the voice of Christ, the Good Shepherd, and to the precious flock, I chose the picture of Christ in John 10, with his insistence that the sheep hear his voice, as the Father from heaven sealed the ministry of Jesus at the Transfiguration: "This is my beloved Son; listen to Him." Any voice other than Christ's is deceptive and destructive. "It is required of stewards that they be faithful." This is especially true of the "stewards of the mysteries of God," the under-shepherds called to feed the precious flock with the pure Word and Sacraments. How blessed is the flock which has such a pastor!

Heralds of the Cross

You are the stars that stud the spacious skies,
and by your bright reflected light we chart
eternal voyages, and earthbound eyes
of worn, world-weary souls at length take heart
to find their way to beatific rest.
There were you set to occupy the height,
to mark the road to life's most urgent quest,
to shine the brightest in the darkest night.

Though passing clouds may hide and mundane lights
obfuscate your pure gleams and you are spent
in seeming unregarded labor, shine!
and, shining, pierce through these terrestrial nights
until one day your Author will enshrine
your orbits in a glorious firmament.

Meter	Sonnet
Based on	Daniel 12:3
Theme	Ministy/Witness
Written	26 March 1942

While a student at Concordia Seminary, St. Louis, Missouri (1939–45), I was asked to write a pageant for the annual Concordia Day festival, an event which was meant to publicize the seminary to its local supporters, a day of athletic contests and campus tours, highlighted by the evening's pageant. The director of the pageant was our recently called homiletics professor and my mentor in many ways, Dr. Richard Caemmerer. At his encouragement I wrote the historical pageant, ending it with this sonnet dedicated to all ministers of the Gospel, past, present, and future—and by extension to all witnesses to the Gospel, clergy and lay. It was a special thrill to receive Dr. Caemmerer's commendation for the pageant and to have him direct the speech choir in reciting the sonnet at the evening's climax. This took place in the spring of 1942, just prior to our class's departure for a year of vicarage.

Here Is the Living Proof, Good Lord

Here is the living proof, good Lord,
of what our faith can do;
see what our efforts can achieve
when they are blessed by You.

This house we hallowed to Your name,
where swallows make their home,
where those are blessed who meet You here
and pray, "Your kingdom come!"

You, Jesus, are the living proof
that all our debts are paid,
that all we owed and could not pay
on You, God's Lamb, were laid.

You carried every debt we owed
to cross and death and grave,
and so what we could never pay
You graciously forgave.

Make us the living proof, good Lord,
of what Your Word can do,
to show the world the Way, the Truth,
and Life that come from You.

To all whose debts by You are paid
You set forth one more goal:
"Owe no one anything but love"
till all the world is whole.

Great triune God, inhabit us
and fill us with Your grace,
that we who meet You in this house
may one day see Your face!

Meter	CM
Based on	1 Samuel 7:12; Acts 20:28; 1 Peter 1:18, 19
Theme	Mortgage burning
Written	20 April 1987
Suggested tunes	ST. ANNE
	ST. PETER

St. Lucas Lutheran Church, St. Louis, requested a text to a familiar tune on the occasion of its mortgage burning on April 26, 1987. The parallels with our indebtedness to God, and the atonement for all our debts by the blood of Christ were obvious, as well as the injunction to owe no one anything but love (Romans 13:8). The hymn was sung to *ST. ANNE* for its suggested reference to "O God, our help in ages past."

Holy Spirit, Gift of God

(Six Hymns on the Third Article)

Opening stanza:
Holy Spirit, Gift of God,
spread Your grace and peace abroad;
plant the seed of life in all
doomed to death in Adam's fall.

(Insert appropriate stanzas. See below.)

Closing stanza:
Praise the Father, praise the Son,
praise the Spirit, Three Yet One!
Never-ending glory be
to the blessed Trinity!

Hymn stanza insert 1:
Long before I knew Your name,
in my heart You lit Your flame;
by the Water and the Word
my adoption was conferred.

Best Gift God the Father gives,
who receives it dies and lives.
Ask—It will not be refused!
Pray—how is It to be used?

Hymn stanza insert 2:
One is nevermore alone
who is kin to God's dear Son;
all are joined in unity
in God's timeless family.

New in outlook, new in hope,
heightened vision, broadened scope;
in them glows a love divine,
through them Jesus' virtues shine.

Hymn stanza insert 3:
Not by human mind and skill
can we know God's holy will;
only through the Spirit's eyes
we see what is true and wise.

Everything becomes brand-new,
what we want and what we do,
just like being born again,
confident to say "Amen!"

Hymn stanza insert 4:
Melter of the hardened heart,
show all who have grown apart
what it means to be forgiven
and to be an heir of heaven.

Ever since the Spirit came,
we are freed from guilt and shame;
Spirit-led and Spirit-fed,
free to follow Christ our Head.

Hymn stanza insert 5:
Show the love, the cross, the grave—
show all Christ has done to save;
show the resurrected Word;
cry in us: "My God! My Lord!"

Christ who lived for us and died,
by the Spirit was revived;
by that Spirit we shall too
rise from death to life anew.

Hymn stanza insert 6:
From the Spirit comes the breath—
breath that will not end in death,
but revives to breathe the air
of a bliss beyond compare.

What creation could have been,
unstained by the curse of sin,
we shall know in fullest bloom
in our promised perfect home.

Meter	7.7.7.7.
Based on	The Third Article of the Apostles' Creed
Theme	Called by the Spirit
Written	26 August 1990
Suggested tune	SONG 13 by Orlando Gibbons

The Department of Stewardship of The Lutheran Church—Missouri Synod, in preparing a study guide on the Third Article of the Apostles' Creed on the theme "Called by the Spirit," requested a hymn related to each of the six parts of the Article on the Holy Spirit. My response took the form of a six-part hymn with an opening and closing stanza bracketing two stanzas for each part of the Article.

The choice of the tune, *SONG 13* by Orlando Gibbons, was the familiar and readily accessible melody associated with the well-known hymn to the Holy Spirit by Samuel Longfellow, "Holy Spirit, Truth Divine."

How Could I Hurt You So

How could I hurt you so,
whom once I called my friend,
forgetful of my pledge to you,
your gifts misspent!
For you I thirst,
my bones are dry,
and I am as you found me first.

How could you love me so,
whom once you called your friend,
forgetful of my faithlessness
for years on end?
I claim no grace,
but for your cross
restore my joy in your embrace.

Meter	6.6.8.4.4.4.8.
Based on	Matthew 26:75; Psalms 32 and 51
Theme	Penitence/Restoration
Written	23 June 1980
Suggested tune	LOVE UNKNOWN

A spontaneous composition for no special occasion. A song that expressed my thoughts as I reviewed the enormous number of wasted opportunities and regretted denials of my Lord's friendship over six decades. This song was inspired by John Ireland's plaintive tune, LOVE UNKNOWN.

How Meager and Mundane

How meager and mundane
our view of heaven is
before we see God's majesty
or we are his;
So lift your eyes,
my soul, and see
the sapphire throne and realms of bliss!

How futile and morose
our daily life must grow
when all we have is what we grasp
down here below;
so set your heart,
my soul, on things
above where lasting treasures glow!

How aimless and ingrown
our pilgrimage becomes
when in this passing place we build
our lasting homes;
so set your feet,
my soul, upon
the road to yon palatial domes!

Meter	6.6.8.4.4.4.8.
Based on	Luke 12:15–21; John 14:1–4; Romans 8:16–23
Theme	Eternal values/Heaven
Written	27 June 1980
Suggested tune	LOVE UNKNOWN

Life is never the same after a close encounter with death. As a pastor, I witnessed mortality and how individuals dealt with it. And when I myself suffered cardiac arrest, my own values were tested, and my life and career fell into eternal perspective. This text was my observation of the shortsightedness of a life that does nor look to eternity. It is not an escape from reality, but an infrequent acknowledgment that this life is temporal and that it must be lived in the hope that transforms death from a dead end into the launching of the eternal adventure for which we are preparing. I did not know in 1980 that I would undergo three major operations in the next six years and a second cardiac arrest. The extension of life I was graciously granted allowed me to write many of the hymns in this collection. This song was also inspired by *LOVE UNKNOWN*, the John Ireland melody, and was set to that tune's meter.

How Pleasant, Lord, When Christians Live

How pleasant, Lord, when Christians live
in peace and unity,
when in your children your own love
the world can feel and see.

But we confess our wanton ways,
no one is innocent;
who has not sinned, has not forgiven?
Our fellowship is rent.

In shame and near despair we cry,
have mercy, Lord, forgive!
Unworthy all, we claim your grace,
then judge if we should live.

Repair the fabric of your church
which we have torn apart,
the garment of your peace and love,
as living as your heart.

Accusing falsely, wrongly hurt,
we sulk the years away,
suspicious of each other's aims,
we cannot even pray.

The whitening harvest waits and rots,
the sheaves we bring are small;
your judgment clock moves fast to strike,
we slumber through your call.

Bind up the fractures, heal the wounds
that break your heart and ours;
speak your strong reconciling word,
restore our waning powers.

Upon your dear afflicted Bride
come place your healing hand;
renew the love we once avowed
and make us one again.

Meter	CM (8.6.8.6.)
Based on	Psalm 133:1; John 17:20–23; Ephesians 4:1–16
Theme	Church/Unity/Peace/Renew
Written	11 January 1971
Suggested tune	ST. PETER or other CM

On the eve of the split in The Lutheran Church—Missouri Synod, as the storm clouds were gathering, I was moved to write this hymn, echoing Christ's passionate high priestly prayer in John 17, the strong exhortations of St. Paul to the Ephesians (chapter 4) and Psalm 133:1, which my mother used to quote when my brothers and I would quarrel, and the Slovak hymn based on that verse, which I translated as "How lovely and how pleasant". To my knowledge this hymn has not been sung, though its subject matter still applies in a fractured church.

I Have a Father You Would Like

I have a Father you would like
To be your Father, too.
There's no one like Him in the world
To do what He can do.

He understands me when I cry,
and when I'm all alone;
He lets me know He's there nearby
As well as on His throne.

My Father is a King, you see,
The greatest King of all,
And yet when His own Son was born,
He shared a cattle stall.

He came because He cares for me,
And so He loves you, too.
Do you know any other friend
Who'd live and die for you?

Now wouldn't you like to be God's child,
With Jesus as your Friend,
Someone who cares so much for you,
Whose love will never end?

Meter	CM
Based on	Matthew 11:25,26; 21:15; 2 Kings 5:1–4
Theme	Children/Witness/Evangelism
Written	15 September 1981
Suggested tune	Extant or new CM tune

I must have remembered George Shibata, a Japanese-American (Nisei) seminary classmate of mine, who, I learned, had become a Christian as a nine-year-old boy in California, when a Christian playmate invited him to Sunday school. After graduating from the seminary in 1945, Shibata spent most of his ministry serving the Japanese people, and at this time is stationed in Okinawa. And there are the biblical examples of Naaman's maid recommending the God of Israel to her master, and the little children singing hosannas to Christ on Palm Sunday. These instances of child "evangelism" were in the back of my mind as I wrote this simple song in response to a stated need for a children's personal evangelism program the church was planning, though it has remained unused to date. It can be sung to any suitable common meter melody until a new one is written for it.

I Praise You, Lord, in Every Hour

I praise you, Lord, in every hour
With all my power,
Since you have heard my crying;
Your arm has vanquished all my foes
With all their woes,
Their victory denying.
Dear God, I plead
From my deep need,
And to my cries
Your mercy flies;
Your grace relieves my sighing.

Praise God, all you who call him Lord,
He keeps his word:
Remember how he saved you.
His anger lasts a moment brief,
Soon comes relief;
You know that He forgave you.
Your holy God
Withdraws his rod;
You go to bed,
Your eyes still red,
But waken free and joyful.

Lord, you are patient, I am weak,
Until I seek,
And then I find you waiting;
You build my confidence and strength,
And I, at length,
See all my fears abating.
How should I not
Praise you, my God?
Your life I see
Begun in me,
New joy and hope creating.

Meter	8.4.7.8.4.7.4.4.4.4.7.
Based on	Psalm 30
Theme	Praise/Restoration
Written	27 February 1986
Suggested tune	ICH PREIS DICH, HERR

This contemporary paraphrase of Psalm 30 was prepared for the Becker Psalter series and was first presented at Grace Lutheran Church, River Forest, Illinois, on March 16, 1986. For additional commentary on the series, see notes under "Before Your Awesome Majesty."

In Darkest Night

In darkest night, the heavens declare your majesty,
Your wisdom, power, glory, and charm for all to see.
Where Abram gazed in wonder, we stand in awe today,
as stupefied and challenged as he by that display.
Still there, in all their splendor, the stars proclaim your might,
still there your faithful promise beams love and life and light.

Then to this darkened planet you sent your Morning Star,
the Light of light from heaven, to lead us where You are;
from that Judean atom a constellation burst,
each star a shining angel announcing peace on earth.
Look down with joy from heaven, dear God, be pleased to see,
piercing our earthly darkness-your global galaxy!

Here shine as cheerful heralds, a sparkling diadem,
announce Messiah's coming at night in Bethlehem;
reflect the love that made you and set you where you are,
that honored you and chose you to be a guiding star;
entice the wise and wary to permanent domains,
that nightless new creation where God in glory reigns.

Meter	13.13.13.13.13.13.
Based on	Job 38:7; Psalm 138:1–5; Daniel 12:3; Matthew 2:2; Hebrews 11:12; Revelation 1:20; 22:16
Theme	Mission/Witness/Epiphany
Written	18 November 1988
Suggested tune	THAXTED by Gustav Holst

To commemorate the 75th anniversary of Bethlehem Lutheran Church, Saginaw, Michigan, in 1989, a hymn for use by the church at large was requested, focusing on the star of Bethlehem which inspired the visit of the Magi, and is the subject of the Bethlehem Star window of the commissioning church. The inscription of the window identifies the theme: "Jesus Christ is our bright and Morning Star, now and forever."

This theme shared a number of references in "Heralds of the Cross," a sonnet I composed for the 1943 Concordia Day pageant at Concordia Seminary in St. Louis, based on Daniel 12:3. Other allusions to stars in the Scriptures suggested the glorious position and purpose of the witnesses to Jesus Christ, the Morning Star.

An indirect reference to the 75th "diamond" anniversary of Bethlehem congregation may be found in the image of a diadem usually made of diamonds of star-like quality. The unusual metrical pattern of the text, six 13-syllable lines, was dictated by the recommended tune, *THAXTED,* by Gustav Holst, for which Sir Cecil Spring-Rice wrote a national hymn, "I vow to thee, dear country."

In Hopelessness and Near Despair

In hopelessness and near despair,
I cry to you, my Savior!
My guilt is more than I can bear,
I have not earned your favor
You know me as I really am:
How much is truth, how much is sham;
Why should you heed my pleading?

I see my heart's condition now
My heart's diverse affections.
Why do I love the things you loathe;
I'm torn in two directions:
Now prodigal, now pharisee,
O God, be merciful to me;
Who else but you can help me?

I tremble as I feel your hand,
Expecting retribution,
Yet hear no curse or reprimand,
But grace and absolution:
With you there is forgiveness, Lord,
You speak the sweet, consoling word,
And I am sure you love me!

Forgiven, free of guilt and shame,
Grant me some time to render
A gift to glorify your name,
Love to reflect your splendor:
This world must know what I have learned,
That you bestow what none has earned:
The joy of full forgiveness!

Meter	8.7.8.7.8.8.7.
Based on	Psalm 130
Theme	Repentance/Forgiveness
Written	9 December 1985
Suggested tune	AUS TIEFER NOT

This contemporary paraphrase of Psalm 130 was also prepared for the Becker Psalter series and was first presented at Grace Lutheran Church, River Forest, Illinois, on February 16, 1986. For additional commentary, see notes on "Before Your Awesome Majesty."

In the Streets, in Home and Workplace

In the streets, in home and workplace,
everywhere Your Name is said,
turn the thoughtless, flippant phrases
into earnest praise instead.
    YaHWeH, true, most holy Lord,
    be our choice four-letter Word!

O my God, I die without You,
O my God, see my despair!
O my God, how much You love me!
O my God, how great You are!
    Move me, help me to reclaim
    Your most holy, precious Name!

Jesus Christ, the world's Redeemer!
Jesus Christ, God's holy Son!
Jesus Christ, my Intercessor!
Jesus Christ, the Judge to come!
    Move me, help me to acclaim
    Your most holy saving Name!

For Christ's sake, have mercy on me!
For Christ's sake, forgive my sin!
For Christ's sake, bring peace among us!
For Christ's sake, new life begin!
    Move me, help me to proclaim
    Yours the only saving Name!

Meter	8.7.8.7.7.7.
Based on	Exodus 20:7; Acts 4:12; Philippians 2:9,10
Theme	Reverence for God's Name
Written	20 December 1992
Suggested tune	KOMM, O KOMM DU GEIST DES LEBENS

For years, and increasingly of late, I have been distressed by the profanation of God's name in nearly every area of life and every segment of society, including the youngest of children. Can any person or society be blessed that treats the holiest name so frivolously? Can a God whose name (i.e. person) is so glibly and disrespectfully used be reverenced and loved as He deserves? Has God rescinded the commandment that holds anyone guilty who takes that holiest of names in vain?

To protect that holy name, God's chosen people of the Old Testament did not utter the Tetragrammaton, the four letters, YHVH, lest they take it in vain. Our use of anyone's name bespeaks our attitude toward that individual's personhood and identity. Next to ingratitude, the daily, universal abuse and blasphemy of God's name reveals one's stance toward the only Being whose grace alone can change our curses into blessings, beginning with the Creator and then proceeding to those created in His image.

I knew a reverent Christian who bowed his head every time he heard or said the name of Jesus. Suppose every grateful creature would even now bow the knee at the name of Jesus, as every creature in heaven and on earth will one day do? Must the Lord wait until then to be recognized and revered as He deserves?

Jesus, Come and Crown This Day with Blessing

Jesus, come and crown this day with blessing,
Every thought and act our thanks expressing;
Show us how
We can now
Keep our vow;
Cheerfully your rule of love confessing.

Gracious God, of all the gifts You give us,
Your vast love and mercy will outlive us;
Every day
Come what may
On the way
You are always waiting to receive us.

You led us to find a life-companion,
Someone special in a holy union,
Someone who
Loves like You,
Faithful, true,
Closest when we kneel in blest Communion.

Modeled by Christ and the Church's pairing,
Each the other's joys and sorrows sharing,
Hearts entwine
Love divine,
Glow and shine
Like Yours, for the loved one nothing sparing.

Meter	10.10.3.3.3.10.
Based on	Ephesians 5:17–33
Theme	Christian Wedding Anniversary
Written	28 June 2002
Suggested tune	NYNÍ, Ó DRAHÝ JEŹISI

Having celebrated our own Golden Wedding anniversary five years earlier, the request by the family of Thomas and Louise Daniel for a 50th anniversary hymn for their parents provided an opportunity to compose an authentic Christian marriage anniversary hymn for longtime pastoral ministry. The marrriage St. Paul defines and advocates, patterned on the union between Christ and His Bride, the Church, is the model for all marriages with its special divine purpose: to pass on the legacy of faith to the next generation.

The request for a Slovak melody was exactly the one that came to mind as expressive of the love of sacred music by both our families. The haunting melody by Slovak church musician and historian, Adam Sultéty (1748–1803), in his hymn-tune collection, *Partitúra,* 1798, composed for a morning hymn by hymnwriter Joachim Kalinka (1611–78), seemed a naturally fitting vehicle for heirs of the same rich spiritual and musical heritage.

Jesus, Immanuel

Jesus, Immanuel,
Come and among us dwell
As You once came.
Who else but You alone
Would leave a heav'nly throne
And do what You have done
To earn that Name?

As You were prophesied,
You took our flesh, defied
Sin, death, and hell.
In ev'ry century
You set the captives free
And prove Yourself to be
Immanuel.

For all for whom You care
Your love moves You to bear
One saving Name.
One Friend who died for us,
One Friend who lives for us,
One Friend who prays for us,
Always the same.

(Optional)
God Father, Lord of all,
Bless all who heard Your call,
Hallowed Your Name,
Who saw Your will begun,
Witnessed it gladly done,
Rejoiced as one by one
Your kingdom came.

Christ Jesus, ever near,
Your Spirit and good cheer
Our fears dispel.
As in our yesterdays,
Help us to find new ways
To live and sing Your praise,
Immanuel!

Meter	6.6.4.6.6.6.4.
Based on	Isaiah 7:14; Matthew 1:22,23; 9:2; 14:27; Luke 11:2; John 17:20, 21, 26
Theme	Church/Anniversary/Church Growth
Written	16 July 1997
Suggested tune	ITALIAN HYMN

Immanuel Lutheran Church in St. Charles, Missouri, celebrating its 150th anniversary in the same year as The Lutheran Church—Missouri Synod, commemorated the milestone with a hymn expressing the congregation's anniversary theme: "Jesus Christ, the same yesterday, today and forever." The implications of the church's name—Immanuel—inspired the text of the anniversary hymn.

Jesus, Take Us to the Mountain

Jesus, take us to the mountain,
where, with Peter, James, and John,
we are dazzled by Your glory,
light as blinding as the sun.
There prepare us for the night
by the vision of that sight.

What do You want us to see there,
that Your close companions saw?
Your divinity revealed there
fills us with the selfsame awe.
Clothed in flesh like ours You go
matched to meet our deadliest Foe.

What do You want us to hear there,
that Your dear disciples heard?
Once again the Voice from heaven
says of the Incarnate Word:
"Listen, listen, everyone,
This is My beloved Son!"

Take us to that other mountain
where we see You glorified,
where You shouted "It is finished!"
where for all the world You died.
Hear the stunned centurion:
"Truly this was God's own Son!"

We who have beheld Your glory,
risen and ascended Lord,
cannot help but tell the story,
all that we have seen and heard;
say with Peter, James, and John:
"You are God's beloved Son!"

Meter	8.7.8.7.7.7.
Based on	Psalm 2:6–12; Luke 9:28–36 and parallels; John 1:14; 17:1, 5, 22 etc.; 2 Peter 1:16–19, James 2:1, etc.
Theme	The Transfiguration of Our Lord
Written	18 January 1991
Suggested tune	SILVER SPRING by Carl Schalk

To commemorate the 50th anniversary of St. Luke Lutheran Church, Silver Spring, Maryland in 1991, a hymn on the Transfiguration was requested. The hymn writer is as much at a loss for words contemplating the glory of the transfigured Christ as were the disciples. The references to the hidden glory of the Son of God and the endorsement of the Father are too numerous to be included in one hymn. A hymn on this theme is fitting for many worship occasions throughout the church year which the above listing only begins to suggest.

There is an unexpected connection between this text and "Peace Came to Earth," written almost exactly 7 years earlier to honor Pastor Theodore Schneider, at that time pastor of The Lutheran Church of the Good Shepherd in Lancaster, Pennsylvania, and now pastor of St. Luke Lutheran Church, the congregation which commissioned this hymn. "Peace Came to Earth" was composed on Pastor Schneider's (and my) favorite theme, the Incarnation of Our Lord. The name Immanuel occurs eight times, and the first stanza's line alludes to the hidden glory of our Lord, "And God embodied love and sheathed his might." On the mount of Transfiguration that glory was momentarily and partially revealed to the inner circle of the Twelve, a glory they were to see behind the gory visage on Mount Calvary shortly thereafter, and in all the following dark moments of their lives.

Jesus, When You Preached

Jesus, when you preached revealing
what God promised to fulfill,
bringing life and hope and healing
to the blind, the deaf, the ill,
helpless like the rest you found me
captive in the chains that bound me,
only you could cure my soul—and make me whole.

Jesus, stop to help this beggar,
open these blind eyes to see,
eyes to recognize my Savior
sent to heal the world and me.
Through these eyes I see the others,
lost and lonely, poor and dying.
Cure the blindness of my soul—and make me whole.

Jesus, tell me that God loves me,
open my deaf ears to hear
words of comfort and forgiveness,
peace and hope and life and cheer.
Let me hear the cries of others,
pleading, suffering, despairing.
Cure the deafness of my soul—and make me whole.

Jesus, heal this paralytic,
raise me up to follow you;
free my hands and arms for serving,
legs and feet to run life's race;
With your Spirit's power fill me,
activate my total being.
Cure the palsy of my soul — and make me whole.

Jesus, hear my pleas for mercy,
turn them into shouts of praise,
telling how you came from heaven,
died for all and rose again.
Loose my tongue to bless and comfort,
teach and pray: your caring witness
singing, "You have healed my soul—and made me whole!"

Meter	8.7.8.7.8.8.8.7.4.
Based on	Psalm 41:4, 147:5; Isaiah 53:5; Luke 4:18 & parallels
Theme	Christ, the Healer
Written	20 October 1996
Tune	SUNSET HILLS by Kim Kolander

Prompted by the need for a hymn on the healing of a friend's critical illness, the theme was expanded to cover the universal need for healing graciously provided by Christ, the divine Healer. Our Lord's first sermon identifies him as the fulfiller of Isaiah's prophecy of the Messiah in Isaiah 61:1–3.

This hymn may serve as the Hymn of the Day on the Third Sunday after the Epiphany, Series C.

The text was metrically and melodically inspired by Kim Kolander's tune, *SUNSET HILLS*, originally composed for the hymn, "Source of Breath from Time's Beginning" (1988).

Just As a Happy Bride

Just as a happy bride
recalls her wedding day,
like Eve, we fondly note your side
and know we once were clay.
You chose us for your own
to share a throne with you;
we owe this all to you alone,
for you make all things new.

Out of a bursting heart
your choosing love has thrilled,
O Christ, for every day's fresh start,
for promises fulfilled,
we sing to praise our prize:
a constant feast with you,
a dying love that never dies,
for you make all things new.

From a baptismal womb
we came, your precious wife,
and when you rose from death's strong tomb,
you filled us with your life.
Renew us day by day
and keep us true to you,
remember us if we should stray,
for you make all things new.

One of the crowns you own
you wear with special pride,
make us a diamond in that crown
you wore when crucified.
Dear Father, now ours too,
dear Bridegroom, always true,
dear Spirit, we live, thanks to you,
for you make all things new.

Meter	SMD
Based on	Revelation 21:2, 5, 9; 22:17; Ephesians 5:25b–27; Genesis 2:21–24
Theme	The Church/Renewal/Anniversary
Written	25 September 1982
Suggested tune	DIADEMATA

Prompted by a request for a text commemorating the 75th anniversary of Gloria Dei Lutheran Church, St. Paul, Minnesota in 1983, on the theme, "Behold, I make all things new" (Rev. 21:5), I composed this text, centering on the imagery of bride and bridegroom suggested by the Revelation passage.

The hymn suggests a number of comparisons between marriage and Christ and his church. Her very origin is from Christ, from his pierced side as Eve's was from Adam's. Christ is the Second Adam, and the holy catholic church is the Eve that Eve would have been had she not sinned.

Other marriage images follow. The crown refers to the rule of Christ, in which the Bride will share. She is a diamond in that crown. A congregation celebrating its 75th diamond anniversary can find special meaning in that reference.

The text is set to the meter and tune of *DIADEMATA*, so that when sung to that tune (or even combined with that text), it may draw on that magnificent melody's background and lead the singers into positioning their existence and experience as Christ's Bride into that royal, exalted and jubilant setting.

Leap, World, for Joy

Leap, world, for joy, and hell be filled
with terror at the birth of Jesus,
who takes a body to be killed
and from our fears and loneness frees us.
Sing, country, city, rich and poor,
your Savior comes, despair no more.
Across vast boundaries of space
he saw us lost and blindly groping.
Consumed by love for our mean race,
he sought us far beyond our hoping,
among us came, among us dwelt:
before such love who would not melt?

Let manger, star, and angel choir
unhinge us from our sleep and sorrows;
let callous hearts and cold take fire
with glories for remaining morrows.
O pampered one, it is for you
God gave this gift, his Son, anew.
Endearing Father, thanks and praise
for so preparing our salvation;
beloved Son of God, we raise
our hands to you in adoration;
and with the Holy Spirit too
be love and glory sung to you!

Meter	8.9.8.9.8.8.D
Based on	Hebrews 2:14,15 and Christmas texts
Theme	Incarnation/Redemption
Written	September, 1964
Suggested tune	by John Boda, 1964

Inspired by the rugged character of Robert Southwell's (c. 1561–95) "This little Babe so few days old," this text was written for the Christmas (December) 1964 issue of *This Day* magazine, which I was editing at the time. The words "man" and "thee" in the original version betray the time of composition in the 70's and 80's. Hence, I have updated these "exclusive" words in this revised version.

John Boda, a childhood friend, composer, conductor, pianist and professor, prepared a melody for the text, which then appeared in the magazine. He also composed a cantata-style choral and orchestral setting of the text, presented in concert by the University of Florida, Tallahassee, orchestra and chorus.

Let All Who Captive Lie

Let all who captive lie
in chains of any kind,
look up, look up, our help is here,
here what we seek we find.
        Take heart, take heart,
        our caring Lord is near.

Defender of the weak,
Protector of the wronged,
who else but Christ can end the grief
so painfully prolonged?
        Take heart, take heart,
        our caring Lord is near.

As those whom Christ redeemed,
we know what freedom is:
a fellowship of faith and love,
a daily feast of grace.
        Take heart, take heart,
        our caring Lord is near

Christ visits when we do,
He has no feet but ours,
no hands but ours to help and heal,
and open prison doors.
        Take heart, take heart,
        our caring Lord is near.

Forever in His heart,
and never out of sight
we children of a loving God
find songs to fill the night.
        Take heart, take heart,
        our caring Lord is near

Meter	SM and Refrain
Based on	Matthew 25:31–40; Luke 4:16–21
Theme	Social Concern
Written	15 May 1989
Suggested tune	MARION

The Lutheran Ministries Association of St. Louis, Missouri was celebrating its 90th anniversary in 1989, a long and illustrious record of social services to the sick, the lonely, the imprisoned, the elderly, and those confined to institutions. A hymn to commemorate this milestone and to inspire the services of God's people in this worthy cause was commissioned by the LMA.

The first sermon of our Lord and the revelation of the Last Judgment provided the theme of the hymn, with a focus on Christ as deliverer, advocate, and servant, and our calling to continue His ministry in our time and place. Selecting the familiar tune *MARION* determined the metrical structure of the text.

Let Us All Give Thanks and Sing

Let us all give thanks and sing
Every time these church bells ring,
For this house, our ancestry,
And this year of jubilee: Alleluia!

Refugees for years oppressed,
Yearning for a place of rest,
"People of the Word" they came
Here to share their Savior's Name: Alleluia!

Here our Father made them His
Children, heirs of promised bliss,
Gathered here our Lord to meet
And a meal of love to eat: Alleluia!

What a favor to receive,
What a legacy to leave:
Knowing Him who hears our pleas,
Blessing us with perfect peace: Alleluia!

Praise the Father, praise the Son,
Praise the Spirit, Holy One:
One with all who've gone before,
One Whom all the saints adore: Alleluia!

Meter	7.7.7.7.4.
Based on	Isaiah 55:11–13; Matthew 28:18–20; Acts 16:9
Theme	Slovak American Lutheran church anniversary
Written	10 April 2000
Tune	SONNE DER GERECHTIGKEIT

This hymn celebrates two 2000 A.D. Slovak American Lutheran Church anniversaries: the 100th anniversary of the Synod of the Evangelical Lutheran Churches (SELC) District of The Lutheran Church—Missouri Synod, and the 95th anniversary of St. Lucas Evangelical Lutheran Church, St. Louis, Missouri. Both church bodies were founded by Slovak Lutheran immigrants from the former Austro-Hungarian Empire in the last quarter of the 19th century. These refugees were a few of the one-third of their nation's population, fleeing a thousand-year occupation of their homeland with only a trunkload of possessions, but including a Bible, a Catechism, and their 250-year-old hymnal, the *Cithara Sanctorum* (Harp of the Saints).

In the course of a century, most of the congregations have dropped Slovak services and have absorbed through intermarriage, transfers, and conversions a multi-ethnic membership, united in the proclamation of the universal Gospel which traveled from Jerusalem via St. Paul to Macedonia, then via the Greek missionary brothers, Cyril and Methodius, in 863 A.D., to the people occupying Central Europe for the next eleven centuries.

The phrase "People of the Word" in the second stanza hints at the possible reason this particular Slavic nation has the name "Slovak." It is surmised that the name was derived from the Slavic word for "word": "slovo" referring to the first sentence of the Bible translated into their language codified by Cyril and Methodius was, "In the beginning was the Word, and the Word was with God, and the Word was God." (John 1:1)

The melody to which this text was written dates back to the Bohemian Brethren 1566 *Kirchengesang*, the third edition of Johann Horn's (Jan Roh) 1544 hymnal. Horn was a contemporary and friend of Martin Luther. The tune is composed in the distinctive Slavic Mode, and is connected to the German text "Sonne der Gerechtigkeit" (Sun of Righteousness).

Let Us Praise Our Gracious God

Let us praise our gracious God,
Children of an alien sod:
God has made this dwelling place
Haven for a scattered race:
Alleluia!

Sons and daughters, greatly blessed,
Of a nation long oppressed;
Like our ancestors may we
Seize the Gospel hungrily:
Alleluia!

Precious altar, precious font,
Life and food for ev'ry want:
Here our parents, here may we
Know the truth that makes us free:
Alleluia!

Here, where many years have passed,
Ev'ry promise still holds fast.
May these gifts we have from You
Richly bless our children, too:
Alleluia!

Loving Father, meet us here,
Risen Savior always near,
By the Spirit kept alive,
We can sing, survive, and thrive:
Alleluia!

Meter	7.7.7.7.4.
Based on	Psalm 34:17–22
Theme	Commenoration/Church in the New World
Written	7 October 1983
Tune	SONNE DER GERECHTIGKEIT

Beginning in the 80s of the last century, one-third of the population of Slovakia emigrated from their homeland, mainly to America, to escape more than nine centuries of political oppression and economic distress. Whether Roman Catholic or Lutheran, they brought with them a strong set of Christian values and a devout faith and established congregations soon after their arrival. For the commemoration of the first Slovak Lutheran congregation's 100th anniversary in the New World, Holy Trinity Lutheran Church of Streator, Illinois, requested a commemorative hymn. The choice of the hymn tune was guided by the fact that Holy Trinity congregation traces its roots to the Slavic Reformation, whose Bohemian Brethren branch produced many hymns and melodies, one of the most festive of which is *SONNE DER GERECHTIGKEIT.*

Some of the references in this hymn coincide with those explained in the notes on the translation of the Slovak hymn "Christians, Let Us Remember."

Light the Candle

Advent 1:
Light the candle of LOVE today,
the Giver of love is here!
Welcome the love we live and die for,
but only Christ can give.
Flicker and flame and glow with love,
Light up the world around you.

Advent 2:
Light the candle of PEACE today,
the Giver of peace is here!
Welcome the peace we fight and cry for,
but only Christ can give.
flicker and flame and glow with peace,
light up the world around you.

Advent 3:
Light the candle of JOY today,
the Giver of joy is here!
Welcome the joy we crave and pray for,
but only Christ can give.
Flicker and flame and glow with joy,
light up the world around you.

Advent 4:
Light the candle of HOPE today,
the Giver of hope will come!
Welcome the hope we long and wait for,
but only Christ can give.
Flicker and flame and glow with hope,
light up the world around you.

Christmas:
Light the candle of CHRIST today,
the Giver of light is here!
Welcome the light we grope and sigh for,
but only Christ can give.
Flicker and flame and glow with light,
light up the world around you.

Meter	8.7.9.6.8.7.
Based on	Advent texts
Theme	Advent Candle-lighting
Written	20 September 1987
Suggested tune	ADVENT CAROL by Carl Schalk

Since many churches observe an Advent candle-lighting ceremony the four Sundays before Christmas, a "carol" was requested to accompany the lighting based on the themes of love, peace, joy, and hope. The stanzas may be sung cumulatively or separately each Sunday, ending with the Christ candle on Christmas Eve and Christmas Day.

Lord, As You Taught Us Once to Pray

Lord, as you taught us once to pray
So teach us now in love to live.
From heaven you brought the better way,
You sought us lost and fugitive.
You changed our wills from "must" to "may,"
You calm us with your "I forgive,"
And all our fears are soothed away
It is by love that we survive.
Lord, as you taught us once to pray,
So teach us now in love to live.

As you for love were crucified,
So teach us, Lord, that way to peace.
You healed the hurts of those who cried
You made the griefs of mourners cease,
Gave Satan's prey a place to hide.
Who sees you on your cross-bound knees,
Sees love that cannot be denied.
This kind of love in us increase.
As you for love were crucified,
So teach us, Lord, that way to peace.

As you were moved by love toward man,
Make us such vessels of your grace.
We need no other reason than
That we reflect our Father's face.
Show us the depth and height and span
Of love that spares no sacrifice,
And we shall do what you began:
Reach to the world with your embrace.
As you were moved by love toward man
Make us such vessels of your grace.

Lord, as in love you saw God's will,
So make that love, that will, ours too.
This world in endless dryness still
Will die and dies without your dew.
Since God is love, and angels thrill
To find this wonder ever new,
His gracious will help us fulfill
And join his joyful retinue.
Lord, as in love you saw God's will,
So make that love, that will, ours too.

Meter	10 lines of 8'
Based on	Luke 11:1–4; John 15:12–17
Theme	Love Divine/Unity in Christ
Written	30 January 1978
Suggested tune	ANNIE LYTLE by Lloyd Pfautsch

This was one of three hymns commissioned by the Hymn Society of America in 1978 in memory of Annie Lytle Miller (1918–77) and set to a tune by Lloyd Pfautsch. The theme was one of my favorites and one, I feel, has to be constantly re-emphasized in the Christian community: love for one's neighbor inspired by God's love for us and our love for God. If we love the God whom we do not see, how should we not love our neighbor whom we can see?

The repeated refrain in each stanza bears traces of the villanelle, which I would some day like to see used in its full form in a sacred song. I would hope to be forgiven the use of the generic word for humankind in stanza three for the sake of succinctness and rhyme in the third stanza. I have not yet found an adequate poetic substitute for 'man" that does not sound artificial while drawing undue attention to itself and diverting attention from the rest of the poem.

Lord, I Must Praise You

Lord, I must praise you when I stand in wonder
At your mighty works and splendor
There is no other God, no one above you,
Yet so close to those who love you.
O Lord, have mercy!
All your works declare your majesty
In an endless grand doxology;
Even more would I praise
Your compassion, love, and grace.
O Lord, have mercy!

Nothing but good you give to those who fear you,
Ever near those who revere you.
To you the hungry come for daily feeding,
And the poor for justice pleading.
O Lord, have mercy!
All your deeds are honest and sincere,
All your vows as true as they appear;
Perfect love, rarest kind,
All I need in you I find.
O Lord, have mercy!

You sent your people long-desired salvation,
Making us a blessed nation.
You are the Rock: on You our hopes are founded,
Safe we dwell, by love surrounded.
O Lord, have mercy!
Make us wise to follow in Your ways,
And receive our sacrifice of praise.
We are Yours, Yours to use
For your dream as You may choose.
O Lord, have mercy!

Meter	Irregular
Based on	Psalm 111
Theme	Praise/Gratitude/Trust
Written	4 December 1985
Suggested tunes	ICH WILL VON HERZEN DANKET GOTT GOTT SEI GELOBET

This contemporary paraphrase of Psalm 111 was one of eight requested for the Becker/Schuetz cantata series and was presented for the first time at Grace Lutheran Church, River Forest, Illinois, on January 12, 1986. Background notes on the series may be found at "Before Your Awesome Majesty."

Lord Jesus Christ, Your Presence Here

Lord Jesus Christ, Your presence here
as prized and honored Guest
adds special luster to our cheer
and makes us truly blest.

What better model could we find
than Your dear Bride and You,
what stronger kind of love to bind
two hearts that vow, "I do!"

Your dream is far more glorious
than for ourselves alone;
this day can bring more happiness
than just for two made one.

As You once gave Yourself to serve,
so raise our fallen race,
our lineage of love start here,
a life to sing Your praise.

Meter	CM
Based on	John 2:2; Ephesians 5:21–33; Revelation 19:7–9
Theme	Marriage/Wedding
Written	28 August 1993
Suggested tune	DUNLAP'S CREEK

Marie Rubis, whose acquaintance I made through the Association of Lutheran Church Musicians, asked to have a hymn written for her marriage to Michael Bauer, also a church musician, to be solemnized at Trinity Lutheran Church, Mission, Kansas, on November 27, 1993.

Lord of Lords, Adored by Angels

Lord of lords, adored by angels,
is that You with towel and basin
washing Your disciples' feet!?
Like the Twelve, we stare in wonder,
Jesus, Word of God eternal,
do You stoop to wash ours too!?

As you shed your earthly garments,
so you laid aside your glory,
so you shed your life as well.
Let the towel and the basin
be the symbols of our service;
let your mind be in us all.

Moved by your devotion toward us,
honored to be called your servants,
we have joined you in your Way
Hesitant, we gird the towel,
fill the bowl with cleansing Water,
and begin to know your joy.

Serving Savior, Model Servant,
for the joy you set before us,
make your Way our history
till we hear your commendation:
"Well done, good and faithful servant,
come and share my joy with me!"

Meter	8.8.7.8.8.7.
Based on	John 13:4,5; Hebrews 12:2; Matthew 25:21
Theme	Joy in faithful service/Maundy Thursday
Written	10 May 1988
Suggested tune	FAITHFUL SERVANT by Tom Leeseberg-Lange

This text was commissioned to commemorate the retirement of Pastor Donald L. Krueger and to acknowledge his example of faithful service during 35 years in the Lutheran ministry and 20 years as pastor of Holy Trinity Lutheran Church in South St. Louis County.

The text uses as its source of inspiration a sermon delivered on John 13:4,5 by Dr. Eugene C. Bay on February 28, 1988 at Bryn Mawr Presbyterian Church and by my lifelong fascination with Christ's footwashing. I was particularly struck by the connection between John 10:18, John 13:4 and John 19:24.

Usually I do not draw attention to the structure of a text, except when it serves a subliminal influence on the theme. In this case, the expected rhyme in the last line of stanza one is missing, just as the footwashing action was totally unexpected. The rhyme begins to appear in the second and third stanzas, but imperfectly, to reflect our growing but incomplete conformity to Christ's example of servanthood. Finally, in the last stanza there is a true rhyme, indicating the arrival at the state of perfection, of complete conformity to God's will.

I debated whether the hymn should be in the singular or plural, settling on the plural because the foot washing was done for the entire group of disciples, and the corporate worshiping body should identify with the servant role as the Body of Christ serving humanity in his name.

Finally, this incident is usually identified in the pericopes with Maundy Thursday, whereas it is an ongoing theme for the church and should not be tucked away in that day when it is subordinate to the commemoration of the Lord's Supper. Hearing the text on February 28 impressed me with its relevance on any other worship day, and added to its shock value by its message at that unexpected time. Worship planners might consider assigning this text and theme to a Sunday emphasizing Christian service.

Mark This Moment and This Place

Mark this moment and this place
with God's many gifts of grace.
Wonder why and how we got here,
what moved us to cast our lot here,
why does this one school exist,
and, if not, would it be missed?

Think of those who thought of you
when these halls were freshly new,
set a higher goal than knowledge
one might find in any college,
who would plan and sacrifice
for this kind of enterprise!

Students, teachers, journey-mates,
each and all with special traits,
here begin to probe the mystery
how true wisdom changes history,
how we fit in God's great scheme,
find life's purpose, live its theme.

Youthful minds, a fertile ground,
youthful spirits heaven-bound,
Christ the Wisdom, Christ the Power,
sow the seed and watch it flower,
Spirit-led, minds full of facts,
here begin your Book of Acts!

Meter	7.7.8.8.7.7.
Based on	Job 28:28 & parallels, Romans 11:33; 1 Corinthians 1:24
Theme	Higher learning/Institutional Anniversary
Written	18 October 1993
Suggested tune	by Donald Busarow

Upon the request of the 150th Anniversary Committee of Wittenberg University, Springfield, Ohio, this hymn was written to mark the special features of this school, echoing the focus of its Reformation namesake, where generations of scholars and spiritual leaders were introduced to its Gospel center, from which all learning radiated.

Central to the education advocated by the Scriptures is the Wisdom of God, identified as Christ, the Wisdom and Power of God, which gives meaning to all learning, and applies it to the glory of God and the welfare of humanity. Every aspect of the arts and sciences is given value beyond mere factual knowledge as God's wonderful works and resources are mined with proper acknowledgement and appreciation.

We are indebted to the visionary and dedicated pioneers who founded Christian higher institutions of learning in order to keep the center of all learning in the Wisdom of God.

The Bible demonstrates various disciplines discovering God's footprints in nature and in the cosmos, planted there to entice the wisdom-seeker to search for the divine Author and the reason for their existence. (Acts 14:24–28) Many of the characters in the Bible were not apostles or prophets, but individuals in various walks of life whose search for wisdom led them to follow their talents' leading to the discoveries and developments of arts and sciences. The conclusion of the hymn suggests that every Christian writes a Book of Acts, as did St. Luke, MD, in recording the far-reaching, God-pleasing, society-enriching activities in the Acts of the Apostles. One would be amazed at the Books of Acts of Wittenberg (USA) students and faculty over the past century and a half.

Professor Donald Busarow was asked to compose a new melody appropriate to the uncommon meter, for which only two hymns are found in Lutheran hymnals, *DELIG ER DEN HIMMEL BLAA* and *WEIL ICH JESU SCHAFLEIN BIN*, both of which convey a different mood.

My Crown of Creation

My crown of creation, you were there at the start,
When I dreamed of a world, you were there in my heart,
You were made for the center of the garden I planned,
Your name is forever written on my hand.

Refrain:

> Take heart, the best is yet to be!
> If you can see what you mean to me,
> You will know the truth, and it will make you free,
> Once you see, my child, what you mean to me.

You left me to wander, and the pain began;
Imagine my grief when I called you and you ran!
I searched for you everywhere, at what a cost!
My coin, my sheep, and my child—all lost!

Refrain

I heard you there cheering when they waved their palms;
I gave you healing when you begged for alms;
And there at the hanging, did you hear me cry:
I am here for you, and for you I die?

Refrain

You thought we were finished when I lay quite dead,
But deep in grief you remembered what I said:
No grave can contain me, I will rise again!
And now that I live, you can sing Amen!

Refrain

I will move even heaven and the earth, I will,
If you believe every promise I fulfill;
No threat can tear us apart, you'll see:
Haven't I proved what you mean to me?

Refrain

Meter	Irregular
Based on	Jeremiah 31:3; John 3:16; 8:31,32
Theme	God's love in Christ/Trust/Post-Easter
Written	17 December 1987
Suggested tune	SIMPLE GIFTS

Following a hymn festival at Holy Trinity Lutheran Church, St. Louis County in the fall of 1987, Charles Ore suggested a new text for the Shaker tune, "The Gift to Be Simple" upon which Sydney Carter based "The Lord of the Dance." I had long felt another text should be written for this popular tune in still another adaptation and variation. The result was "My Crown of Creation," which Ore arranged for mixed choir and premiered on an early 1988 choir tour through Kansas, Oklahoma and Texas by the Seward, Nebraska Concordia Teachers College choir.

The object of this text was to tie the redemption of the long-promised Messiah to the love of God as its most convincing evidence and the basis for the individual believer's hope. That promise reaches back into eternity and culminates in eternity, binding the believer to the eternal God.

Not in Lightning, Storm, and Thunder

Not in lightning, storm, and thunder
Do we find your heart, O God;
All who come to know that wonder
Treasure it, forever awed:
Yearning heart of love and grace,
You reveal it in this place.

Time and space cannot contain you,
Silent, You seem cold, austere,
Yet our sins and sorrows pain You,
And You come among us here.
Who on earth would not rejoice,
Called to come and hear Your voice!?

Daily mercies, each more gracious,
As You mold our mortal clay,
And the One by far most precious
Is the One You gave that day
When by Water and the Word
Our adoption was conferred.

By your messengers' bold preaching
Of your faith-creating Word,
By Your self-revealing teaching
Life is fed by what is heard.
Answering Your fervent "Come!"
In Your house we find our home.

To your table You invite us,
Savior, sinner, side by side;
In one body you unite us,
Faithful Bridegroom, grateful Bride.
Waiting Father, Serving Son,
Sealing Spirit, keep us one!

Meter	8.7.8.7 7.7.
Based on	Psalm 122; Isaiah 55:1–6; Luke 15; Matthew 11:28; 25:34; Revelation 22:17, and parallels
Theme	Invitation to worship
Written	4 June 1994
Suggested tune	BOEHRINGER by Tom Leeseberg-Lange

Faith Memorial Lutheran Church, Valparaiso, Indiana, planning to mark Pastor Hans Boehringer's 40th anniversary of his ordination, commissioned a hymn on the theme of Psalm 122, opening with David's words, "I was glad when they said to me, 'Let us go to the house of the Lord.'"

Having been inspired by this sentence to write "Now the Silence" in 1968, and not having exhausted the subject of worship at that time, this request offered an opportunity to re-examine this profound subject still experiencing a crisis in the Church 25 years later. Now even the basic doctrine of the Trinity is being reconstructed and, some say, denied and discarded. All the more reason to reaffirm the creeds of the Church in hymnody, which expresses the faith of those who sing the liturgy.

Now, at the Peak of Wonder

Now, at the peak of wonder,
Sing your new song of praise,
Tell all the world He loves you,
Lord of your years and days.
Caught by His glory, shine with its splendor,
Now, while your heart's ablaze.

For the sad world around you,
Helpless and terrified,
Dying for want of rescue,
Watching you from outside:
Here is the water, here is the banquet,
Here is the Lamb that died.

Garden of children growing,
Help those who crawl to walk,
Feed them the Bread from heaven,
Teach those who lisp to talk:
Tell them the story, show them the glory,
Sheep of the Shepherds flock.

Make this a place so winsome
Jesus is almost seen,
Sinners and angels searching,
Find here a joy serene:
Filled with the Spirit, glow with the glory,
Glory of pastures green.

Now at the Savior's impulse
Touch with His healing hand
All those who suffer, hunger,
Mourn, or wear Satan's brand.
Friend to the lonely, God's earthly angels,
Strong with the wronged to stand.

Now to the caring Father,
Now to the risen Son,
Now to the cheering Spirit,
Now to the Holy One:
Sing alleluias, live alleluias,
Never the song be done!

Meter	7.7.7.7.5.5.6.
Based on	1 Peter 2:9, 10
Theme	The Christian Community/Anniversary
Written	20 August 1981
Suggested tune	SAPPINGTON by Richard W. Gieseke

To mark the 25th anniversary of its organization, the Lutheran Church of the Resurrection in Sappington, Missouri, commissioned this hymn to depict the purpose and activities of a Christian congregation. The hymn's use is not restricted to the anniversary of a church, though it can be used as such for anniversaries other than the 25th, or to celebrate the community of Christ in mission.

Richard W. Gieseke, while organist and choir director at Resurrection Church, prepared a concertato arrangement of the hymn for congregation, choir, timpani, organ, and brass, and named it SAPPINGTON after the church's location.

Now the Silence

Now the silence
Now the peace
Now the empty hands uplifted

Now the kneeling
Now the plea
Now the Father's arms in welcome

Now the hearing
Now the power
Now the vessel brimmed for pouring

Now the Body
Now the Blood
Now the joyful celebration

Now the wedding
Now the songs
Now the heart forgiven leaping

Now the Spirit's visitation
Now the Son's epiphany
Now the Father's blessing

Now   Now   Now

Meter	Irregular
Based on	Habakkuk 2:20; Psalm 122:1
Theme	Entrance/Worship/Communion
Written	12 March 1968
Suggested tune	NOW by Carl Schalk

If there was one hymn text that proved a catalyst for my hymn writing, it was "Now the silence,' already alluded to in the introduction to this anthology. And Carl Schalk must be given the credit for recognizing the potential of this unusual text as a hymn. Its subsequent acceptance convinced me (and evidently many others) that hymns could take on new forms and yet perform their function in congregational worship. In the nearly three plus decades since the text came to me while shaving, I have been discovering roots and hints in past experiences and Scriptural passages and stories. The opening line of one of Hviezdoslav's lyrics, 'Wish me silence, wish me peace,' surfaced 25 years later as 'Now the silence, now the peace.' And the reverse order of the Doxology/Benediction not only expressed the order in which I pictured the Trinity coming to us in worship, but also the order in which the Incarnation took place: the visitation of the Virgin Mary by the Holy Spirit, then the Son's epiphany as the incarnate Word, followed by the universal blessing that is bestowed upon all in whom this same process occurs.

O Day of Days, the Day I Found

O day of days, the day I found
The love that had been seeking me;
More than a word, more than a sound,
That Word was God and set me free.

O day of days, the day I found
That Word a body on a cross;
No sacrifice of friend has bound
Me to him by so great a loss.

O day of days, the day I found
A life to live that's more than me,
A blessing for the world around,
A cause to serve, a way to be.

O day of days, the day I found
Your people raised like me to sing;
Now one with them and those beyond
I look for ways to thank our King.

Stand by me, Father, Flesh, and Flame:
Embrace, embolden and increase
Your child reborn to bear Your name,
Another messenger of peace.

Meter	LM (8.8.8.8.)
Based on	John 1:35–51; Galatians 1:11—2:21
Theme	Discipleship/Commitment/Confirmation/Rededication
Written	5 October 1972
Suggested tune	WINCHESTER NEW

Now and again the remembrance of God's grace in Christ stuns me into an awareness and appreciation of the relationship I enjoy with God. This hymn is meant to jog my memory and that of other children of God and prompt thanksgiving and rededication. It can also serve as a hymn for confirmation and commitment to service.

O Dearest Friend

O dearest Friend, my nearest and most faithful Friend,
Do not discard me though I grieve you much.
I look for you at every cliff-walled trail's end,
In crowds and lonely rooms, to feel your touch.
I mourn the vows of love I made but have not kept,
I call you from a heart you made your own.
Remember me as one who in the Garden slept
While you were on your way to earn my fadeless crown.

Create in me a heart as clean as newest born,
A heart, my God, that beats for you alone;
Make it a temple your free Spirit would adorn,
With living flesh replace my heart of stone.
Restore to me the joy of your salvation,
Recapture, oh, the thrill of our first love,
Securely hold me, mold me your creation,
Delight me yet again with such disarming love.

Meter	12.10.12.10.12.10.12.12.
Based on	John 21:15–17; Psalm 51
Theme	Repentance/Restoration/Commitment
Written	24 January 1976
Suggested tune	LONDONDERRY AIR

When I was five, and we lived in Racine, Wisconsin, my father took me to Milwaukee to hear a concert by Fritz Kreisler, renowned as one of the world's greatest violinists. As I shook the hand of the virtuoso backstage, I was determined to play the violin, too. In a few weeks I was taking lessons on my three-quarter-size violin. Seven years later my teacher assigned me Kreisler's poignant transcription of Londonderry Air, which has haunted me ever since. Fifty years after the Kreisler concert I was moved by that bittersweet Irish air to write a text depicting that deeper relationship between the Christian and his/her dearest Friend and the vulnerability of that friendship as it experiences closeness and disappointment, with always the hope of restoration. This was illustrated for me at least in the Garden test of Peter, the chosen friend who let down his dearest Friend and yet could hope to be given another chance. The first stanza can stand by itself, or, combined with the second, can echo the similar experience of David as expressed in Psalm 51. It was the weekly singing of the Offertory based on Psalm 51:10–12 that became my frequent penitential prayer.

O God, Eternal Father, Lord

O God, eternal Father, Lord,
Creator by your mighty Word,
Be now by us and all adored. Alleluia.

O Son, still God today as then,
In flesh like ours, true God and Man,
You served and died and rose again. Alleluia.

O Spirit, God, Iconoclast,
By Blood and Water cleanse our past,
The life you seed, make grow and last. Alleluia.

Meter	8.8.8. and Alleluia
Based on	Revelation 4:11; John 14:26; 1 Peter 1:2
Theme	Holy Trinity/Credo/Doxology
Written	20 June 1969
Suggested tune	GELOBT SEI GOTT

Inspired by numerous versified Credos that occupy so many liturgical hymnals, this abbreviated three-stanza "credo" can serve as a brief confessional or doxological minute in one's daily devotions. Line 2 in stanza two still uses the generic word for humanity, betraying the date of its composition.

Of All God's Gifts

Of all God's gifts, the best is yet to come:
A feast befitting God's new heaven and earth,
A celebration only God could plan:
The marriage of the Lamb and cherished Bride!

What comfort for despairing prodigals?
Is there a chance of coming home again?
Look at the outstretched hand, the yearning love,
The cross, the triumph over death and hell!

God sees the outcasts, orphans, and the lost,
Invites them all to fill the banquet hall;
The poor become the kingdom's royal heirs,
Their names recorded in the Book of Life.

Come, join those loved ones who have gone before,
Remember where we heard this call of God;
What we have now, God wants the world to have:
The gifts of life and love and peace and joy!

Meter	10.10.10.10.
Based on	Matthew 22:1-13; Revelation 19:7, and parallels
Theme	The Church/Relationship with Christ/ Anniversary
Written	5 March 1994 / 21 April 1994

The University Lutheran Church of Hope, Minneapolis, commissioned this hymn for the commemoration of its 90th anniversary in April, 1994. This congregation, like all other faithful Christian communities takes its place in the unbroken line of God's worshipping people beginning with Pentecost and thereafter witnessing to the Lord in all parts of the world. The present generation — the third since the congregation's founding — is a link in that chain, carrying the Gospel from parent to child, ultimately aiming for that everlasting goal of the Church, the wedding of the Bride of Christ with her divine Groom, the Lamb of God.

Jesus' parable of the King's son's wedding forms the basis for the hymn. The echoes in the Book of Revelation end the Biblical record, the original purpose of creation being fulfilled by the restoration of the relationship broken by the Fall. The Church will spend eternity contemplating the magnitude of that redemptive love of God.

A new melody was composed for the hymn by the congregation's music director, William Beckstrand.

One by One the Spirit Calls Us

One by one the Spirit calls us,
Andrew, Simon, James, and John;
With the love of God enthralls us,
Wins, adopts us, one by one:
Precious daughter, precious son.

Day by day the Spirit moves us
From the old to the new way,
Patiently improves us, proves us,
Forms, transforms us, day by day,
Breathes life into mortal clay.

Year by year the flock increases,
Sharing mercy, hope, and cheer;
Finding, knowing what true peace is,
Growing closer year by year.
Christ was right: "The Kingdom's here!"

See the sign of God in action:
Word and water, bread and wine;
All who want true satisfaction,
Life and mercy — see the sign!
Trace the branches to the Vine.

Someday soon we saints will gather
All around the Lamb's high throne,
Praising Spirit, Son, and Father,
All together — someday soon:
One with God, forever one.

Meter	8.7.8.7.7.
Based on	Acts 2:36–47; 1 Corinthians 6:11; Revelation 7:9–17
Theme	The Church/The Communion of Saints
Written	30 January 1993
Suggested tune	LINCOLN by Carl Schalk

To celebrate the 40th anniversary of Faith Lutheran Church and School, Lincoln, Nebraska, the congregation requested a hymn based on the theme for Easter 3, Series A, modeled on the baptismal life of the first Christian church.

The description of the early church in Acts 2 is one of "more than an emotional Pentecostal experience, but rather a new life centered in "Word and Sacrament as our source of faith and hope, rest and renewal." (Cassie McMahan) This was a welcome assignment, converging on my special focus on baptism and the baptismal life. The "Christened" believer begins a union with the Trinity through his/her union with Christ; as well as a communion with all others "washed, sanctified, and justified in the name of the Lord Jesus, and by the Spirit of our God." (1 Cor. 6:11) One hymn can cover only a few dimensions of this vast subject; it can only suggest the contemplation of other aspects of this divine/human relationship.

A poetic device was created to suggest the unity of the individual members of the Body of Christ by the repetition of the opening phrase at the end of the fourth line, and by rhyming lines two and five with that phrase. A fifth line expands and underscores the thought of the preceding quatrain.

Pass in Review

Pass in review, ambassador of Christ:
Pass in review, each sacrifice and prize,
Pass in review, the sowings of the Word,
Pass in review, the harvest gleaned and stored.

Vessel of clay for mysteries divine,
Chosen to join the apostolic line,
Given your heritage, your gifts, your call,
Your place as sentinel on Zion's wall.

Servant of sinners, though yourself the same,
Partner in sorrow, yet with hope aflame,
Cheering the lonely, Gospeling the poor,
Leading your precious flock through Christ the Door.

Pass in review, slaves ransomed and set free,
Pass in review, one noble company,
Pass in review, your victor's banner raise,
Pass in review, your life a song of praise.

Meter	10.10.10.10.
Based on	Isaiah 62:6; 2 Corinthians 5:20; Hebrews 13:17
Theme	Ministry/Anniversary
Written	2 April 1986
Suggested tune	OLD 124TH

For more than a generation, pastors' ordinations and installations in our church have used one of the few available hymns pertaining to the office of the holy ministry, "God of the prophets, bless the prophets' sons," to *OLD 124TH*. Even fewer hymns were available for ministers celebrating anniversaries or retirements. So I welcomed the request to write a hymn for the golden (50th) anniversary of Dr. John Kovac at St. Lucas Lutheran Church, St. Louis, on May 25, 1986. Various aspects of the holy ministry are reviewed as the life and career of God's servant are commemorated. The text was set to OLD 124TH, which in turn was to call up associations with the Denis Wortman text, "God of the prophets."

Peace Came to Earth

Peace came to earth at last that chosen night
When angels clove the sky with song and light
And God embodied love and sheathed his might—
    Who could but gasp: Immanuel!
    Who could but sing: Immanuel!

And who could be the same for having held
The infant in their arms, and later felt
The wounded hands and side, all doubts dispelled—
    Who could but sigh: Immanuel!
    Who could but shout: Immanuel!

You show the Father none has ever seen,
In flesh and blood you bore our griefs and pain,
In bread and wine you visit us again—
    Who could but see Immanuel!
    Who could but thrill: Immanuel!

How else could I have known you, O my God!
How else could I have loved you, O my God!
How else could I embrace you, O my God!
    Who could but pray: Immanuel!
    Who could but praise Immanuel!

Meter	10.10.10.8.8.
Based on	Luke 2:14; Galatians 4:4; Ephesians 2:14
Theme	Incarnation/Christmas
Written	24 January 1984
Suggested tune	SCHNEIDER by Paul Manz

As Pastor Theodore E. Schneider's congregation, The Lutheran Church of the Good Shepherd in Lancaster, Pennsylvania, was preparing to celebrate the 25th anniversary of its spiritual shepherd's ordination, Dr. Karl F. Moyer, organist and choir director, requested a hymn based on a memorable sermon Pastor Schneider had preached on an earlier Christmas Eve on Galatians 4:4. The hymn was to laud the Incarnation rather than the charms of Christmas, and was to be presented as a gift to the church and to Pastor Schneider at the anniversary service on Trinity Sunday, June 17, 1984. 1 was able to attend the commemorative service, one of the few times I was privileged to witness the introduction of a new hymn.

Since Pastor Schneider's favorite theme also happened to be mine, I was pleased to write a text that would explore more of the implications of the Incarnation than are ordinarily found in Christmas texts; for example, the communion that takes place in the Sacrament of the Altar, and the incorporation of believers into the Body of Christ. One is dealing with the very essence of Christianity, in which the Incarnation is absolutely essential to the world's redemption and the union of the creature with the Creator and Redeemer. The repetition of Immanuel is meant to impress its literal meaning on the singer of the hymn with its numerous implications.

Readings from Acts, Versified

SERIES A

Second Sunday of Easter *Acts 2:14a, 22–32*

The One who died by sinners' hands
On brutal Calvary
Was God's own Son, confirmed by death,
To set us sinners free.

So sure was David of his hope
That his great Son would rise
He lived and died sure that he too
Would live in Paradise.

Doxology:
Now sing the mighty acts of God,
Now make his mercy known,
Now mark the triumph of his love,
Now gather 'round his throne.

The risen Christ, the ruling King,
The coming Judge and Lord,
Be welcomed, praised, obeyed, and served,
And evermore adored.

Third Sunday of Easter *Acts 2:14a, 36–47*

The Man we crucified is made
By God the Lord of all;
He chose this way to justify
The victims of the Fall.

What shall we do to show our true
Repentance for this crime?
Be cleansed by him and tell his love
Until the end of time.

Doxology:

Fourth Sunday of Easter *Acts 6:1–9; 7:2a, 51–60*

The kingdom, like a mustard seed,
Began with just a few,
But these, devoted to their Lord,
Miraculously grew.

And other seeds, like Stephen, fell
Into the ground to die,
But from them sprang a line of trees
Whose branches touch the sky.

Doxology:

Fifth Sunday of Easter *Acts 17:1–15*

First to the Jews and then the Greeks
Christ's messengers proclaimed
The Risen Savior of the world,
By God himself acclaimed.

And some believed, and some did not,
And some just turned away,
But those who took the word to heart
Found their own Easter Day.

Doxology:

Sixth Sunday of Easter *Acts 17:22–31*

All have a god whom they revere,
To whom they give their due,
But Christ has come to show the One
Whom we proclaim to you.

He is the Father of mankind
And of a Son divine,
Who, though a man, will judge all men,
Whom no grave can confine.

Doxology:

Seventh Sunday of Easter *Acts 1:(1–7) 8–14*

This parting word the Savior spoke
To his assembled band:
"Go forth and make me followers
In this and every land.

"Baptize and teach what I have taught,
And I will be with you!"
With this he raised his hands and rose,
And disappeared from view.

Doxology:

SERIES B

Second Sunday of Easter *Acts 3:13–15, 17–26*

God's power still indwelling him,
Bold Peter dares Christ's foes:
"How could you kill the Prince of life,
Whom Abraham's God chose?

But God restored him back to life—
And you can still repent;
This time accept with grateful hearts
The Gift that God has sent.

Doxology:
O Spirit of the Risen Christ,
O Savior, Victor, Friend,
O smiling Father, ever our
Beginning and our End.

Combine our song of worship with
Your angel choirs, that when
We reach your presence we may join
Their glorious Amen!

Third Sunday of Easter *Acts 4:8–12*

The courts of evil still condemn
The guiltless Son of Man;
So will it be, so is it now,
And was since time began.

Before Christ's judges Peter stands
For healing one born lame,
Proclaiming that salvation comes
By none but Jesus' name.

Doxology:

Fourth Sunday of Easter *Acts 4:23–33*

As Christ, their Master, once condemned,
Was by the grave released,
So Peter, John, could not be held
By prison or high priest.

They had to tell what God had done
And what he still can do,
To make the Gospel known to all:
That Word makes all things new.

Doxology:

Fifth Sunday of Easter *Acts 8.26–40*

Not for Jerusalem and Jew
Alone did Jesus die;
Go, Philip, greet the African
And give him God's reply.

Isaiah pictures God's meek lamb
For sinners sacrificed,
And sinners recognizing him
Would ask to be baptized.

Doxology:

Sixth Sunday of Easter *Acts 11:19–30*

The blood of martyrs is not shed
In vain, but sows the seeds
Of valiant new disciples whom
The world wants not but needs.

Death turns to life, and scorn to praise,
By God's strange alchemy;
The Gospel fathers a new breed
Of heavenly ancestry.

Doxology:

Seventh Sunday of Easter *Acts 1:15–26*

The chosen Twelve, now lacking one,
Met to replace their loss;
In prayer they sought the will of him
Whose throne replaced the cross.

To prove his care for every need,
He made their number whole,
So all who take each step with him
Will reach their glorious goal.

Doxology:

SERIES C

Second Sunday of Easter *Acts 5:12, 17–32*

How futile of the grave to try
To hold the rising lord!
How useless of his enemies
To chain the living Word!

Both tomb and prison must release
That race divinely born;
For those obeying God, not men,
Each day's an Easter morn.

Doxology:

With pulsing, full, and bursting heart,
Repeat the Easter song,
The new life celebrate, the feast
Of victory prolong!

The Father of all life be praised,
The Son who vanquished death,
The Spirit, making all things new,
Adore with every breath!

Third Sunday of Easter *Acts 9:1–20*

Saul heard the cry we all must hear
Before we come to faith:
"Why do you hound me, little one?
Why do you cause my death?"

But when we cry in turn, "O Lord,
What will you have me do?"
He comes in mercy, "Peace!" he says,
"I want to make you new."

Doxology:

Fourth Sunday of Easter *Acts 13:15, 16a, 26–33*

God's promises have never failed,
The Word he speaks holds true,
And whether we believe or not,
God does what he must do.

The faithless Jews reject their Christ,
Fulfilling his true word,
While all believing Israel
Is proud to call him Lord.

Doxology:

Fifth Sunday of Easter *Acts 13:44–52*

The Gospel, like a passing cloud,
Is meant to shower all,
Christ made his sacrifice for each
Lost victim of the Fall.

The Spirit lingers only where
His gift is well received,
Where, on the cross, despite the shame,
One's Savior is perceived.

Doxology:

Sixth Sunday of Easter *Acts 14:8–18*

How like two gods th' apostles seem,
With healing powers endowed;
Yet knowing where they got the gift,
They glorify their God.

In flesh the Son of God appeared,
Here founded his domain;
He chooses vessels made of clay
To magnify his reign.

Doxology:

Seventh Sunday of Easter *Acts 16:6–10*

A voice from Macedonia
Cries: "Come and help us, please!"
And lo, the praying man is heard
While still upon his knees.

No other plea so pleases God
As when his children cry;
Will he not answer them at once
And to their rescue fly?

Doxology:

Meter	8.6.8.6.
Based on	Easter cycle lectionary readings from the Book of Acts
Theme	Easter life
Written	15 September 1980
Suggested tune	Easter Motet Series, by Christopher Tye

Christopher Tye (c. 1505–72), musical tutor to King Edward VI and organist of the Chapel Royal under Queen Elizabeth, rendered the first fourteen chapters of the Book of Acts into meter, which he then set to music. Augsburg Publishing House requested new texts for three sets of six Tye motets each for use on the Sundays of Easter and based on the First Lesson as appointed in the three-year lectionary (all from the Book of Acts) in the *Lutheran Book of Worship* and *Lutheran Worship.* The texts were prepared for a three-set collection published by Augsburg in three successive years under the title Easter Motets: Series B in 1984, Series C in 1985, and Series A in 1986.

Remember, Lord, the Times You Called Me

Remember, Lord, the times you called me
to be your follower and friend?
Your words, your cause, your self enthralled me;
you gave my life a source and end.
My first communion and my vow!
How is our friendship now?

I dare not claim a special favor
for deeds heroic, much less due.
I need an understanding Savior,
I need a patient friend like you.
I need someone to take me back,
restore the joy I lack.

There still are souls and bodies crying
for help and healing, life and peace.
You saved the fruitless tree from dying,
you promised prisoners release.
Like Peter, Saul, and Magdalen,
make me all new again.

Forgiving Father, giving Savior,
renewing Spirit, keep your word:
give me a foretaste of forever,
where love and joy are never blurred.
With pride and weakness gone for good
I'll thank you as I should.

Meter	9.8.9.8.8.6.
Based on	Psalm 51; Luke 13:6–9; Revelation 21:5
Theme	Repentance/Renewal
Written	6 December 1987
Suggested tune	ICH WILL DICH LIEBEN

For its 1988 Lay Renewal program, Concordia Lutheran Church, Kirkwood, Missouri, requested an appropriate text incorporating the themes of the conference: Reflection (Recollection), Repentance, and Recommitment. The hymn attempts to reflect the thoughts and feelings of most disciples of the Lord, who once made a commitment to follow him, but who have all experienced loss of ardor or loyalty and wish to be renewed by the Spirit who called them and created in them the spark of faith. The hymn refers to several of many followers of Christ whose flickering faith was revived or renewed by him who makes all things new. The fruitless tree is an allusion to the fig tree in Christ's parable in Luke 13.

The text is set to the meter of the familiar hymn, "Ich will dich lieben, meine Starke," by Johann Scheffler, which Catherine Winkworth translated so beautifully as "You will I love, my strength, my tower." The hymn deals with related themes, and the use of the familiar tune associated with it may serve to underline the theme of the present text which the tune seems to fit quite comfortably.

Rock-a-bye, My Dear Little Boy

Rock-a-bye, my dear little Boy, dear little Boy,
Wonder of wonders, my blessing and joy:
Slumber as I gently hold you,
Let my tender love enfold you,
Gift of God to me and the world,
Here in my arms lies so peacefully curled.

Little Jesus, Infant divine, Infant divine,
One with the Father, yet born to be mine:
As I rock you calmly sleeping,
Angel guards their watch are keeping;
Precious Child, one day we shall see
What love has destined for you and for me.

Meter 12.10.8.8.8.10.
Based on Luke 1:46–55, 2:51
Theme Christmas/Mary's Lullaby
Written 6 July 1987
Suggested tune Czech Carol "Hajej, nynjej" (ROCKING)

The charming Czech Christmas carol traditionally known as *ROCKING* translated into English a half century ago has captivated me for many years. I was, however, disappointed in the lightness of its content, pretending as it does to be sung by the maiden who composed the Magnificat. Wondering what kind of lullaby the mother of the Savior might have sung to "that holy Thing" she had borne, I wrote a new text moving the content of the carol closer to a hymn while trying to keep the simplicity and intimacy of the traditional carol.

Furthermore, since Mary was the kind of mother who "kept all these things in her heart," it is likely that she mulled over the message of Gabriel, the greeting of Elizabeth, and the prophecy of Simeon as she rocked the Infant to sleep, and wondered, as most mothers do, what would become of this special child, and what the "sword" was that would one day pierce her heart.

Still another variation occurs in the composition of this new text to an old tune: each note in the carol is given a syllable instead of the numerous slurs that appear in *ROCKING*.

See Mary Setting Out at Dawn

See Mary setting out at dawn
for Zion with her six-week Son,
and Joseph, turtle-doves in hand,
to carry out the Lord's command.

There faithful Mary, meek, demure,
has come to be acknowledged pure,
then dedicates the Holy One
by whom God's perfect will is done.

When Mary brings Messiah there,
God answers Simeon's lifelong prayer
for peace for him and everyone
who prays in faith, "Your will be done."

Because she brings the Savior there,
grey Anna has a Gift to share.
Had she not prayed, "Your will be done,"
who would have met and known God's Son?

All have some special part to play
in God's eternal plan who pray,
"In heav'n, so here Your will be done"
at every rising of the sun.

Meter	8.8.8.8.
Based on	Luke 2:22–24 (40)
Theme	Presentation of Our Lord (February 2)
Written	6 January 1991
Suggested tune	WO GOTT ZUM HAUS

A hymn text on the Presentation of Our Lord was needed for a concertato in the 1991 series of vespers at Grace Lutheran Church, River Forest, Illinois, to go with the chorale tune, *WO GOTT ZUM HAUS.* Because no text existed on the subject in that meter, I had an opportunity to delve more deeply into that significant event for Mary and her son, Jesus. After numerous inadequate starts I came upon what seemed to be the key to Mary's and Jesus'—and, in fact, all children of God—character: willing submission to the will of God. Beginning with the Magnificat and ending with Christ's Gethsemane prayer, this theme is central to faith and life.

See This Wonder in the Making

See this wonder in the making:
God himself *this* child is taking
As a lamb safe in his keeping,
His to be, awake or sleeping.

Miracle each time it happens,
As the door to heaven opens
And the Father beams: "Beloved,
Heir of gifts a king would covet!"

Far more tender than a mother,
Far more caring than a father,
God, into your arms we place *(him/her/them)*,
With your love and peace embrace *(him/her/them)*.

Here we bring a child of nature,
Home we take a newborn creature,
Now God's precious son or daughter,
Born again by Word and Water.

Meter	8.8.8.8. Trochaic
Based on	Romans 6:3–6; Colossians 2:12; James 1:18; 1 Peter 3:2; Titus 3:4–7
Theme	Infant Baptism/ Regeneration
Written	5 August 1984
Suggested tune	TRYGGARE KAN INGEN VARA

Hymnody can help restore Baptism to its central place in the life and worship of God's people. As such, it can open the mind and heart to a range of considerations of this sacramental means of grace often forgotten, overlooked, or ignored by too many Christians, whereas it can and should be the source of daily comfort and an incentive to daily repentance and the renewal of one's membership in the Body of Christ and participation in the crucifixion/redemption of Christ, as attested to by such important passages as those listed above, the contemplation of which can open floodgates of inspiration for other hymns on the subject of Baptism.

The validity of Baptism as a sacrament has served God's children, infant, young, and old, since apostolic times, and has proved to be a refuge and an earnest of their divine regeneration and adoption.

Lines 1 and 2 of the fourth stanza translate the thought of an old European folk saying associated with infant baptism: "We took you to church a heathen; we brought you home a Christian."

This particular hymn text was prompted by a long-standing need for more contemporary baptismal hymns, and as a substitute for "Children of the heavenly Father," set to the charming Swedish folk tune usually only indirectly related to the rite of baptism. This new text, specifically connected with Baptism and tied to the Swedish tune, affords an opportunity to define how that familial relationship comes about.

Shine Like Stars

See how the galaxies are always there,
Made by the One whose glories they declare,
Signs of a God with might and care to spare:
Shine like those stars!

So we are made to occupy a place
Within a firmament of time and space,
Each one enlightened with a special grace
To shine like stars.

Who were the stars God gave us in our youth,
Who led us to the Way, the Life, the Truth?
Now when we show our children that same route,
We shine like stars.

Who are those loved ones always at our side,
Who walk before us, each a trusted guide,
Who give us only what true friends provide,
Who shine like stars?

Here by our faith and hope and love we shine,
Revealing by our deeds a power divine,
One almost hears God saying, "You are mine,
You shine like stars!"

Though passing clouds may for a moment hide
Our gleams of faith, God's promises abide:
One day our orbits will be glorified —
So shine like stars!

How many have been led to Bethlehem
To see the Morning Star arise for them?
Now glitt'ring diamonds in his diadem,
They shine like stars.

There we are set to occupy the height,
To glow the brightest in the darkest night,
That many still may know the world's true Light,
Shine, shine like stars!

Meter	10.10.10.4.
Based on	Phlippians 2:15,16; Matthew 5:14–16; Daniel 12:3; John 1:6–12; et al.
Theme	The Great Commission
Written	28 April 1993
Suggested tune	STARS by Carl Schalk

The 1993 Great Commission Convocation of The Lutheran Church—Missouri Synod selected as its theme, "Shine Like Stars," based on Philippians 2:15,16. This hymn was commissioned for the assembly in Minneapolis, October 7–10. The stated purpose of the convocation was "to enable participants as partners in the Gospel to share their faith and to involve their congregations in the task of teaching, reaching, and caring for all people in our changing world."

Four emphases were designated for the convocation: Shine like stars in family and friendships/in the Church/in Society/in the World.

The assignment echoed a sonnet I had written 51 years earlier for a pageant at Concordia Seminary, St. Louis, entitled "Heralds of the Cross," based on Daniel 12:3.

The favored and familiar theme was now to be applied to the priesthood of all believers, in a strophic form. The decision to use the familiar iambic pentameter was its use in a number of stirring hymns with such moving melodies as *SINE NOMINE* and *ENGELBERG*.

Simon, Simon, Do You Love Me?

Simon, Simon, do you love me?
If you do, then feed my sheep.
Simon, Simon, do you love me?
If you do, then feed my lambs.
Show me that my love has moved you,
imitate how I have loved you.
Simon, Simon, do you love me?
If you do, then feed my flock.

Simon, Simon, do you love me?
If you do, then follow me.
Simon, Simon, do you love me?
If you do, then follow me.
Follow where your faith will take you,
knowing I will not forsake you.
Simon, Simon, do you love me?
If you do, then follow me.

Simon, Simon, do you love me?
If you do, then feed my sheep.
Simon, Simon, do you love me?
If you do, then feed my lambs.
Ponder why I called and trained you,
named you Rocklike, and ordained you,
do you love me, truly love me?
If you do, then feed my flock.

Meter	8.7.8.7.8.8.8.7.
Based on	John 21:1–19; Matthew 4:18–20, 16:15–17; Luke 22:31–34, 54–62; Mark 9:2–10; Acts 2:14–41; 1 Peter 5:1–4
Theme	Commitment/Ministry
Written	9 March 1997
Suggested tune	LAESCH by Carl Schalk

One of the most poignant episodes in the ministry of our Lord took place in that forty-day period between Easter and the Ascension when Peter was reinstated into his apostleship. How he must have despaired of forgiveness for his denials in the Court of Caiaphas. How he hurried to the empty tomb, hoping ferventlyy that the report of the women was true. Would he get the absolution that would restore him to the closest circle of friends and followers of the Messiah? Could he be counted on to face his own crucifixion without flinching or deserting the Son of God? If Simon was to be called Peter again, he would have to re-examine his dedication to the One for whom he had once left everything.

What a list of "threes" that encounter on the shore of Galilee would recall for Simon Peter! The 3-year companionship and tutorship with Jesus. The inner circle of 3 disciples. One of the 3 invited to witness the Transfiguration, facing the Son of God flanked by Moses and Elijah, a dazzling threesome. A member of the trio asked to accompany their Master during his agony in the Garden of Gethsemane, and being awakened 3 times. The 3 questions in the high priest's courtyard, and the 3 denials. The report of the Resurrection 3 days later. The 3 questions and the 3 replies forming the basis of this hymn. And the confirmation of his reinstatement on the Day of Pentecost when 3,000 witnessed the bold public testimony of the one renamed Peter.

The text with the tune *LAESCH* was composed for Dr. Theodore Laesch upon his retirement as President of the Northern Illinois District of The Lutheran Church—Missouri Synod, culminating a shepherding ministry advocated by St. Peter in his First Epistle, chapter 5:1–4.

So Much to Sing About

So much to sing about,
so much to praise you for,
so much I cannot live without
and so much more:
at which display
of majesty
the very stones are moved to shout.

So much to sing about:
once orphaned and alone,
how could I dare believe the news
that you would come
to live and die,
for me, for me!
and so make sure my welcome home.

So much to sing about:
your wisdom, might and love,
that even three-score years and ten
are not enough
to count your gifts
and search beneath
the surface of your treasure-trove.

So much to sing about:
all I have seen and heard,
your glory in my talents' use
my best reward:
that others see
what I have seen
and sing with me: "It is the Lord!"

Meter	6.6.8.4.4.4.8.
Based on	Psalm 90; Matthew 24:14–21; Luke 19:40; Psalm 116:12–19
Theme	Stewardship of talents/Music
Written	26 April 1989
Suggested tunes	LOVE UNKNOWN MANZ by Paul Weber

Paul Manz, world renowned organist, improviser, composer, and teacher, was celebrating his 70th birthday on May 10, 1989. A hymn commemorating this milestone in his dedicated career was commissioned by the Lutheran School of Theology at Chicago, where Dr. Manz was about to conclude his teaching career. As a friend and contemporary of Manz, I was asked to write a text befitting a citation he was to receive as Confessor of Faith at the Chicago seminary.

Rather than write an explicit birthday hymn or one spelling out the many sacrifices a dedicated servant of Christ makes in the confession of his faith, I chose to focus on the inspiration and motivation a Christian follows in the use of one's special talents, in this case in the area of worship and music. Echoes of the scriptural passages appear in the text, coincidentally mentioning the biblical "three-score years and ten" Manz was celebrating, yet with which every reader of Psalm 90 can identify in noting the limited opportunities one has for developing and using one's talents to the glory of God. The text ends with John's exclamation of recognition in the post-resurrection appearance of Christ at the Sea of Galilee.

After trying several different metrical forms, I kept returning to one of my favorite tunes, *LOVE UNKNOWN* by John Ireland, to which the text fits comfortably The metrical pattern for "My song is love unknown" is usually given with different line lengths, although the total number of syllables is equivalent and conforms to the phrasing of Ireland's haunting melody.

Marking my own 70th birthday twelve days before Manz, I wrote the kind of hymn text that would express my own feelings about the urgent but happy use of one's talents to the glory of God as centered in the Gift of gifts, Jesus Christ.

Someone Special

Someone Special, I know who:
That Someone, my God, is You!
Who could make a world like this
And a heaven full of bliss;
Someone special I must be,
Since You made it all for me!

Someone Special, that You are,
To create the Christmas Star,
Heralding the Savior's birth,
Bringing peace and joy to earth.
Someone special I must be,
Since You made that Star for me!

Someone Special, who would give
His own Son that all might live,
And by Him would set us free
From all sin and misery.
Someone special I must be,
Since You gave Your Son for me!

Someone Special, who would send
His good Spirit for a Friend,
Faith Creator, Light and Guide,
Always standing at my side.
Someone special I must be,
Since You gave that Gift to me!

Someone Special—God and man,
You were there when I began,
You'll be there when I depart,
For You live within my heart.
Someone special—now I see,
That someone is really me.

Meter	7.7.7.7.7.7.
Based on	Romans 8:14–17; 1 Peter 2:9, 10
Theme	Children/Self-esteem
Written	30 October 1978
Suggested tune	EISENBERG by Carl Schalk

In preparation for the Year of the Child in 1979, the Board for Parish Education of The Lutheran Church—Missoui Synod commissioned this hymn for children, to relate the Christian child to the various seasons of the church year, and hereby to the life of Christ. It was introduced at the 1979 general convention of the LCMS in St. Louis, where a children's choir sang certain stanzas in German, Spanish, and Chinese. It has been used in various curricular materials and at parochial school teachers' conferences. Three additional stanzas were composed for the Southern California Lutheran Teacher's Conference in 1986.

Carl Schalk composed a very suitable melody for the text. The hymn was dedicated to our three grandchildren, Daniel, Joel, and Jonathan Raedeke, whose parents are Christian day school teachers.

Someone Special

(Stanzas for Teachers)

Teachers Past

Someone special, teachers past
Teaching truths that last and last,
Planting seed they prayed would grow,
Yet not reaping what they sowed,
Someone special they must be,
For those seeds bore fruit in me.

Teachers Present

Someone special, teachers now,
Teaching God's own "why' and "how,"
Pointing to the Word who came,
Everlastingly the same:
Someone special they must be,
In whom creed and life agree.

Teachers Future

Someone special still to come,
Marching to a distant drum,
Children now, some day mature,
What they teach will long endure:
Someone special they will be,
Every one a fruitful tree.

Meter	7.7.7.7.7.7.
Written	17 June 1986
Suggested tune	EISENBERG by Carl Schalk

At the request of the Southern California Lutheran Teachers Conference, I wrote three additional stanzas that include the religious teachers of our children, who are special in their own fight. These stanzas are useful for occasions remembering the involvement of our children's spiritual tutors.

Son of God, Which Christmas Is It?

Son of God, which Christmas is it
that we share this year?
Will it glow with new reflections,
will it bring You near?
Will I marvel:
what a favor! what a gift
only God can give!

Jesus, bless the one who told me
how You came to earth,
why You left Your heavenly dwelling
for a human birth.
Do I marvel:
what a favor! what a gift
only God can give!

Jesus, bless the ones who taught me
all the songs I sing:
of the angels, and of Mary,
and the Savior King.
Do I marvel:
what a favor! what a gift
only God can give!

Jesus, bless the ones who hurry
from the stable light
with the story of Your glory,
brightening the night.
Share the marvel:
Love's best favor! Love's best gift
anyone can give!

Meter	8.5.8.5.4.7.5.
Based on	Luke 2:1–20; 2 Timothy 1:5
Theme	Christmas
Written	16 November 1990
Suggested tune	MONTGOMERY by Carl Schalk

Prompted by a request from Our Redeemer Lutheran Church, Montgomery, Alabama, honoring Karl Albrecht, church organist for more than 25 years, this text evolved.

As I observed my wife, first with our own children, and then with our granddaughter, playing and singing the traditional Christmas carols as they could share the piano bench with her, I remembered my own introduction to the glorious story of the Incarnation by my mother and father. There is that passing reference in Paul's Second Letter to Timothy, where he implies the same kind of passing of the heritage of faith from generation to generation. Simultaneously, the best Christmas Gift is being given—a Gift that never stops giving, whose culmination extends into eternity.

Source of Breath from Time's Beginning

Source of breath from time's beginning,
Source of faith till time shall end,
Seeking, striving, life-sustaining,
Ever-giving, never spent:
Gift of gifts no one can merit,
God-revealing Holy Spirit,
Like the Father with the Son,
you make us one.

O my sister, O my brother,
See what we have lived to see!
One with Christ and one another,
Joined as we were meant to be:
One because one God so loved us,
One because one Spirit moved us,
One because one Savior prayed
and we obeyed.

Here our common faith unites us,
Closer than the closest twins,
Here the love of Christ ignites us,
Here our unity begins.
Bring back home the lost and scattered,
Bind up those whose lives are shattered,
Show the world what Christ has done
to make us one.

Meter	8.7.8.7.8.8.7.4.
Based on	John 17:20–23; Ephesians 3:14–21; 4:1–7, 11–13; Colossians 3:12–16
Theme	Unity rooted in faith and love
Written	14 August 1988
Suggested tune	SUNSET HILLS by Kim S. Kolander

This text answers a request by St. Thomas/Holy Spirit Lutheran Church, Sunset Hills, Missouri, for an original hymn celebrating the tenth anniversary of a successful merger of two congregations. The theme is the unity of faith within the Una Sancta expressed in a visible unity between two formerly separate Christian congregations. The merged congregation's logo for this special commemoration depicted the leading of the Spirit as believers are called to unity, rooted in love, and renewed for mission in response to Christ's high priestly prayer.

The names of the united congregations are implied in the text, the Holy Spirit being mentioned by name as the source and sustainer of unity, and St. Thomas by the reference to the closeness of twins. Nevertheless, the hymn is meant to be useful for the theme of unity at any suitable time during the church year and by other congregations.

St. Thomas/Holy Spirit's musical director composed the tune *SUNSET HILLS.*

Spirit, God, Eternal Word

Spirit, God, Eternal Word,
what was that first song you heard
when the newborn planets sang
and the vault of heaven rang?
In that choir enlist me, too,
        to sing to you.

Let me raise my voice to you,
be my theme song all life through,
Love and mercy capture me,
awesome grace enrapture me,
songs of gratitude and praise
        fill all my days!

Through the dark of doubt and fear
let me feel you always near.
Certain of your faithfulness,
knowing you will heal and bless,
I can lift my heart again
        and sing Amen.

With my talents, skills, and time
realize your will sublime:
let the world around me hear
wisdom, hope, and Gospel cheer,
and my love for you remain
        my life's refrain.

Meter	7.7.7.7.7.4.
Based on	Job 38:7; Psalm 40:1–3; Luke 2:13, 14; Revelation 7:12
Theme	Song of the Saints/Music in the Lord's Service
Written	3 July 1992
Tune	LEESEBERG-LANGE by Kim Kolander

Friends of Tom Leeseberg-Lange, recognizing twelve years of music ministry at Holy Trinity Lutheran Church, South St. Louis County, requested a hymn on a topic of general use to honor him and to reflect his ardent interest in hymnody as an expression of faith.

The four passages above provided the framework for a contemplative yet firm expression of the believer's theme song—the praise of the Holy Trinity by creation, by the announcement of the Eternal Word's Incarnation, and by the new life in Christ created by the Spirit. This is the song God puts into the heart of every saint throughout time and eternity.

Kim Kolander, St. Louis organist, choir director, and long-time colleague of Tom's, was asked to compose an appropriate melody for the new song, and was inspired to write *LEESEBERG-LANGE,* presented to the honoree at a special service at St. Thomas/Holy Spirit Lutheran Church July 26, 1992.

Stand Before Me, Lord

Stand before me, Lord, in power,
that I know whom I can trust:
Light and Life I take for granted,
yet without you nothing is.
Strength for good, for change, for justice,
everything comes from your hands:
you're the kind of God I long for,
make of me the child you want,

Stand before me, Lord, in mercy,
that I know whom I may trust.
I could spend my life repenting,
but for mercy, I am lost.
Prodigal, you saw me drifting,
from a cross you called me home.
You're the kind of God I long for,
make of me the child you want.

Stand before me, Lord, in wisdom,
that I know whom I should trust.
Wisdom looks beyond this moment,
wisdom takes you at your word.
Be my map, my star, my compass,
use my days in useful ways.
You're the kind of God I long for,
make of me the child you want.

Stand before me, Lord, in glory,
that I know whom I may trust;
glorious in love and beauty,
grace and holiness and truth.
Now that I have seen my Savior,
I know what true glory is.
You're the kind of God I long for,
make of me the child you want.

Meter	8.7.8.7.D.
Based on	1 Corinthians 1:24; Revelation 6:9–12, passages regarding power, mercy, wisdom, and glory
Theme	Trust/Renewal/Dedication
Written	7 August 1990
Suggested tune	BEACH SPRING

Inspired by the thought of one's confrontation with God either by a specific intervention by God in one's life or by one's search for God, I found the revelation of God at such a time to be a preview of the song of the company of the redeemed in Revelation 7:9–12, where this earthly experience comes to full fruition. Though mercy is the one attribute not mentioned in that celestial song of the redeemed, it is personified in the Lamb enthroned to whom the song is directed.

I find it difficult to pinpoint a single theme for this hymn nor the numerous passages of Scripture dealing with the four subjects. Perhaps response to God's revelation may be the closest to the purpose of the hymn. The metrical pattern was suggested by *BEACH SPRING*, though a new tune may be composed for it.

The Best of Gifts

The best of gifts, the gift of peace,
first known, then lost, in Eden,
could never ever be retrieved
by wish or force or pleading.
The God of peace, by mercy moved,
prepared the surest way to prove
a caring heart, a heart of love,
a heart for sinners bleeding.

None but the Prince of Peace could end
the enmity and warfare
that tore our ties to God and friend
and doomed our common welfare.
None but the Prince of Peace could still
our inner storms, the stubborn will,
the clutching fears, the urge to kill,
and make of us peace-bearers.

The Spirit changes fear to faith
in every age and nation,
and those immersed in Jesus' death
emerge a new creation.
With sin forgiven, dread removed,
we need not strive to be beloved,
but, armed with peace, by God approved,
begin a new vocation.

Among us here may many find
the peace they thirst and strive for,
a blessing to all humankind,
the loftiest cause to live for.
The God of peace is with us now,
the Prince of Peace lives for us now,
the Spirit's peace unites us now;
the gift goes on forever.

Meter	8.7.8.7.8.8.8.7.
Based on	Ephesians 4:1–16; Colossians 3:15; and parallels
Theme	The peace of God/The Church in the World
Written	31 August 1989
Tune	SALEM NEW by Carl Schalk

This hymn text dedicated to Salem Lutheran Church, Tomball, Texas, on the occasion of the building of a new sanctuary was inspired by the name of the church, Salem, the English word for "shalom," which means peace. In researching the concept of peace in the concordance, I realized again most forcefully that this is the central theme of the Scriptures, of Christian doctrine, and of our relationship to God. No hymn, however long, can exhaust this subject, while it can occupy the study, the contemplation and the thanksgiving of a church and its members for a lifetime.

The Friend I Need

The friend I need
is the friend I have
when I have You for a friend;
who else would bleed
out of selfless love
and stay my friend to the end?

"I call you friends,"
says the Son of God,
to tell you how much you are worth."
The Father sends
what no one else could:
his gift of peace to the earth.

I look at You
whom I call my friend,
to know what friendship should be;
now born anew
like the Child God sent,
I start to be what I see.

I look around
with my newborn eyes
and see so many alone.
The love I found
and the Lord I prize
can draw us all into one.

Meter	4.5.7.4.5.7.
Based on	John 15:12–17
Theme	Friendship, Divine and Human/Youth
Written	19 March 1983
Suggested tune	AMIGO by David Christian

Illustrating the theme of Friendship ("Amigos de Christo") for the 1983 Youth Convention of The Lutheran Church—Missouri Synod in San Antonio, Texas, this hymn takes its inspiration from the statements of Christ in John 15:12–17, where Christ introduces himself as the ideal friend and the model for true friendship, inspired and motivated by Jesus, who is addressed in the hymn.

The Greatest Joy of All

The greatest joy of all
comes from the Source of all,
the God who has the best in mind—
a paradise for humankind—
the greatest joy of all.

What joy to have a God
who shares our flesh and blood,
Someone who listens to our cries,
keeps every promise, never lies—
is there a better God?

No other joy is more
worth living, dying for,
than that which God's own Son derives
from loving, serving, saving lives:
that joy is ours and more.

Now blest with love to spare
for those who need our care,
we share the joy that Jesus brought,
the joy his death and rising bought:
the joy beyond compare!

Meter	6. 6. 8. 8. 6.
Based on	Luke 2:10,11; John 15:11; 17:13; Hebrews 12:2; Matthew 25:21, 23, 34–40, and parallels
Theme	Charity/Service/Joy
Written	1 December 1998
Suggested tune	ADDISON by Carl Schalk

Reviewing the remarkable beginning and growth of Lutheran Child and Family Services of Illinois over the past 125 years, suggested tracing the motivation for all Christian charities: the joy for which the human race was created, redeemed, and destined for eternity. That joy is restored by Christ and motivates the followers of Christ to serve others with the joy the birth of the Messiah brought to the world and the gift of everlasting joy bought by God's beloved Son and sealed by His resurrection. That vision is shared when the love of God is brought to those in any need.

The Holy Innocents

Rachel will not be comforted this night
When even Rama's empty streets convulse
With sobs. Salvation has been put to flight—
And Herod reigns, God's finger on his pulse.

Meter	10. 10. 10. 10.
Based on	Matthew 2:16–18; Jeremiah 31:15–17; 1 Peter 4:12
Theme	The Holy Innocents, Martyrs/Massacre of innocents
Written	3 January 1943

Shocked once again by the briefly reported (and just as quickly forgotten) massacres of innocent civilians by ruthless rulers and conscienceless followers, I was again reminded of the Massacre of the Innocents observed on the liturgical calendar on December 28, a commemoration generally overlooked and unobserved even in liturgical churches. The continuous repetition of this horror in holocausts, ethnic cleansings, and forced migrations of millions of innocent parents and children is a reason for pause by fellow-believers and the composition of a threnody to stir their hearts and prayers.

The Commemoration in Lutheran hymnals amounts to one stanza in "For All Thy Saints in Warfare" and among the many carols, the Coventry Carol deals with this earliest Satanic attack on the newborn Messiah.

My own apathy toward these tragedies is typical of most unaffected people inside or outside the Church. Situations that bring the Son of God to tears and to the cross, move only a handful of fellow-humans to relieve the suffering with self-sacrificing ministry.

It has taken me 52 years to suggest a litany or a hymn on this subject, using the text of a quatrain composed in the afterglow of the 1942 Christmas holiday while vicaring in a Western Pennsylvanian mining town.

Some composer may be inspired by this recapitulation of Herod's edict with a choral Kyrie-type setting in the mood of the Coventry Carol, to be rendered during the Christmas season.

The Ordinary in Hymn Form

1. Kyrie

Look down in mercy on us, Lord,
receive our prayers and praise,
Eternal Father, Spirit, Word,
for your amazing grace.

CM

2. Gloria in Excelsis

Angels, sing, and earth, reply:
"Glory be to God on high!"
God who flung the stars in space,
God who formed the human race,
God the mind and God the cause,
God the source of nature's laws,
God of wisdom, power, and love,
God of gods, all gods above.
Angels, sing, and earth, reply:
"Glory be to God on high!"

Angels, sing, and earth, reply:
"Glory be to God on high!"
God who saw your creatures fall,
loved them still, and loved them all,
gave your only Son to prove
what is mercy, what is love;
and the Spirit, given free,
recreates your family.
Angels, sing, and earth, reply:
"Glory be to God on high!"

7.7.7.7.D and Refrain

3. Credo

Great God, our creator, from whom all receive
their being and blessing, in you we believe.
Almighty, all-knowing, all-gracious, all-true,
Provider and Father our trust is in you.

And you, Jesus Christ, we affirm as our Lord,
true Son of the Father, by angels adored;
Redeemer incarnate, you paid for our sins,
and, joined in your rising, our new life begins.

Free Spirit of wisdom and power and love,
on us, as on Christ, you descend from above;
you call us, you cleanse us, you open our eyes,
you keep us in peace, you restore paradise.

11.11.11.11.

4. Sanctus

"Holy, holy, holy!" all the saints in glory
fill your temple with their song around your golden throne;
"Holy, holy, holy!" with them we adore you,
God in three Persons, all in Christ as one.

11.12.12.10.

5. Agnus Dei

Meek, slaughtered Lamb of God,
bearing the sinners' load
to buy our peace:
now risen and enthroned,
with life and glory crowned,
to all the lost and found
please grant your peace.

6.6.4.6.6.6.4.

Meter	Various meters	
Based on	Scriptural texts of the liturgical Ordinary	
Themes	Kyrie, Gloria in Excelsis, Credo, Sanctus, Agnus Dei	
Written	21 January 1990	
Suggested tunes	Kyrie	NEW BRITAIN
	Gloria in Excelsis	MENDELSSOHN
	Credo	ST. DENIO
	Sanctus	NICEA
	Agnus Dei	OLIVET

Prompted by a request from the Commission on Worship of The Lutheran Church—Missouri Synod for five hymn texts on the subjects covered in the Ordinary of the liturgy (see listing above), the following texts were submitted for consideration by the Commission. The texts were being solicited from several hymn writers for a Divine Service III project that would offer in English an order of service similar to Luther's well-known "Deutsche Messe."

The Wedding Starts

The wedding starts:
Two racing hearts
Prepare to merge at this time in this place.
Now comes the bride,
Soon at her side
Her groom will join her on this day of days.

Here, too, among all called to attend
Stands their most honored Guest and (dear) Friend.
Here, in God's presence, solemn vows are spoken,
Rings are exchanged as love's pledge and token.
Here is the One who binds and makes them one,
Then adds the gift of joy here begun.

"Husband and wife,
Now one for life,
Care for each other wherever you go;
God be with you,
Ever be true,
Pray for the promise of love God wants you to know."

Meter	Irregular
Based on	Genesis 2:24; Mark 10:9; Ephesians 5:22,25; 1 Peter 3:7
Theme	Christian Wedding
Written	30 October 1999
Tune	Wagner's *Lohengrin* "Bridal March"

Responding to a request from Dr. David H. Stohlmann, pastor of Mount Olive Lutheran Church, Sebastopol, California in March 1997 for a Christian text for Wagner's popular *Lohengrin* "Bridal March," honoring Maria Schmidt on her 100th birthday, the request was considered seriously, then tentatively set aside for later consideration. Dr. Stohlmann pointed to other secular music to which sacred words had been set; e.g., Beethoven's "Ode to Joy," *AUSTRIA, NATIONAL ANTHEM, THE ASH GROVE,* and folk tunes such as *AR HYD Y NOS* and *TRYGARRE KAN INGEN VARA*. Upon reconsideration, the present text was written, offered for consideration, and accepted in October 1999, with the hope of providing a Christian view of the marriage ceremony set to a popular melody.

Then the Glory

Then the glory
Then the rest
Then the sabbath peace unbroken

Then the garden
Then the throne
Then the crystal river flowing

Then the splendor
Then the life
Then the new creation singing

Then the marriage
Then the love
Then the feast of joy unending

Then the knowing
Then the light
Then the ultimate adventure

Then the Spirit's harvest gathered
Then the Lamb in majesty
Then the Father's Amen

Then Then Then

Meter	Irregular
Based on	1 Corinthians 2:9; 2 Corinthians 4:13–18
Theme	Resurrection/Eternal Life
Written	17 February 1970, revised 10 January 1986
Suggested tune	NOW by Carl Schalk

Subsequent to the writing of "Now the silence" I wrote this "sequel" to the hymn that summarizes the elements of a worship service. If all that (in "Now the silence") is happening in our worship of the Lord here, what awaits us in our worship when we reach the end of our redemption in the glory of the world to come? One can only begin to imagine in a hymn of this kind some of the wonders C. S. Lewis explores in *The Weight of Glory*.

There's a Gathering of Daughters

There's a gathering of daughters,
Hearts set on life's highest goal
Who have found the living waters
Meant for every thirsting soul;
Sisters moved to share God's favor
With their siblings everywhere,
Spirit-linked to Christ their Savior,
Living out His daily Prayer.

Every meeting a reunion
Rich in memories and dreams
Of a close world-wide communion
Binding dedicated teams.
Like their mentors since creation,
So God's daughters still today
Practice their unique vocation,
Caring in their special way.

Picture that exciting meeting
With their risen, reigning Lord,
Every saint the others greeting,
Perfect love and joy restored,
Everything alive and thrilling,
Everlasting peace begun;
See God's boundless grace fulfilling
Every promise one by one.

Many wait to be invited,
All of whom are loved to be
In one family united
For a deathless destiny,
Singing glory, Alleluia,
To the Father, to the Son,
Honor, blessing, Alleluia,
To the Spirit—Holy One!

Meter	8.8.8.8.D
Based on	Matthew 28:1–10; Revelation 7:9–17
Theme	Women's Mission
Written	28 May 2001
Suggested tune	GALILEAN

Upon a request from the Lutheran Women's Missionary League for a 50th Anniversary Convention hymn, set to an existing melody, the traditional mission hymn, *Hark! The Voice of Jesus Calling* came to mind as an urgent call to harvest the mission field, which is the central purpose of LWML.

The theme for the hymn is the mission the first witnesses of the Resurrection were to perform. The women were told by the Angel and by Jesus Himself to tell the disciples and others that Christ, the Savior of the world, had risen from the tomb.

Since not all the members of the LWML are single or wives or mothers, they are all daughters, children of the heavenly Father, and siblings to the other children in God's family.

The Revelation 7 passage and reverence anticipates the result of the Gospel's accepted invitation: everlasting peace and joy in the presence of God by the Atonement of the Lamb of God.

This Child of Ours

This child of ours
—this miracle—
You have a dream and plan for it:
You wash it clean,
You cradle it,
You bless it and You call it Yours:
this child of ours,
this child of Yours.

This child of Yours
—this miracle—
reborn of Water and the Word;
the Book of life
records its name,
You smile and angels celebrate:
this child of Yours,
this child of ours.

This child of ours
—this miracle—
whom Christ would die for, we may love,
and train and raise,
and teach and praise,
and watch the Spirit mold a life:
this child of ours.
this child of Yours.

Meter	8.8.8.8. Refrain
Based on	John 3:5; Matthew 18:10; 19:14
Theme	Baptism
Written	5 August 1984
Suggested tune	THIS CHILD OF OURS by Richard W Gieseke

A baptismal hymn for their child Sarah was requested by Richard and Susan Gieseke while Richard was organist and choirmaster at Resurrection Lutheran Church in Sappington, Missouri, a suburb of St. Louis. I wanted to point out the dual parentage of our children as the result of Baptism. Though our child becomes God's child by means of the washing of regeneration, it still remains our child, but with much more significance than it would have as just a human offspring, though that is miracle enough. Combine that wonder with the miracle of spiritual rebirth, and the worth of the child increases fantastically.

This House with All Its Parts

Opening and Closing Stanza: *(optional)*

This house with all Its parts
reflects in faithful hearts
the glory of the Lord.
What memories are stirred
by sight and sound and word
to glorify the Lord.

The Font

Here at the font we pause
to mark the start and cause
of our new life in Christ.
We are new creatures now,
co-heirs of God's sure vow:
Where God is, there is life.

Each time the sign is made,
each time your name is said,
when fear or pain is rife:
recall whose child you are,
that God is never far:
Where God is, there is life.

The Altar

"Come home," our Father calls,
"beloved prodigals,
come to the happy Feast."
See everything prepared,
no cost, no effort spared:
Where God is, there is peace.

Once lost, now reconciled,
each one God's precious child,
the blessings never cease
in God's close family
of caring unity:
Where God is, there is peace.

The Pulpit

The Word who made all things,
whose praise creation sings,
who sends the Spirit-Dove,
reveals the heart and mind
of God for humankind:
Where God is, there is love.

God's angels still proclaim
that One, that saving Name,
in whom we live and move;
who hears them and believes
eternal life receives:
Where God is, there is love.

Meter	6.6.6.6.6.6
Based on	Exodus 40:44; John 3:5; Galatians 2:27,28; 1 Corinthians 20:16,17 and parallels
Theme	Dedication of church, font, altar, and pulpit
Written	6 October 1992
Tune	LAUDES DOMINI

At the request of Concordia Seminary, St. Louis, Missouri, I was asked to write a hymn (or stanzas) for the dedication of the Chapel of St. Timothy and St. Titus and of the font, altar, and pulpit, to take place November 15, 1992. This was an occasion I never expected to see 48 years after my graduation from the seminary, nor to be living in St. Louis at the time.

The hymn turned out to consist of an introductory and closing stanza, and three two-stanza segments pertaining to the three dedications. The melody *LAUDES DOMINI* was selected by the seminary dedication committee, headed by Dr. James Brauer, dean of the chapel.

The hymn was first used at the dedication service November 15, 1992 by an overflow gathering of more than 1500.

This Is a Time for Banners and Bells

This is a time for banners and bells,
For trumpets and festive throngs;
This is a time for holiday frills,
For worship and marching songs:
Come, sing to the Lord,
Give thanks to the Lord,
For he makes all things new,
For he makes all things new.

Think of the time when we were alone,
A nobody, weak and small,
Christ sought us out and made us his own,
The Bride of the Lord of all:
Come, sing to the Lord...

Cherish the time we spent in his grace,
The ones with the dream and we,
Sheltered and fed and loved in this place
By him who has made us free:
Come, sing to the Lord...

Live for the time of glory to come,
His pennant of love unfurled,
Cross-bearing pilgrims, heading for home,
Whose faith overcomes the world:
Come, sing to the Lord...

+Gloria Dei, Christ is alive,
And we, his beloved Bride,
Creature so rare, now seventy-five,
A diamond he wears with pride:
Come, sing to the Lord...

+ (stanza optional)

Meter	9.7.9.7. Refrain
Based on	Revelation 21:5; 2 Corinthians 5:17
Theme	Commemoration/Church Anniversary
Written	20 February 1983
Suggested tune	GLORIA DEI by Paul Manz

Gloria Dei Lutheran Church of St. Paul, Minnesota, built its 75th anniversary celebration in 1983 around the theme: "Behold, I make all things new" (Rev. 21:5), a refrain of Paul's statement in 2 Cor 5:17. The Church is Christ's Bride, his new creation, and the community of believers is witness to that regenerating power of God and the transforming power of Christ. This hymn can serve any congregation marking an anniversary by omitting the fifth stanza, which compares the diamond (75th) anniversary to a diamond in Christ's crown.

This Is a Time to Pause and Ask

This is a time to pause and ask;
"Why was I born, and for what task,
Why in a certain time and place,
And on which road to run life's race,
The calling on that new birthday
By Christ, the Life, the Truth, the Way?"

Remember what you once received
When called to faith and you believed:
What tested you, what strengthened you,
What Spirit's act made all things new.
Reborn, adopted Child of God,
Set out with Him on paths untrod.

Now carry out at any cost
A rescue mission to the lost
Before this time of grace runs out:
This is what life is all about.
God's loving plan is there for all
Who heed the Savior's urgent call.

God bless you for your faithfulness
And have you know the joy and bliss
Of greeting Jesus face to face,
And hear fulfilled the pledge of grace:
"Well done, good servant, welcome home!
Rejoice to see God's kingdom come!"

Meter	8.8.8.8.8.8.
Based on	Matthew 28:18–20; Romans 8:28 ff.; 10:10–18; 1 Peter 2:9,10; Philippians 3:12–14; et al.
Theme	Called to Serve; Recognition of Service
Written	31 October 2001

The request for a hymn marking the retirement of Dr. Stephen Carter as President of Concordia Publishing House provided an opportunity to compose a suggested review of any Christian's life and faith as a part of God's plan for time and eternity. This review does not have to wait until one's life is ending, but it can move us to use what time we have left in carrying out the mission for which we were called. A recommitment to the call to serve as members of the Body of Christ can result in the discovery of unused talents and new opportunities for living a fruitful life.

Martin Luther summarized the plan of God and its fulfillment in the meaning of the Third Article of the Apostles' Creed.

This Love, O Christ

This love, O Christ, is so much like your own,
This love of husband for his wife
A new creation molded into one,
Self-giving, sharing bread and breath,
No sacrifice too great, not even death,
One love, one promise, one for all of life

This love, O Church, is so much like your own,
This love of bride for her dear groom:
A new creation molded into one,
Devoted, faithful unto death,
Entwined together like a living wreath,
To scent this life with love's divine perfume.

Meter	10.8.10.8.10.10.
Based on	Ephesians 5:21–33; Revelation 19:7–9
Theme	Wedding/Marriage
Written	1 July 1977
Suggested tune	THIS LOVE by Donald Busarow

In an age when secular models for marriage are selfish and romantically unrealistic, when the meaning of marital love is diluted and distorted (as it is in most popular songs), I welcomed the opportunity to hold up for the Christian couple exchanging vows the model set by the Scriptures: the totally committed union between Christ and his Bride, the Church, as depicted in Isaiah, the Song of Solomon, Hosea, Ephesians 5 and Revelation 19. Surely the power to achieve an approximation of that ideal union is available from the One who designed marriage and blesses the couple who commit themselves to its ideal and purpose. The practice of daily confession in the home is the mark of the Spirit's presence and activity. In displaying and nurturing this model for marriage, the Church is as much a savior in respect to this fundamental element as it is in its concern for peace and justice, for the poor, the homeless, and the hungry. In a Christian marriage these virtues and values are nourished for the happiness of families and the health of society.

This wedding song was requested by Concordia Publishing House for a collection of wedding hymns, and Donald Busarow was asked to set the text to music.

One small revision should be noted in 2:4. The line originally read: "Admiring, trusting, faithful unto death," which had two extra syllables.

This Time of Rest

This time of rest, this time for thought,
When days are long and numbered,
Help me review my story's plot
In peace and unencumbered.

What have I learned in all these years
That Your sheer mercy gave me?
That of Your love through smiles and tears
You keep me and You save me.

You chose me once, You hold me now,
And always You are near me;
You made and kept Your faithful vow,
You promised You would hear me.

What shall I leave this world, my heirs,
What legacy, what vision,
What wise advice, what fervid prayers,
What help for life's decision?

Dear Father of my risen Lord,
My Shepherd and my Savior,
May many share my faith's reward:
Your life and You forever.

Meter	8.7.8.7.
Based on	Psalm 90 and parallels
Theme	Advanced age/Retirement
Written	24 October 1994

Having been retired for eight years and having passed the biblical "threescore years and ten," this hymn grew out of contemplation of the transitoriness of life and its meaning for the child of God: a versified prayer for elderly Christians.

This Touch of Love

This touch of love,
this taste of peace,
how can it last and still increase?
I cannot bear
to have this air
of wonder cease.

This happy feast,
this friendly bond,
how can I keep it long beyond
this fleeting hour,
this surge of power,
this treasure found?

This glow of joy,
this glimpse of light,
this momentary pure delight,
I dread to leave
to fret and grieve
and die in night.

This freshly washed,
this feeling free,
I need to know that this can be;
make me believe
what I receive
is meant for me.

Christ Jesus, you
are what I need,
the Bread and Wine on which I feed,
no friend so true,
no life so new—
I'm rich indeed.

O Savior, now
my spirit raise,
give new direction to my ways,
in all I view,
in all I do,
to give you praise.

Meter	4.4.8.4.4.4.
Eased on	Matthew 26:26–29; Luke 22:14–20
Theme	Post-Communion
Written	3 March 1971
Suggested tune	COMMUNION by Carl Schalk

Not always, not even often, much less often enough am I aware of what is happening in that high and tender meeting between my Lord and myself in the Sacrament of Holy Communion. I would hope that a hymn of this kind would heighten the consciousness of those who have just communed of the special nature of the occasion.

Though Mountains Quake and Oceans Roar

Though mountains quake and oceans roar
And lightning cracks the heavens,
Though nations rage in ruthless war,
We still have one last haven:
Our God still is God;
High above the flood,
This God's in control
From pole to trembling pole:
The Lord of hosts is with us.

There is a city where God dwells,
Where peace flows like a river;
Beyond the reach of death and hell,
It stands secure forever.
There, held in his arm
Like sheep safe from harm,
All promises kept,
Yes, even while we slept:
So great a Savior loved us!

Attention, nations, friend and foe:
Hear God himself appealing:
All who are tired of hate and woe,
Come to his Son for healing!
What we could not do,
Live and hope anew,
The Devil's head crushed,
Our every terror hushed,
God does, and he is with us!

Meter	8.7.8.7.6.6.6.6.7.
Based on	Psalm 46
Theme	Trust
Written	29 September 1985
Suggested tune	EIN FESTE BURG

At the risk of presumption, this contemporary paraphrase of Psalm 46 was requested for the Becker Psalter series of cantatas presented at Grace Lutheran Church, River Forest, Illinois, on October 27, 1985. I trust it may claim a place, though inferior, next to the Reformer's with gratitude for the use of his mighty melody. Additional notes on the cantata series may be found under "Before Your Awesome Majesty."

Through the Din of Life Around Me

Through the din of life around me
comes a haunting song of love.
One can hear it glowing, growing
like a rainbow through the clouds,
made in heaven, full of promise,
bringing peace and joy and comfort.
Let me learn that song of praise—and sing along.

Listen closely to the lyrics,
recognize them as a prayer
echoing the composition
of the very Son of God,
when his close companions begged him:
"Teach us how to pray sincerely."
"God's dear children, pray like this — and God will hear!"

Witness and review the wonders
all around, above, within,
gather instruments and voices,
loft the song around the world,
Spirit-led, with Christ arisen,
in that realm of love and glory,
joining all whose song I heard—who heard mine, too.

Meter	8.7.8.7.8.8.7.4
Based on	Luke 11:1–4; Colossians 3:15–17; and parallels
Theme	Worship/Hymns/Music
Written	24 October 1996
Suggested tune	SUNSET HILLS by Kim Kolander

Considering a subject and format for a hymn requested by Gethsemane Lutheran Church, St. Louis, honoring church musician Kim Kolander on the 20th anniversary of his music ministry, the endlessly fascinating and inexhaustible Prayer of prayers offered the most appropriate outline of subjects for corporate or private worship. It describes the relationship between the children of God and their heavenly Father, and proposes a list of concerns for worshipers: reverence, the goal and mission of life, dedication, confession of faith, trust, daily devotion and petition, repentance, forgiveness, trials and spiritual struggles, thanksgiving, praise, etc.

In some hymns, the words come first and melodies are composed to give them a musical expression. Other times, certain tunes inspire fitting words. In this instance, having written a hymn text, "Source of Breath from Time's Beginning," for which Kim Kolander composed a fitting tune, that tune in turn inspired the format of the text for this hymn.

To Know God's Love, Behold the Cross

To know God's love, behold the cross!
Who else would suffer such a loss?
What gift is there of greater price
Than this astounding sacrifice?!
        Lord, have mercy!
        Christ, have mercy!

Who else could possibly atone
For all the world, but you alone?
None but a perfect Lamb could bear
The curse that dooms all to despair!
        Lord, have mercy!
        Christ, have mercy!

Like that amazed centurion,
We too exclaim: "You are God's Son!"
Who else in heaven or earth but you
Would do what only God could do?
        Lord, have mercy!
        Christ, have mercy!

Unless you were to rise again,
That Friday would have been the end;
The creatures whom you came to save
Would join you in your death and grave.
        Lord, have mercy!
        Christ, have mercy!

Each time we meet, you come to us
Across the gulf of time and space:
Your children here—you everywhere,
You in your Word—we in our prayer:
        Lord, have mercy!
        Christ, have mercy!

Meter	8.8.8.8.4.4.
Based on	John 3:14–17; Romans 5:8; Ephesians 2:4,5; 1 John 3:16; 4:9; and parallels
Theme	The Gospel/Lent/Good Friday
Written	28 May 1997
Suggested tune	JEZISI, DRAHY POKLAD MOJ

This alternate text with a Lenten theme was requested for a concertato composed by Cantor Mark Sedio, as an alternative to Sedio's translation of the beloved Slovak hymn, "Jezisi, drahy poklad moj": "My Dearest Treasure, Jesus Christ," published by Concordia.

The origin of the Slovak original text is uncertain. It is first found in Vaclav Kleych's hymnal of c. 1726, with a superscription, "Salve cordis gaudium,"suggesting a possible paraphrase of an older Latin hymn.

To the Everlasting Hills

To the everlasting hills I lift my eyes,
For I know, the One who made them hears my cries.
When despondent and afraid,
Where else can I turn for aid?
Who is more able to help me,
Who is more willing to help me?

Would the Lord who made us ever let us fall;
Won't the Lord who chose us answer when we call?
Guide by day and Guard by night,
Superhuman care and might:
More than a sufferer aches for,
More than a sinner could ask for.

Go and come in peace, no evil shall come near,
God will stand between you and the things you fear
Cling to this eternal Friend,
With you always, without end:
Trust such a Keeper to love you,
Trust such a Keeper to save you.

Meter	11.11.7.7.8.8.
Based on	Psalm 121
Theme	Trust
Written	27 February 1989
Suggested tune	Setting of “Zu dem Bergen hebet sich ein Augenpaar” by Peter Cornelius

A new hymn based on Psalm 121 was sought by MorningStar Music Publishers to fit a musical setting by Peter Cornelius (1824–74) on a German paraphrase. “Zu dem Bergen hebet sich ein Augenpaar.” The metrical pattern of the German text and choir setting dictated the rhyme and meter of the requested hymn. Rather than restricting the composition to a metrical paraphrase of Psalm 121, of which there are so many in existence already, including some that have become classic, I chose the characteristics of a hymn prompted by the imagery of the biblical Psalm.

The unique metrical pattern restricts this text to this melody or to another which would replace the Cornelius setting.

To Those Who Seek God's Kingdom First

To those who seek God's kingdom first
great blessings multiply.
Their deepest hunger, longest thirst
God vows to satisfy.
Faith puts the promise to the test
and proves God's will is best.

Because a single pioneer
set out in faith and prayer,
God's answer still surrounds us here
with precious love and care.
Because a planter sowed good seeds—
what crowds their harvest feeds!

How many more may still be blest,
who pray "Your kingdom come!"
and find their haven and their rest,
their safe and friendly home,
where grace and goodness, joy and peace
are nurtured and increase!

How many lives are moved to sing
a song of thanks and praise
for those who brought them to the King,
whose mercy fills their days,
the Bridegroom we can hardly wait
to greet at Heaven's gate!

Meter	8. 6. 8. 6. 8. 6.
Based on	Matthew 6:33; 2 Corinthians 9:6–11; John 3:29–36; Revelation 19:5–9 and parallels
Theme	Fruitful faith/The Church/Anniversary
Written	1 September 1997
Suggested tune	BROTHER JAMES' AIR

Prompted by the 50th anniversary of Lutheran Haven, a retirement center of the SELC District of The Lutheran Church—Missouri Synod, in Oviedo, Florida, the hymn describes the fulfillment of Matthew 6:33, the dominating motto of its founders in 1948.

The Haven's beginnings go back to 1911, when Andrew Duda, Sr. immigrated with his wife and four children from Slovakia to a farm in Cleveland, Ohio. The next year he moved to central Florida with several other Slovak Lutheran families from Trinity Lutheran Church. A four-year stay failed, and the farmers returned to Cleveland for a decade. Upon their resettlement in Florida, the colony organized a congregation and met in a frame bulding for services without a resident pastor for 22 years. In 1948, the Duda family donated land and funds to the church and Synod to provide "an orphanage and an old folks' home for retired pastors." Under the direction of their resident pastor, Stephen M. Tuhy, and a board of directors, the project soon expanded into a church edifice, a residence for children, a Christian day school, and a retirement village for Lutheran retirees, now numbering more than 300 residents

The ministry of the Slavia/Oviedo settlers is evidence of the fulfillment of our Lord's injunction in Matthew 6:33: "Seek first the kingdom of God…"

The closing reference to the Bridegroom identifies the faithful followers of Christ as members of the Una Sancta—the Bride of Christ practicing faith and love and awaiting her marriage to the Lamb of God mentioned in Revelation 19:5–9, a glorious reunion of those whose faith and membership in the Body of Christ resulted from the sowing of the Word.

BROTHER JAMES' AIR suggested itself as a fitting melody echoing the 23rd Psalm as a description of the relationship between the King of love, the Good Shepherd and his flock.

Today Again, the Gift of Life

Today again, the gift of life:
from whom, if not from You?
Eternal and righteous,
majestic and holy,
creator of wonders,
wishing Your creatures the best:
But more than a wish, a promise,
more than a promise, an oath,
more than an oath—a seal!
You are the one, the only God,
There is no God like You!

Today again, the gift of love:
from whom, if not from You?
Compassionate seeker,
self-giving redeemer,
revealer of heaven,
giving Your creatures the best:
but more than a gift, a person,
more than a person, Your self,
more than Your self—Your all!
You are the one, the only God,
there is no God like You!

Today again, the gift of peace:
from whom, if not from You?
Inviting, forgiving,
consoling, restoring,
adopting, rejoicing,
all to remind us of You:
but more than a thought, an impulse,
more than an impulse, a song,
more than a song—a life!
You are the one, the only God,
there is no God like You!

Meter	Irregular
Based on	Psalm 71:15–24
Theme	Devotion/Service to God
Written	2 January 1989
Suggested tune	TURCO by Carl Schalk

The First Presbyterian Church of Dearborn, Michigan requested a hymn honoring Alexander J. Turco on his 25th anniversary as Director of Music on the themes of devotion and service to God.

The resulting text was inspired by Psalm 71:15–24 in the New English Bible translation. The passage is one of several impressed by God's uniqueness ("Who is like you, O God"), which in turn moves the creature to awareness, awe, and appreciation. Each new day provides a reason for gratitude and praise, with some of it expressed in song, but all of it in a life of devotion and service to God.

Triumphant Lamb and Lord of All

Triumphant Lamb and Lord of all,
Receive the highest crown!
No one who ever ruled on earth
Could do what You have done—
Create a realm of love and peace—
No one but You alone!
To You, eternal King of kings,
Your blood-redeemed creation sings:

Refrain:
The Kingdom, the Power, and Glory are Yours
forever and ever. Amen.

All might is Yours to own and wield,
You save us when we cry;
Our fiercest foes, and Yours as well,
Assail us till we die;
Defeated by Your cross, they fall,
And where You rose, they lie!
Now, with Your victory complete,
With saints and angels we repeat:

Refrain

Is there for You and everyone
A greater joy than this:
Your plans and promises fulfilled,
An endless life of bliss?!
The glory You prepared for all
You want no one to miss.
Because You are the One God sent,
We too shall sing at this event:

Refrain

Meter	8.6.8.6.8.6.8.8. Refrain
Based on	Daniel 7:13,14; Matthew 6:13b; 25:31; 1 Timothy 5:15,16; Revelation 1:4b–6; parallels and pericopes
Theme	Christ the King
Writtcn	13 September 1994
Tune	by Kenneth T. Kosche

Coinciding with a hymn festival at Concordia University, Mequon, Wisconsin, on Christ the King Sunday (November 20, 1994), was the request for a Hymn of the Day to be introduced that day. In a review of the numerous Old and New Testament references to the crowning of Christ the King, the doxology of the Lord's Prayer—though not appearing in certain manuscripts—nevertheless sums up the song of the saints and heavenly hosts at the coronation of our much-undervalued and underestimated Savior of the world. This doxology was chosen as the framework of this new text. The resulting hymn tries to tie the Church Militant to the Church Triumphant, which, from the viewpoint of our supraspace and supratime triune God merges into the concurrent events of a "timeless" eternity. In this existence on earth, we operate in created time and space; in our resurrection, all events take place in a continuous Now. We have to believe it to see it.

Up Through Endless Ranks of Angels

Up through endless ranks of angels,
Cries of triumph in his ears,
To his heavenly throne ascending,
Having vanquished all their fears,
Christ looks down upon his faithful,
Leaving them in happy tears.

Death-destroying, life-restoring,
Proven Equal to our need,
Now for us before the Father
As our brother intercede:
Flesh that for our world was wounded,
Living, for the wounded plead.

To our lives of wanton wandering
Send your promised Spirit-Guide,
Through our lives of fear and failure
With your power and love abide:
Welcome us, as you were welcomed,
To an endless Eastertide.

Alleluia, alleluia,
Oh, to breathe the Spirit's grace!
Alleluia, alleluia,
Oh, to see the Father's face!
Alleluia, alleluia,
Oh, to feel the Son's embrace!

Meter	8.7.8.7.8.7.
Based on	Luke 24:50–53; Acts 1:9–11
Theme	Ascension (Hymn of the Day)
Written	25 May 1973
Suggested tune	ASCENDED TRIUMPH by Henry V. Gerike

During the preparation of the *Lutheran Book of Worship* (1978), Augsburg Publishing House asked for an Ascension hymn to go with *OUR LADY TRONDHEIM,* hence the metric structure of the text. Into that format I gathered a number of implications of the Ascension as they apply to the followers of Christ, who recall his departure and await his promised return. Taking the Scriptural phenomenological viewpoint, I originally began the text with the word "Up." The publishers, however, preferred to avoid the three-tiered universe imagery and so substituted the word "There," in which version they published a setting by Carl Schalk. When the Inter-Lutheran Commission on Worship chose the text as the hymn of the day for Ascension, the original opening preposition was restored and a last-minute substitution for both *OUR LADY TRONDHEIM* and the Carl Schalk tune was made: *ASCENDED TRIUMPH* by Henry V. Gerike, the festive tune almost always used with the text since that time.

Walls Crack, the Trumpet Sounds

Wails crack, the trumpet sounds,
the day of jubilee explodes.
The night of feardom gone,
old jails erupt in dancing crowds.
The freedom we parade for
is the freedom Jesus paid for,
so sing a life of gratitude:
        Alleluia!

Christ comes, the Servant-King,
to do what we could never do,
to break our binding chains,
our dead and dying hopes renew.
The freedom we were made for
is the freedom Jesus paid for,
so sing a life of gratitude:
        Alleluia!

Believe the slate is clean,
enjoy God's year of jubilee;
explore with fresh new hearts
the vast bright fields of liberty.
The freedom that we prayed for
is the freedom Jesus paid for,
so sing a life of gratitude:
        Alleluia!

Stand fast, the demons lurk
to trap us in the death we left.
Christ lives, and so do we,
with power to keep and share the gift.
The freedom we were freed for
is the freedom Jesus paid for,
so sing a life of gratitude:
        Alleluia!

Meter	6.8.6.8.7.8.8.4.
Based on	Leviticus 25:8ff., Isaiah 61:1–3; Luke 4:16–21
Theme	Spiritual liberty
Written	19 February 1990
Suggested tune	MISSION by Carl Schalk

Inspired in part by the 50th (Jubilee) anniversary of Trinity Lutheran Church, Mission, Kansas; by Leviticus 25:8ff., Isaiah 61:1–3 and its fulfillment in Luke 4:16–21; by the many passages defining the glorious liberty of God's children; and not least by the tumultuous events transpiring in Eastern Europe at the time, this text came into being. The richness of the subject cannot adequately be covered in one hymn. One can only suggest by inference the connection between the name of Christ (literally, the Anointed One) and the identity of the "anointed" one in Isaiah's prophecy who was "to proclaim liberty to the captives." Significantly, the first day of the year of jubilee ("the acceptable year of the Lord" in Christ's first sermon) was to take place on the Day of Atonement, heralded by a trumpet call. How fitting then to tie Jesus (literally, Savior) and his work of atonement to that unbelievable freedom by repeating that fact in the hymn's refrain. The worshiper can make further connections between St. Paul's exhortation to the Galatians to "stand fast in the liberty by which Christ has made us free" and the warning of Jeremiah (34:8–11) to God's people not to lose their liberty by slipping back into the old bondage, and even worse, to abuse their freedom by oppressing their neighbor, as Jesus warned in the Parable of the Unmerciful Servant.

The text is not meant to be restricted to the jubilee of a congregation, but can be used by Christians at any time to remind them of the precious freedom they enjoy, and their mission to share that freedom with so many still in captivity.

Weep with Us, Jesus

Weep with us, Jesus, at our loss,
as once you wept for Lazarus.
Who knows but you how deep our grief,
Who else but you can bring relief?

Console us, Jesus, with your touch,
lest we be burdened overmuch.
Cry to these graves, "Release your prey!
Your grip was loosed on Easter Day."

You do not leave us comfortless,
you have a word to speak to us:
"All who believe in Me shall live,
all rise with Me from death and grave."

Assure us who are left to weep:
"Your precious ones are just asleep;
I shall awaken them one day
where all God's children laugh and play."

"Some good will come from this, I swear;
till then rest on My Spirit's care.
With joy your wept-out eyes will glow
to see the bliss your loved ones know."

Meter	8.8.8.8.
Based on	John 11:35(43,44), Matthew 19:13–15
Theme	Requiem for children's death
Written	10 July 1991
Suggested tune	LM

During the Hymn Society of America's annual conference at St. Olaf College, Northfield, Minnesota, July 7–10, 1991, Edward J. Mikel, Jr., a conferee from Riverside, Illinois, met me in a dormitory corridor. In the course of our conversation, he shared the story of a haunting experience that occurred three years earlier in the town of Riverside, a tightly-knit community. On May 8, the first day of the Little League season, a car whose driver suddenly blacked out, plowed into a dozen children sitting on a bench on the third base line of the field, killing three and injuring eight. The tragedy left the families of the children and the community in shock. Three funeral services and a memorial service attempted to console the mourners. Mikel suggested the composition of a hymn for such inexplicable occurrences.

The report of that tragedy and its personal impact on so many people embedded itself into my consciousness, and the night the conference ended the thoughts of this hymn began to form. A month later the text suggested itself as a requiem for similar occasions, and possibly for the memorial service conducted annually in Riverside on May 8.

Welcome in the Name of Christ

Welcome in the name of Christ
who has sent you to us!
Come, ordained to be our guide,
lead our Alleluias.
Come, the answer to our prayers:
shepherd, teacher, feeder,
by the Spirit of the Church
called to be our leader.

In this place and for this time
help us write our diary.
We would be your joy and crown,
and your hope and glory.
By your words and by your works
show us Christ our Savior;
serve us with the Bread of Life,
Life that lasts forever.

For the righteous few who pray,
God will spare the city;
for the cries of those who care,
God will hear and pity.
Here a harvest to be gleaned,
here a field for sowing;
here the empty come to find
blessings overflowing.

Send us, Christ, as You were sent,
Your lost sheep to gather,
God's own family to be:
mother, sister, brother.
Keep us warmly one with you,
safe, alive, and growing,
give what only You can give:
peace beyond all knowing.

Meter	7.6.7.6.D
Based on	Matthew 10:40, 41; 1 Thessalonians 2:19, 20; Matthew 6:34; John 6:27, 47; 20:21–23.
Theme	Installation of a pastor
Written	9 April 1989
Suggested tune	GAUDEAMUS PARITER

Holy Trinity Lutheran Church, St. Louis (see "God who built this wondrous planet") requested a hymn for the installation of its newly-called pastor, in June, 1989. Having had this experience three times, I could recall my thoughts and feelings as I joined a calling congregation in their ministry. Then, tracing the vocation of the Christian pastor to the calling of the disciples and their apostleship, I found a number of parallels between a congregation and its pastor in the New Testament record that still apply.

The Christian pastor's ministry is an extension of Christ's ministry, his compassionate gathering of "sheep without a shepherd." Our Lord's commissioning of the apostles to "make disciples of all nations," one sowing, another watering, still another harvesting the regenerative seed of the Word, and many other images of disciples "serving the Bread of Life" sufficient to feed the multitudes of the world, the gathering of the nameless into God's family as Jesus' "brother, sister, mother," the influence of the faithful few on the community, the leading of the Spirit, and so on could have added more stanzas to accommodate the multi-faceted glory of the holy ministry.

GAUDEAMUS PARITER by John Roh (Horn), a Bohemian Brethren pastor and hymn writer (c.1490–1547), a contemporary of Martin Luther, was selected. This melody is associated with "Come, you faithful, raise the strain," a cheerful Easter hymn. The tune not only dictated the meter of the text, but suggests the central message of the risen Christ, whose coming was heralded at his birth as One who would bring peace. Our Lord's post-resurrection greeting was "Peace be with you." The hymn ends with the fulfillment of that promise.

What Are You Looking for, Magdalen?

What are you looking for, Magdalen, Magdalen,
What are you looking for, Magdalen?
Object of shame and scorn,
By seven demons torn,
What are you looking for, Magdalen, Magdalen,
What are you looking for, Magdalen?

When Jesus Christ appears,
you are healed, you are healed,
When Jesus Christ appears, you are healed;
When he removes your fears,
You wash his feet with tears,
When Jesus Christ appears,
you are healed, love is sealed,
When Jesus Christ appears, you are healed.

On dreadful Calvary, when he died, when he died,
On dreadful Calvary, when he died,
You and your sisters three
Stood watch beneath that tree
On dreadful Calvary, when he died, crucified,
On dreadful Calvary, when he died.

Too late you came with balm, Mariam, Mariam,
Too late you came with balm, Mariam,
When from the grave he came
Alive, he spoke your name,
Alive, he spoke your name, Mariam, Mariam,
Alive, he spoke your name, Mariam.

You were the first to know Jesus lives, Jesus lives,
You were the first to know Jesus lives!
You were the first to go
To spread the Easter glow
That everyone may know Jesus lives, Jesus lives,
That everyone may know Jesus lives!

Meter	12.9.6.6.12.9.
Based on	Luke 8:2; Mark 15:40; 16:1, John 19:25; 20:11–18; Luke 7:38
Theme	Commemoration of Mary Magdalene, July 22
Written	17 March 1992
Suggested tune	WONDROUS LOVE

At the request of the planning committee for the ALCM Conference in Austin, Texas the summer of 1992, a hymn text commemorating Mary Magdalene was written to be introduced at the conference on July 22.

The text was to be written to the tune *WONDROUS LOVE*, hence the folk-like structure of the text.

Although Mary Magdalene probably was not the sinful woman of Luke 7:38, nor the Mary mentioned in John 11:2, nevertheless her gratitude and devotion figuratively matched that of the other two women who washed Christ's feet with their tears and dried them with their hair. More important for the commemoration of Mary Magdalene was her presence at the cross and her being the first to see the risen Christ and thereby the first "apostle to the apostles" sent to announce the Resurrection of her Lord and ours. The New Testament pronunciation of her name is used in the hymn to echo the saying of her name as she may have heard it.

What Would the World Be Like?

What would the world be like,
if You were known the one true God,
if we gave up our proud facade,
and knelt before You meek and awed—
what would the world be like?

What could the world be like,
if all received and loved Your Son,
Your kingdom came, Your will were done,
and envy, lust, and greed were gone—
what could the world be like?

What blessings would we know,
if everyone sought truth and peace,
saw justice rule, and good increase,
and lifelong captives found release—
what blessings would we know?

What joy would fill Your heart,
if we loved You as You love us,
had faith in all Your promises,
were like You: helpful, generous—
what joy would fill Your heart?

What would our lives be like,
if every day began with thanks,
and every gift received with thanks,
and every day were closed with thanks—
what would our lives be like?

Meter	5.8.8.8.5.
Based on	Mark 1:14,15; 2 Timothy 1:9, 10 and parallels
Theme	Conflict/Crossroads/Gospel of the Kingdom
Written	8 December 1991
Tune	DES MOINES, by Carl Schalk

At the request of the planning committee for the 1992 conference of American Lutheran Church Musicians Region III in Des Moines, Iowa, this hymn was written to express and apply the theme of the conference, "Worship and World: Conflict and Crossroads" and dealing with the influence of culture on worship.

The Gospel comes with a message and values to every culture, setting up a contra-ideal, resulting in tension and conflict. Christ came preaching the Gospel of the Kingdom of God, a vision of a lost paradise that God promised to realize for everyone who received the Savior in faith.

Christ comes to deal with the causes of human conflicts and misery: ignorance (Eph. 4:18), pride (Gen. 3:5; 1 Peter 5:5), envy (Mt. 27:18), lust (Js. 4:1), and greed (1 Tim. 6:10). In the Kingdom of God, these destroyers of peace and relationships are replaced by love, peace, and joy that come from reconciliation with God and the new birth.

This hymn asks the worshipper to visualize the promise and potential of the Gospel's power in the individual, in society, in culture. It is available, it is as free as love itself. And there is only now for our decision to accept or reject it.

When God's Dread Judgment Bursts Abroad

When God's dread judgment bursts abroad,
when heavens burn and this earth quakes,
who shall be then yet serving God
and loving until that Day breaks?

What kind of people should we be
who see the nearness of the end,
while Christ is dying and unfree,
naked and hungry, without friend?

Safe as we are, elect in grace,
hopeful of standing at your throne,
give us the time to show your face
to others doomed to grope alone.

Let none despair or loving shirk
because remaining days are few,
but in these hours of waiting work
the work of Him who sent us too.

So come, Lord Jesus, come with speed
to consummate your kingdom new;
and while we wait and warnings heed,
let us still living live for you.

Meter	LM
Based on	Matthew 24:3–14, 36–51
Theme	The Day of Judgment
Written	21 November 1964

Going through my files of earlier poetry, I came across this hymn written in November 1964, and found it particularly befitting the turbulent years 1989–90. The text seemed especially appropriate for the threatening weeks of August 1990, during the Persian Gulf crisis.

When the Seed of Faith Is Planted

When the seed of faith is planted,
even angels are amazed.
Lest we lightly take for granted
such a wonder, God be praised!
After all, remember Who
made the seed and makes it grow.

So the Church is generated
by the Spirit with the Word,
as a few, in faith united,
act upon the Word they heard,
and the Lord who told them "Go!"
multiplies the seed they sow.

Now a global generation
numbers millions who confess:
"Christ the joy of our salvation,
source of lasting happiness,
You our Bridegroom, we Your Bride,
what love — that for us You died!"

Heaven knows no greater pleasure
than the prodigal's return,
and we have no greater treasure
than the joy no one can earn.
Now that we have found our rest,
we can bless as we were blest.

All-creating, All-redeeming,
All-renewing God and Lord,
Joyfully, with mercy beaming,
harvesting Your fruitful Word:
as our faith and love increase,
make us planters of Your peace.

Meter	8.7.8.7.7.7.
Based on	Luke 2:10; John 15:11; 17:13, 17, 18; Matthew 13:23; 28:18–20; Romans 10:8ff. and parallels
Theme	Church/Mission/The Word/Joy
Written	13 June 1996

Requested by the Commission on Worship of The Lutheran Church—Missouri Synod to commemorate the Sesquicentennial of the Synod in 1996–97. Among many possible themes, the purpose, origin, and mission of the Church was chosen. Beginning with the announcement of the angel of the Lord to the Bethlehem shepherds: "Fear not! For, behold, I bring you good tidings of great joy, which shall be to all people," the Gospel becomes the theme of Christ's mission and, in turn, the theme of the Great Commission. The Gospel produces faith, and faith results in joy, joy in the heart of the God of love, joy in the rescued believer, joy in heaven among the angels over one repentant sinner. The chain continues through all the generations of the human race and culminates in eternity.

Other implications and ramifications of the theme can be found in many parallel passages, making it difficult to restrict the hymn to five stanzas.

When You Woke That Thursday Morning

When you woke that Thursday morning,
Savior, Teacher, faithful Friend,
thoughts of self and safety scorning,
knowing how the day would end;
Lamb of God, foretold for ages,
now at last the hour had come
when but One could pay sin's wages:
you assumed their dreadful sum.

Never so alone and lonely,
longing with tormented heart
to be with your dear ones only
for a quiet hour apart:
sinless Lamb and fallen creature,
one last Paschal meal to eat,
one last lesson as their teacher,
washing your disciples' feet.

What was there that you could give them
that would never be outspent,
what great gift that would outlive them,
what last will and testament?
"Show me and the world you love me,
know me as the Lamb of God:
Do this in remembrance of me,
eat this Body, drink this Blood."

One in faith, in love united,
all one body, you the head,
when we meet, by you invited,
you are with us, as you said.
One with you and one another
in a unity sublime,
see in us your sister, brother,
one in every place and time.

One day all the Church will capture
that bright vision glorious,
and your saints will know the rapture
that your heart desired for us,
when the longed-for peace and union
of the Greatest and the least
meet in joyous, blest communion
in your never-ending feast.

Meter	8.7.8.7.D.
Based on	Communion narratives in Matthew, Mark, Luke, and St. Paul
Theme	The Eucharist/Holy Communion
Written	25 February 1991
Suggested tune	IN BABILONE

The Commission on Worship of The Lutheran Church—Missouri Synod, wishing to recognize the 25th anniversary of its current executive director, Dr. James L. Brauer's ordination, commissioned a communion hymn for the occasion. The theme happened to coincide with my near-obsession with worship and the centrality of the Word and Sacrament and the significance of Holy Communion for the strengthening of the Body of Christ, some of which I stated in my comments on 'This Touch of Love." As I delved into the Institution of the Lord's Supper, I discovered and rediscovered many implications of that awesome event so lightly regarded by so many of our Lord's followers—too often including myself. One among many insights that surfaced in the preparation of the text was the fulfillment of Christ's last recorded words to his disciples in Matthew 28: "And lo, I am with you always to the end of the age." Isn't this pledge fulfilled in the Sacrament of the Altar for those who believe in the Real Presence?

Where Shepherds Lately Knelt

Where shepherds lately knelt,
and kept the angel's word,
I come in half-belief,
a pilgrim strangely stirred;
but there is room
and welcome there
for me.

In that unlikely place
I find him as they said:
sweet newborn Babe, how frail!
and in a manger bed:
a still small Voice
to cry one day
for me.

How should I not have known
Isaiah would be there,
his prophecies fulfilled?
With pounding heart, I stare:
a Child, a Son,
the Prince of Peace—
for me.

Can I, will I forget
how Love was born and burned
its way into my heart—
unasked, unforced, unearned,
to die, to live, and not alone
for me?

Meter	12.12.10.10.
Based on	Luke 2:8–18
Theme	Christmas
Written	9 July 1986
Suggested tune	MANGER SONG by Carl Schalk

Another request from Augsburg Publishing House for a Christmas song for their Christmas Annual, this time for the 1987 edition, like that which resulted in "Before the marvel of this night" in the 1981 annual, prompted the composition of this hymn on the adoration of the Christ Child in the manger. Once again I wondered what fresh approach and contemporary application could be made of that central event in history. Rather than report the event again in the third person, as so many Christmas songs do, I placed myself in spirit at that poor manger bed and reviewed the implications of that visit in my life and future and in that of my fellow human beings. I have struggled, and more so as I grow older, with the incomprehensibility of that event and of my connection with it, and with each commemoration of that miracle becoming more routine, though its impact on God's heart remains the means of my salvation. I pictured myself at the opposite side of the event from Isaiah and his prophecy (9:6, 7), applying the same promise to myself as a late-arriving pilgrim.

Where the Swallow Makes Her Nest

Where the swallow makes her nest,
There God's people find their rest.
Who can count the lavish blessings
God has poured upon this flock?
Who remembers what refreshings
Flow to all from Christ the Rock?
Where the swallow makes her nest,
There God's people find their rest.

Pause amid the rush of time,
Ponder mysteries sublime.
Who we are and how we got here,
Why God chose us long ago,
Still sustains our blessed lot here,
Gives us all we need to grow.
Pause amid the rush of time,
Ponder mysteries sublime.

What if someone had not cared,
What if someone had not dared?
Would we still be trapped in blindness,
Lonely, hopeless, and afraid?
Would we know God's grace and kindness,
Or this refuge ready-made?
What if someone had not cared,
What if someone had not dared?

What a treasure to receive!
What a legacy to leave!
Here the Word invited, saved us,
Gathered us—one family,
On the hand of God engraved us,
Made each one a fruitful tree.
What a treasure to receive!
What a legacy to leave!

Eyes upon our home above,
Thank and praise our God of love.
Test the challenge and the vision
Of a world yet to be won,
And with boldness and decision
Build on what was here begun.
Eyes upon our home above,
Thank and praise our God of love.

Meter	7.7.8.7.8.7.7.7.
Based on	Psalm 84 and parallels; Matthew 28:19,20; Rev. 3:11
Theme	The Church Militant/House of Worship
Written	27 May 1993
Suggested tune	FRANKENMUTH by Carl Schalk

One of the oldest and historic congregations of The Lutheran Church—Missouri Synod, the Evangelical Lutheran Church of St. Lorenz in Frankenmuth, Michigan, commissioned this hymn for its 150th anniversary in 1995. The congregation has a wide reputation for its zeal for worship, fellowship, and missions. Its founders began its history with the building of a log church and school in 1845, with Indian children enrolled in the first school. During its century and a half, it has provided more than 200 'pastors and teachers to the church at large, including presidents of Synod and of the St. Louis seminary, besides supporting a number of missionary families. Its Christian day school is the largest in the Synod. Its third church building and school plant dominate the Frankenmuth community.

Simultaneously, the congregation carries on a wide-ranging spiritual and social ministry, with strong representation and leadership in the community. Rich in musical tradition, the congregation today has some 300 members in two bell choirs, a treble choir, male chorus, and mixed choir.

The anniversary year theme is Revelation 3:11: "Behold, I come quickly! Hold fast what you have, that no one may take your crown."

Where You Are, There Is Life

Where you are, there is life:
the cosmic "Let there be!"
the "Lazarus, come forth!"
Without you nothing is or grows,
your Word umbilical to all.
Where you are, there is life
        and you are here!

Where you are, there is love:
a promise made and kept,
one Son who dies for all,
a love that banishes all fear,
that, like its Father, never ends.
Where you are, there is love—
        and you are here!

Where you are, there is peace:
a resting place at last,
no running anymore;
forgiven and forgiving friends,
the quest of all who share your plan.
Where you are, there is peace—
        and you are here!

True life and love and peace
you are, and we are yours,
Creator, Lamb, and Dove.
Make us partakers of your dream,
see what your heart and hands have done,
and smile and say again:
        how good, how good!

Meter	6.6.6.8.8.6.4.
Based on	John 1:4; 14:6, 23, 27
Theme	New Creation/Union with God
Written	5 December 1982

This is an uncommissioned, unassigned hymn text, for which as yet no tune has been composed. It recalls the union of the believer with God, the first three stanzas referring to the persons of the Trinity, and the last a doxology. I debated about the use of the word "umbilical" in the first stanza, trusting it would not seem to have been chosen for effect rather than meaning. To me it expresses the generating place of the Word in our rebirth as God's children. Lacking rhymes, it is my hope that the rhythm, the refrain, and the melody will take care of that omission.

Who Can Conceive the One True God

Who can conceive the one true God,
before, beyond, above all things,
almighty, awesome King of kings,
whose scepter is a shepherd's rod!
From heaven's throne
this very One
is with us in our gatherings!

Good Shepherd, when you see our race,
a scattered, hopeless flock of sheep,
you have compassion,—and you weep.
But more than that, you take our place!
Love so intense,
love so immense,
enfolds us while we wake or sleep.

You are the promised holy One
God sent the world,—and when you came,
you called your precious sheep by name
and made the long-lost ones your own.
We follow you,
our Shepherd, too,
and find that you are still the same.

Give us true shepherds with your voice
to lead us safely to your fold,
to feed the faith of young and old,
each one a sought and treasured choice,
until the shout
in heav'n rings out:
"One more lost sheep is found! Rejoice!!"

Meter	8.8.8.8.4.4.8. or 8.8.8.8.8.8.
Based on	Psalm 23; John 10:14–17; Luke 15:7; Hebrews 12:2 and parallel texts
Theme	Shepherd/Sheep/Heavenly Joy
Written	1 September 1994

This hymn text was occasioned by the 40th anniversary of Pacific Hills Lutheran Church, Omaha, Nebraska, and scheduled for Transfiguration Sunday, February 26, 1995. A special accent was requested on Christ the Good Shepherd and His call to follow Him for the gift of eternal life.

Following the trail of the Divine Shepherd in the Scriptures, I was again amazed at the inexhaustible references to God's revelation as a self-sacrificing deity filled with the joy of the lost being sought and found: the constant focus of Providence throughout the history of the human race. And I wondered about the possible connection between Luke 15:7 and Hebrews 12:2 as to the joy that impelled the Good Shepherd to risk and sacrifice everything for the lost sheep.

Who Could Have Dreamt a Land Like This?

Who could have dreamt a land like this,
The answer to an exile's prayer,
An Eden in the making?
The thankful find a rare surprise,
Bright bursts of blessing everywhere,
At every new dawn's breaking.
Ring out, sing out,
Hills replying, banners flying,
Bells a-ringing,
Flood our Father's throne with singing.

In deep and honest grief lament
Your glory marred by greed and pride,
The blood for vengeance crying.
Before the Crucified repent
The wasted land, the fratricide,
Your ruthless, selfish vying.
Toll then, toll ten
Bells of mourning, wrath and warning,
Tearful token,
Once for each commandment broken.

God's grace and power remain the same
As when our fathers found this shore,
His Spirit for the asking.
America, invoke that Name,
So shall we all, spared want and war,
In fruitful peace be basking.
Sing out, ring out,
Live in thrilling, dream-fulfilling
Expectation.
Crack new bells in jubilation!

Meter	Irregular
Based on	Proverbs 11:11; 14:34; Deuteronomy 8:10–18; 1 Timothy 2:1-4
Theme	Nation
Written	15 March 1975
Suggested tune	WIE SCHÖN LEUCHTET

Clifton Lutheran Church of Marblehead, Massachusetts, wished to commission a national hymn commemorating the Bicentennial of the Declaration of Independence in 1976, and to dedicate it to the town of Marblehead, where the first German Lutherans landed in 1630, a century and a half before the Constitution was signed. Dr. Cyril Wismar conveyed the request for a hymn to be dedicated to Marblehead in memory of Peter Stengel. I wrote the text to the classic Lutheran chorale *WIE SCHÖN LEUCHTET* for three reasons: 1) It is a strong, stately, and familiar melody; 2) the hymn was commissioned by a Lutheran church to remember the Lutheran immigrants to Marblehead in 1630, for whom this Queen of Chorales recalls the spirit and words of that hymn, and 3) to make this an ethnic tribute to a land of opportunity, where German came close to becoming the official language of the country.

The gifts of freedom, peace, and prosperity are from the hands of a gracious God, priceless gifts to be recognized and received with thanksgiving and responsibility. A national hymn must be honestly patriotic without being jingoistic or blindly chauvinistic. In light of our blessings and privileges, we have much to be humble about. The second stanza strikes the necessary penitential note. That properly recognized, we can go on to celebrate our anniversaries with joy and new dedication to our ideals.

Paul Manz wrote a counter-melody for the chorale tune that can be sung by itself or together with the familiar chorale. Whether intentional or not, the Manz melody begins with the same key notes as "The Star-spangled Banner." The hymn was sung in Marblehead during the bicentennial year as well as throughout the country in Lutheran churches using a special bicentennial order of worship.

Who Is the One We Love the Most

Who is the one we love the most,
the one who has our total trust?
Something or someone is our god,
whose will is willingly obeyed,
to whom we give the years we live:
let that be You, our God, our Lord!

Count every heartbeat, every breath,
trace every step from birth to death,
track every second to its source,
each drop of blood, each blade of grass,
the rising sun, and everyone:
let that be You, our God, our Lord!

Preserve us from all other gods,
all damned, deceitful, loveless frauds;
compare them ruthlessly to You,
the only One, eternal, true
Creator of all life and love:
You are that One, our God, our Lord!

A love no other god has shown,
Your Son upon a cross makes known.
How shall we worship such a God
with more than words and passing nod,
if not with whole heart, mind, and soul,
like Yours for us, our God, our Lord?!

Meter	8.8.8.8.8.8.
Based on	Matthew 6:24; Mark 12:29,30; John 3:16; 1 John 4:7–10, 19; and parallels
Theme	Worship/Devotion
Written	23 January 1997
Tune	by Carl Schalk

The request for an anthem for the 1998 Montreat, NC Conference on Worship and Music on the theme "Worshiping with All Your Heart, Reclaiming the Center," prompted this attempt to express one aspect of my lifelong struggle with worship—an inexhaustible subject. Considering worship as response, whether private or corporate, the worshiper must be aware of the One to Whom he/she is responding. That response is meant to be total, as God's love for us is total. The sacrifice of God's only Son confirms the totality of God's love for all humanity. Any response less than total is lacking in appreciation. Just as tragic is the limited amount of time left to influence and enrich the world with our reflection of God's whole-hearted love and concern, lest anyone perish. God spits out the lukewarm offering as a hypocritical, uncommitted attempt to serve two masters. Only the whole-hearted worship of the one true God satisfies the yearning and longing heart of God whose motivation for the creation, redemption, and sanctification of all creation is LOVE.

Who Is This Who Comes from Nowhere?

Who is this who comes from nowhere,
claims to be the Son of God,
says: "I am the true Messiah,
you can end your waiting now.
Is it love you want—I show it,
is it peace you need—I give it,
is it joy you crave—I vow it,
you can end your seeking now.

"Search instead the sacred Record,
trace my life from crib to cross,
hear me preaching love and freedom,
calling all to God's own cause.
See me give my life for sinners,
see me rise again triumphant,
see me prove God's lovingkindness:
what more can the Savior do?"

See the cosmic plan unfolding,
meant for all to have a part;
someone must believe and play it,
if God's will is to be done.
Someone must continue teaching,
someone must continue serving,
someone must be bold and faithful,
if the kingdom is to come.

Blessed then the poor in spirit,
blest the mournful and the meek,
blest the merciful and righteous,
blest the pure who work for peace.
Patience! we shall stand in glory
thrilled to hear our throned Messiah:
"Welcome, blessed of my Father,
now the joy-full life begins!"

Meter	8.7.8.7.8.8.8.7.
Based on	Hebrews 7; Luke 24:25–27; Matthew 5:2–12; 25:34
Theme	Discipleship
Written	10 February 1987
Suggested tune	PENCHOFF by Bret Heim

When Paul Westermeyer, on behalf of Ascension Lutheran Church, Riverside, Illinois, requested a hymn to mark the congregation's 75th anniversary in 1987, this was one of two texts that I wrote. The other was "Christ Goes Before." The hymn was not to deal specifically with the anniversary, but was meant to hold up to the congregation the mission of the church as it is directed by the ascended Lord. In this text I imagined Christ coming into history and into people's lives as if from nowhere. I thought of the comparison with Melchizedek, the subject of Hebrews 7, the statement of Christ's contemporaries: "Is this not the carpenter's son?" and "What good can come out of Nazareth?" But this is the promised Messiah awaited by Israel and sought unknowingly by pagans. The second stanza summarizes the risen Christ's exposition of the Old Testament prophecies to the dismayed disciples on the road to Emmaus. The third connects the petitions of the Lord's Prayer with the Great Commission, and the fourth ties the Beatitudes to the final commendation of those who follow Christ, who became their Savior in order that their joy might be full.

The lengthening of the third last line of the stanzas was intended to keep the last four lines moving toward the climactic last line.

Witness Our Best Gift from Heaven

Witness our best gift from heaven:
why a perfect world was made;
see the crown of all creation
living happy, unafraid,
everything aglow with glory,
God enjoying, God enjoyed.

What was meant to last forever
would have been forever gone;
but for God's great love and mercy,
death and Satan would have won.
Then, to save a lost creation,
God gave His beloved Son.

Witness Christ, the promised Savior,
hear the angel's news with awe,
wake and wonder with the shepherds,
at the manger kneel and bow.
Hurry then to tell all nations
what great joy you heard and saw.

Witness those who lived before us,
strong in faith, in numbers few,
how the Spirit blessed their witness,
how the Word they planted grew.
Now descendants in the millions
celebrate the joy they knew.

Join the Father in compassion,
join the Son in victory,
join the Spirit in reunion
with the joy-full Trinity.
Witness what the angels witness:
heaven's endless jubilee!

Meter	8.7.8.7.8.7.
Based on	Luke 2:10; John 15:11; 17:13, 17, 18; Matthew 13:23; 28:18–20; Romans 10:8ff; and parallels
Theme	Church/Mission/Joy
Written	24 June 1996
Suggested tune	REAVIS BARRACKS

A hymn was requested by the Commission on Worship of The Lutheran Church—Missouri Synod to commemorate the Sesquicentennial of the Synod in 1996–97. Among many possible themes, the purpose, origin, and mission of the Church was chosen. The theme of joy was traced through the Scriptures and revealed an outline of the Ecumenical Creeds, identifying God's purpose in creation of the world and of humanity and of the plan of salvation, with everlasting joy in eternity. The hymn asks the worshipper to witness the reason for divine and human joy in both senses of the word: witness as observer and witness as testimony. This is really the plan and purpose of the Church. The Good Tidings of Great Joy for all People (the Gospel) is intended by the Risen Savior to be the Great Commission of the Church.

Other implications and ramifications of the theme can be found in numerous parallel passages, making it difficult to restrict the hymn to five stanzas.

Wondering Child of God

Wondering child of God,
keep asking Why.
Why all you see around you,
and why your very eye?
Why beauty, wisdom, love, and breath,
why sin, why sorrow, plague, and death?
What answer from the sky?

Merciful, gracious God,
keep telling Who.
Who always was and will be,
and who alone is true?
Who holy, loving, just, and kind,
who parent, judge, and friend combined?
What answer from the blue?

Comforter sent from God,
keep showing What.
What gives our life its meaning,
and what reveals its plot?
What crucified, incarnate Word,
what risen, life-restoring Lord?
What answer comes from God?

Marveling child of God,
keep learning How.
How you would thank the Giver
of what you are and know?
How you were found and reconciled,
how you became this newborn child?
You know the answer now.

Meter	7.4.7.6.8.8.6.
Based on	Romans 11:33–36; John 14:26
Theme	Holy Spirit/Enlightenment/Assurance
Written	19 August 1989

While working on several commissioned texts, I was diverted by this inspiration. Recently I've been haunted by that childish but profound question which we seem to abandon as we grow older and become obsessed with the "what" and "how" of life, whereas the profound question remains to be answered. Paul turned the question into a doxology at the end of his 11th chapter to the Romans. And Christ promised the Comforter to the perplexed disciples, the Spirit of truth who would teach them everything necessary for their peace and joy. (John 14:26)

You're My Good Shepherd

You're my Good Shepherd, I'm your sheep,
Always within the watch you keep
Over me even while I sleep.
Alleluia! Alleluia! Alleluia!

You led me to a living stream,
I heard your voice give me a name:
"You are my own beloved lamb!"
Alleluia! Alleluia! Alleluia!

Goodness and mercy here surround
Sheepfold and gate and grazing ground;
Every lost sheep is sought and found.
Alleluia! Alleluia! Alleluia!

Gather your flock from everywhere,
Carefree within your loving care,
One Shepherd's life and joy to share.
Alleluia! Alleluia! Alleluia!

Standing alone against our foes,
Who else would take the way you chose:
Willingly died, triumphant rose.
Alleluia! Alleluia! Alleluia!

Guests at your table, help us stay
Bound to our source of life, we pray:
Make every day our Easter Day!
Alleluia! Alleluia! Alleluia!

Meter	8.8.8. Alleluias
Based on	Psalm 23
Theme	The Good Shepherd/4th Sunday of Easter pericope
Written	6 March 1994

Looking for a new Easter hymn which could be sung during the Eastertide, the Episcopal Church of the Good Shepherd, Austin, Texas, requested a text that would apply the name of the church. Two familiar references immediately suggested themselves: the Shepherd Psalm of David, and the Good Shepherd chapter in the Gospel according to John (10). Taking Psalm 23, with its progression of thoughts and comparing them to the self-application of the Psalm by our Lord, the Old Testament reference was fiven a New Testament application and fulfillment, with allusions to the Word and Sacraments as the means of grace. Given the many hymns paraphrasing or applying Psalm 23, this was an opportunity to wed the two passages.

GELOBT SEI GOTT was considered a fairly familiar Easter melody to convey the mood and content of the new hymn.

You Are the King

You are the King Isaiah saw adored
By flaming angels 'round Your lofty throne;
In reverent awe they chorus to their Lord
An endless "Holy, holy, holy One!"

But woe to me! I cannot join that choir;
No sinner can behold that sight and live.
Unclean before that all-consuming Fire,
I cannot be forgiven or forgive.

To my surprise, You stretch Your loving hand
To cleanse my heart, my lips, my eyes, my ears;
You touch me, me! and I see how You spanned
And crossed the gaping gulf to make me Yours.

You call me, Holy Trinity, to be
Your earthly angel? Here am I, send me!

Meter	14 lines of 10’
Based on	Isaiah 6:1–6
Theme	Ministry/Service
Written	20 November 1979
Suggested tune	FAIRMOUNT by Donald Busarow

This text responds to the request of the session and congregation of Fairmount Presbyterian Church of Cleveland Heights, Ohio, for a hymn honoring their dedicated minister of music, Dr. H. Wells Near, to be based on Isaiah 6:1–8. Aware of two great hymns on this text, Luther’s majestic one-stanza narrative hymn, “Isaiah, Mighty Seer” and Reginald Heber’s universally familiar hymn to the Trinity, “Holy, Holy, Holy,” I decided to take a different approach by dealing with God’s call to service in the Kingdom. Having wanted for years to write a hymn in sonnet form, this theme seemed to fit that unusual form admirably: the Shakespearean sonnet of three quatrains and a closing couplet. Since the melody was to be composed after the text, this poetic form was chosen. The hymn is to be understood at different levels, just as the calling of Isaiah came in a vision that lifted him above the act of commissioning to glimpse the very holiness of the triune God and his consuming love for his creatures. One example of a dual meaning is the phrase, “crossed the gaping gulf” referring to the cross as the bridge God provides as the bridge to us and to himself.

You Are the Rock

You are the Rock, and we were hewn
From You, eternal and triune.
To build Your holy Temple here
You chose the tenting pioneer,
Your Spirit setting one by one
As living stone on living stone,
And so this House was raised by You.

Begotten by Your word of grace,
Behold Your family and race:
Its members each a wondrous birth,
Your love embodied here on earth,
One holy, growing miracle.
Add living cell to living cell
Until Your Body fills the world.

As You have blessed us all these years,
Forgiving sins, removing fears,
So may we live as grateful heirs,
Invest the faith that once was theirs,
Your living Word our food and drink.
Add living link to living link
Until the chain of love is forged.

Elect of God, whom God so loved,
Remember how that love was proved;
Elect of God, redeemed by Christ,
Rejoice to be so highly prized;
Elect of God, the Spirit's pride,
Reach out to all who stand outside,
And crown the work so well begun.

Meter	8.8.8.8.8.8.8.
Based on	Ephesians 2:19–22
Theme	Church Anniversary/Commemoration
Written	5 February 1979
Suggested tune	ES IST DAS HEIL

This hymn for the anniversary of a congregation was written to commemorate the centennial of Zion Lutheran Church, Dallas, Texas, in 1979. *ES IST DAS HEIL* was chosen as the melody for its familiarity and associations as a description of the nature and glory of the Gospel, which this church was called to plant and proclaim in the pioneering years of the state of Texas. The text ties that local congregation to the Una Sancta in its purpose and mission, in its recruitment of members for the Body of Christ.

You Are the Shepherd

You are the Shepherd, we your sheep
By Water and the Word;
The promises you make you keep,
And all our cries are heard.

The fearful, helpless, old, and tired
Are cast upon your care
And on the ones whom you inspired
Your love and cheer to share.

What honor and what joy to be
Your hands, your feet, your mind,
To know what makes your children free,
The peace they seek to find.

Bless what we are and what we do,
Good Shepherd, best of friends,
That all your sheep may share with you
The life that never ends.

Meter	CM (8.6.8.6.)
Based on	Psalm 23; John 10:11; 20:16, 17; Acts 20:28
Theme	Social service/Care of the elderly
Written	5 September 1985
Suggested tunes	ST. ANNE
	ST. PETER

The forgotten and neglected elderly people of God are remembered in this text commemorating the 80th anniversary of the Lutheran Altenheim Society of Missouri in 1985. Our care of the elderly should be inspired by the Shepherd who cares for all his sheep, including those who once were with young and who must now be carried by other "shepherds" as they were when they were lambs. *ST. ANNE* was the first choice of tune, because of its familiarity and connotations among the residents of this retirement and nursing facility. The Lutheran Altenheim Society has been a model of Christian charity for eight decades.

You Have a Special Place

You have a special place,
    a purpose and a plan,
for me and everyone You love
    since life began.
Dear loving God,
work out Your plan, achieve Your goal,
    fulfill Your dream.

I learned of You through Christ,
    I came to You through Christ,
Your Spirit made me one with You
    and all in Christ.
Great God of love,
work out Your plan, achieve Your goal,
    fulfill Your dream.

You wrote into my heart
    the pattern for my life,
and parents, teachers, friends,
    all left Your mark on me.
Great God of grace,
work out Your plan, achieve Your goal,
    fulfill Your dream.

How can I thank the ones
    to whom I owe so much?
With Christ in me, may others, too,
    be drawn to You,
as blest as I —
Your plan worked out, Your goal assured,
    Your dream fulfilled.

Meter	6.6.6.6.8.8. or 6.6.8.4.4.8.4.
Based on	2 Corinthians 3:2,3; 2 Timothy 3:14–17; Romans 11:33–36, and parallels
Theme	Christian education
Written	24 May 1996
Suggested tune	DARWALL'S 148th

To mark the 50th anniversary of the Lutheran High School Association, St. Louis, Missouri, a hymn was requested on the anniversary theme, "Written on Our Hearts and Lives," based on 2 Corinthians 3:2, 3, in which the Apostle considers Christians' lives to be letters read by their contemporaries and witnessing to Christ, the wisdom of God and the power of God. The hymn attempts to remind us of the special place, purpose, and plan God has for every person, and how our heavenly Father wants to mold his children into people who leave God's mark on the world by their lives and testimony. Critical in the creation of this new person are parents, teachers, and friends who nurture the faith created by the Holy Spirit.

You Hear the Hungry Crying

You hear the hungry crying
in many a bounteous land,
You see the hungry dying
on barren desert sand;
You tell Your helpless helpers,
"Go, feed the multitude,"
and, while they serve the starving,
You multiply the food.

The hungry still are with us,
though easily ignored,
and You still say, "Go, feed them,"
and You are still the Lord.
Give us Your eyes to see them,
Your ears to hear their cry.
Who, moved by Your compassion,
could coldly pass them by?

With You in us, Lord Jesus,
we feel and act like You;
Your life of love and mercy
impels our mission, too.
Through us pour out Your bounty,
make us Your hands and feet;
in sharing what You give us,
You make our joy complete.

You see more than a body
imploring to be fed,
You see whole persons famished
for You, the living Bread.
In loving one another,
we prove our love for You;
in caring for the needy,
we say our thanks to You.

Meter	7.6.7.6.D.
Based on	John 6 and parallels; 1 John 3:14–24; Luke 6:27–36
Theme	Hunger
Written	9 March 1993
Suggested tune	ANTHES

In planning a World Hunger appeal, The Lutheran Church—Missouri Synod World Relief department requested an appropriate hymn to go with the theme, "Pour Yourself Out for the Hungry."

The assignment proved to be more difficult and challenging than expected. Being told that we will "always have the poor with us," the Christian must constantly be reminded of putting good intentions into practice and "not to grow weary in well-doing." As in any charitable work, the motivation is all-important. And this is supplied by the example of our Lord, the choice of that title being deliberately chosen. It is through the Word, the Son of God, that all things were created (John 1). He is the ultimate provider of life-giving food, and is Himself the Bread from heaven who feeds and sustains our eternal life. If He tells us to pour ourselves out for the hungry, and shows us how that is done, we know what we should do for our hungering neighbor and we will do it for the right reason. And when we do carry out this criterion of the Last Judgment, we will do so out of gratitude rather than for Pharisaic credit.

The text was to be written to fit an extant melody. The closest one to the desired mood of this theme was *ANTHES*, with its "appealing" texts. If another of the numerous 7.6.7.6.D. (iambic) tunes is selected, it should preferably reflect the urgent spirit of the text, avoiding a triumphalistic expression.

You, Jesus, Are My Shepherd True

You, Jesus, are my Shepherd true,
And I your sheep quite helpless;
My ever-loving Guide are you,
Your every thought is selfless;
You feed me, guard me, lead the way
To peace at night and joy by day:
I frolic in your favor.

I follow you. The path you choose,
It is the best way for me;
The lamb you love you will not lose,
You walk the way before me;
And though I pass through death's dark vale,
It is my Lord's familiar trail:
I know its glorious ending.

Surrounded when I am by foes
Who scorn me or ignore me,
In your strong arms I find repose;
You spread a feast before me!
You welcome me! I find a place
Of honor as your heir of grace,
At home with you forever.

Meter	8.7.8.7.8.8.7.
Based on	Psalm 23
Theme	Trust/Guidance/Protection
Written	10 March 1986
Suggested tunes	DER HERR IST MEIN GETREUER HIRT ES IST GEWISSLICH

This contemporary paraphrase of Psalm 23 was one of eight in the Becker Psalter series presented at Grace Lutheran Church, River Forest, Illinois, on April 20, 1986. For additional notes on the series, see "Before Your Awesome Majesty."

You Said, Pray Thus

You said, Pray thus:
"Your kingdom come,
Your will be done"—
and then expect an answer

And so I prayed,
but nothing came,
and, nothing done,
I thought You had not answered,

And yet You had,
for had I not
obeyed in faith
and trusted You to answer?

And someone came,
who prayed the same,
and did Your will,
and was Your answer to me.

And now I know
Your kingdom comes,
Your will is done,
when I become Your answer.

Meter	4.4.4.6.
Based on	Matthew 6:10; Hebrews 1:14
Theme	Service/Dedication
Written	23 December 1989

Having received a letter from a former missionary couple to Liberia, remembering a Christmas when they had no extra money for gifts for their children, a Christmas greeting arrived from my wife with a generous check. It was obviously an answer to prayer, but it struck me that God did not answer the missionaries' prayer by dropping money from heaven in a miraculous way, but by the faith-inspired charity of one of His children. And this is how God seems to have answered my prayers in the past—through one of His children who cared about me.

I was also impressed by the sequence of the petitions in the Lord's Prayer which embodies all of our spiritual and temporal needs. When we truly desire the presence and function of God's Kingdom of grace, power, and glory, we will want to carry out God's good and gracious will on earth as it is done so willingly and joyfully by the angels in heaven. And as we do so, our Father in heaven will be answering someone's prayers through us. And we will be the beneficiaries of angels whom we entertain unawares when they practice brotherly love (Hebrews 13:12).

Zion, Dwelling of the Lord

Zion, dwelling of the Lord
In a warring world,
Where the promised Prince of Peace
Makes all wars to cease,
Where God's creatures, made for living,
Find forgiveness, start forgiving:
        Welcome, welcome peace!

Praise the mercy here bestowed
By a loving God
On a lost, rebellious race
Purely out of grace.
Here begins a new creation,
Chosen, called, a holy nation,
        God's own special race.

Christ, the Church's heart and head,
Risen from the dead:
Keep the witnesses You send
Faithful to the end.
By their living and true teaching
Precious souls for heaven reaching,
        Bless the ones You send.

Heirs of Paradise restored
Thank You, gracious Lord;
Harvests of Your planted Word
Glorify You, Lord.
Where You welcome all believers,
Sainted Gift of Life-receivers
        Ever with You, Lord!

Meter	7.5.7.5.8.8.5.
Based on	Psalm 87; Romans 11:26; Hebrews 12:22–28; & parallels
Theme	The Church/Communion of Saints
Written	5 May 1994

The Slovak Zion Synod of the Evangelical Lutheran Church in America, celebrating its 75th anniversary in 1994, commissioned a hymn to be introduced at its anniversary convention, June 13–15, 1994.

In exploring the numerous references to Zion, the Una Sancta, the holy catholic (Christian) Church, in the Scriptures, I was overwhelmed by the concepts and definitions of Zion, the City of God, the New Jerusalem, the Church Militant and Triumphant, etc. The resulting text alludes to some of the aspects of the Communion of Saints, hoping the singers of the hymn will be moved to pursue the many implications of the theme. Although the hymn was to be introduced at an anniversary service, it is intended to be useful for any occasion remembering and celebrating the New Creation, the Body of Christ.

Translations: Slovak Hymns, Carols, and Songs

A Cuckoo Flew Out of the Wood

A cuckoo flew out of the wood, cuckoo, cuckoo,
Atwitter in holiday mood, cuckoo, cuckoo;
There at the manger, perched on the hay,
Greeting the Stranger born on this day:
Cuckoo, cuckoo, cuckoo…

And, leaving his sheep all behind, cuckoo, cuckoo,
A shepherd the Savior would find, cuckoo, cuckoo;
Singing with joy there with all the rest
To the new Boy there in his crude nest:
Cuckoo, cuckoo, cuckoo…

Now hear the sweet bells as they ring: ding, dong…
In chorus with nature now sing: ding, dong…
Angels and bird there, shepherd and we,
Let all be heard there in symphony:
Ding, dong, ding, dong, ding, dong…

Meter	12.12.9.9.12.
Theme	Christmas
Translated	1965
Translation of	“Hlà, kukučka nechala les” (Slovak carol, origin unknown)

Ascending, Christ Returns to God

Ascending, Christ returns to God: Alleluia.
That we may go the way he trod: Alleluia.

He wears the crown of victory: Alleluia.
From doom and death he set us free: Alleluia.

At his most glorious festival: Alleluia.
Sing, faithful Christians, one and all: Alleluia.

Remember how he told his own: Alleluia.
I go to my dear Father's throne: Alleluia.

Do not depart Jerusalem: Alleluia.
Until the promised Spirit come: Alleluia.

Until you learn all you must know: Alleluia.
To teach the word and where to go: Alleluia.

Without his aid you cannot do: Alleluia.
What I your Lord assign to you: Alleluia.

So kindle, Lord, the Spirit's flame: Alleluia.
And thaw our lives to praise your name: Alleluia.

Until with you, when life is done: Alleluia.
We share the glory you have won: Alleluia.

Meter	8.4.8.4.
Based on	John 20:17; Acts 1:4–12
Theme	Ascension
Written	18 February 1976
Translation of	“Vstoupil jest Kristus na nebe,” Old Czech, 16th cent.
Suggested tune	ZPIVEJMEŽ VŠICKNI VESELE

The Old Czech Ascension hymn from which this translation was made was itself a translation of a Latin original, whose unknown origin obviously antedates the 1636 edition of the *Cithara Sanctorum,* in which the Slovak text appears. In its original form the hymn had 13 stanzas, which I reduced to nine. It was evidently sung to the same melody as “Zpivejmež všickni vesele,” the George Tranovsky hymn which I translated as “Make songs of joy.” (See note at that title)

Christians, Gather Round

Christians, gather round,
Hear the joyful sound!
Christians, gather round,
Hear the joyful sound!
Man by God this night befriended,
Heaven's light to earth descended.
Christians, gather round,
Hear the joyful sound!

Hear we now a voice
Bidding us rejoice.
Hear we now a voice
Bidding us rejoice.
He who in the Godhead rested
Now in flesh is manifested.
Hear we now a voice
Bidding us rejoice.

Glory pure and bright
Breaks upon our night.
Glory pure and bright
Breaks upon our night.
See our fields with splendor blazing,
And our hills in light amazing!
Christians, gather round,
Hear the joyful sound!

Meter	5.5.5.5.8.8.5.5.
Theme	Christmas Eve
Translated	1957
Translation of	“Dobrà novina” (Andrej Ozym, *Kancional*, Turčiansky Sv. Martin, Austria-Hungary, 1805)

Christians, Let Us Remember

Christians, let us remember
Our precious legacy,
And see how we may honor
Our debt most fittingly,
Recalling those who cleansed us
From pagan ways of death
And brought us to the bosom
Of our most holy faith.

For what should one most covet—
Good fortune, fame, or this:
To bear the name of Christian
And claim a certain bliss;
To know the saving Gospel
That multiplies on earth
Faith, hope, and love eternal
The Kingdom's blessed birth?

Ah, we, and we especially,
We daughters and we sons
Of this blest Slovak nation,
We are the blessed ones;
We have a special reason
To thank God for this Gift
And for the way he gave it
And favored us by it.

While others idly waited
To hear the holy Word
And greeted the apostles
With sullenness or sword,
Our nation most sincerely
Desired that priceless Gem,
Invited missionaries,
Revered and welcomed them.

To other people Baptism
Came mixed with blood and force;
Imposed and unrequested,
They had no other course;
But God sent us two brothers
Of winsome friendliness,
Methodius and Cyril,
As saints who came to bless.

Elsewhere for long dark ages
The Word was little known,
And God was worshiped rotely
In language not their own,
Whereas our ancient forebears
Heard from the very start
In sweet maternal phrases
The words that change the heart.

Imagine how our fathers
Must have been overawed
To read in their own language
The mighty acts of God!
The apostolic brothers
So greatly loved our folk,
They learned their tongue and gave them
The word of life, God's Book.

While others boldly flaunted
The banner of the Cross
To plunder rights and freedom,
And gain by others' loss,
Our nation shared its treasure
With meek humility,
Rejoicing when their neighbors
Became newborn and free,

Among us, pagan idols
Fell almost by themselves,
And in their stead grew crosses
And churches by the twelves,
Without the threat of murder.
The lust of greed or gain,
Without the tears of converts
Who traded fear for pain.

Let us, like our ancestors,
Their progeny and heirs,
Use for our own salvation
The means that once were theirs:
The sacraments and Gospel,
The church be our concern;
For God and for our neighbor
Our love with fervor burn!

May we this true religion
In purity preserve,
And spread its grace and power
In heart and life and nerve,
Thus striving to be worthy
To meet our pioneers
And share with them the glory
Of those who persevere.

Meter	7.6.7.6.D.
Based on	Isaiah 51:1; Acts 16:9 ff.; Philippians 1:3–5; 4:15
Theme	Commemoration (Christianization of Slavs)
Written	4 March 1984
Translation of	Pamatujmež krestane, by Ján Kollar, 1842
Suggested tune	VALET WILL ICH DIR GEBEN or HERZLICH TUT MICH VERLANGEN

In contrast to most national heroes, the national idols of the peace-loving Slovak people are two Macedonian missionaries who brought the Gospel to that central European nation in the year 863. In 1983, the Slavic inhabitants of present-day Czechoslovakia commemorated the arrival of Cyril (Constantine) and Methodius at the invitation of the Slovak prince Rastislav, who had erected the first Christian church on Slovak soil in the year 833. The Greek brother missionaries were welcomed and the Gospel embraced, unlike other nations who were converted by force. Despite their struggles with the Western popes, the brothers eventually were granted permission to preach and conduct the liturgy in the vernacular, for which they had created an alphabet and translated the Scriptures. Small wonder they have been revered as the patron saints of Slovak (and Slavic) Christians for eleven centuries. The author of this commemorative hymn celebrates the millennial anniversary of his nation's conversion and the manner in which it was done. One is reminded of a similar conversion of the Macedonians some eight centuries prior to Cyril and Methodius, when the request came to St. Paul in a vision, "Come over to Macedonia and help us" (Acts 16:9 ff.). His response to that invitation marked the beginning of Paul's ministry to his beloved Philippians. By the route of the Macedonian apostles to the Slavs, I trace my own spiritual roots to St. Paul, and consequently was pleased to find this hymn text and to translate it for the millions of English-speaking descendants of that Christian nation, one-third of whose population emigrated to the United States a century ago, bringing their heritage with them.

The Slovak text was written for the 1842 Slovak Lutheran hymnal, the *Zpevnik*, by Ján Kollar (1793–1852), Lutheran theologian, historian, classical poet, and national leader.

Come in Holy Awe and Truth

Come in holy awe and truth,
Brothers, sisters, to the altar:
Children in the bloom of youth,
Elders, come with steps that falter;
All, of great or no renown,
Here, to God, we stand as one.

Those who live by cares oppressed,
Those who scamper through life gaily,
Those who know unruffled rest,
Those who weep in sorrow daily,
Friends and enemies, as one
Boldly come, approach the Throne.

By one cup and by one bread
In one body, Lord, unite us;
By the blood the Savior shed
Now with peace and joy delight us;
Speak the good news once again,
What more cause to sing "Amen!"

By one washing, by one creed,
Each to all one Father binds us,
One the hope on which we feed,
One the grace that seeks and finds us;
Joined in love together so,
To one Table let us go.

Here ourselves we consecrate
To all truth, to love, to justice;
By this action let us state
What a holy people's trust is;
Show to all the Christ who lives,
Eat and drink the food he gives.

Tears of loneliness replace
With new tears of happy laughter,
Children of adopting grace,
See the home the world strives after:
Ours it is when we are one
With the Father and the Son.

Meter	7.8.7.8.7.7.
Based on	1 Corinthians 10:16, 17
Theme	Pre-Communion/Distribution
Written	6 October 1971, rev. 1975
Translation of	"Bližte se s nabožnosti," by Jan Bohumil Ertel
Suggested tunes	GROSSER GOTT
	MEINEN JESUM LASS ICH NICHT

This hymn comes into the English in a roundabout way. It was originally written in German by Johann Friedrich Starke (1680–1756), a German pietist pastor in Frankfurt, whom Julian describes as "a faithful follower of Spener and author of a very popular book of daily devotions (who) wrote 939 pious hymns of no poetic value" (Dictionary of Hymnology, New Dover Edition, 1957, p. 417). The hymn was translated into Slovak in 1745 by Jan Bohumil Ertel, a bilingual pastor in Slovakia and appeared in the 1842 *Zpevnik* (Songbook) as a Communion hymn. Unable to locate the original German text, I assumed this was one of the better hymns of the 939 in Starke's collection, and that it could be further improved poetically by another translation. My interest in the hymn was drawn by its theme of Christian unity and joy and the application of the Sacrament to the life of God's people beyond the sanctuary.

Come Now, Shepherds, Quickly Come

Come now, shepherds, quickly come to Bethl'em's manger lowly,
There for you and for the world is born the Christ Child holy.
At this rare and royal meeting
Sing a song of joyful greeting:
Welcome, King of heaven,
Welcome to the earth!

Born immaculate, the Son of Mary, virgin maiden,
See the manger crude and cold with bread from heaven laden.
Whom the prophets died proclaiming,
She this very night is naming,
Jesus Christ our Savior
Now for us is born!

Blest Redeemer, precious Flower, wonderful Lord Jesus,
Prince of Peace, almighty Savior, from our sins release us!
King of heaven, lord supernal,
Take us to our home eternal.
O beloved Jesus,
Grant us what we pray!

Meter	14.14.8.8.6.5
Theme	Christmas Eve
Translation of	"Pospešte sem, pastuškovia" (Vojtech Wick in *Nebeské Hlasy,* Košice, Czechoslovakia, 1924)

Dear Father God, We Rise to Say

Dear Father God, we rise to say,
Your name be praised for this new day
For health and strength our prayers we lift:
Grant every good and perfect gift.

O God the Son, we pray of you,
May all we plan and say and do
Be ever welcome in your sight,
Be done to your and our delight.

O Spirit God, preserve from fear
All those who fret and sorrow here;
And when the day of days arrives,
With fadeless glory crown our lives.

Based on	Psalm 5:3
Theme	Morning Prayer
Written	30 July 1969
Translation of	“Bože Otťe, buď pochválen,” by Juraj Zábojnik, 17th cent.
Suggested tune	PANE BOŽE, BUDIŽ CHVÁLA, Old Czech

This Trinitarian morning hymn comes to us from the Slovak Lutheran hymn writer, Juraj Zábojnik (1608–72) via later editions of the *Cithara Sanctorum.* The old Czech melody entered the Slovak Lutheran hymnal via the *Cantus Catholici* of 1655. Another tune from a 1576 Bohemian Brethren hymnal is sometimes used with this hymn. Ulrich S. Leopold, editor of *Laudamus*, requested this translation for the 1970 (4th) edition of that Lutheran World Federation tri-lingual songbook. It was reprinted in the 1984 edition.

Dear Little Jesus, We Come to Thy Bed

Dear little Jesus, we come to Thy bed,
Nothing we seek but to be comforted.
Thee we would fondle,
Thee we would cradle,
Thy tender glory around us spread.
Slumber on sweetly now, precious One,
Heavenly Infant, our God's only Son!

Dream, softly dream, Thou blest Flower divine,
Lord of the heavens, asleep in this shrine.
Angels acclaim Thee,
Our God we name Thee,
Born of a Virgin to set us free.
Slumber on sweetly now, precious One,
Heavenly Infant, our God's only Son!

Slumber, Thou Treasure of fabulous worth,
Soft be the straw-bed of Thy lowly birth
Bring us salvation
And consolation,
Grant us Thy blessing while ages run.
Slumber on sweetly now, precious One,
Heavenly Infant, our God's only Son!

Meter	10.10.5.5.9.9.10.
Theme	Christmas
Translation of	“Prišli sme ku tebe, Jezuliatko” (Štefan Pyšný, Ms. Collection in Archives of the Society of St. Adalbert, Trnava, Czechoslovakia, 1932)

Glory Be to You, O Father

Glory be to you, O Father,
and thanksgiving for this food,
set before us by your mercy,
taken from your bounteous good.
Even so before us spread
your own satisfying Bread,
feed us with this heav'nly ration
that we never know starvation.

Father, who in heaven dwelling,
ever hallowed be your name;
in our hearts wield sole dominion,
may your will be all our aim.
Grant our daily bread this day,
take our wretched guilt away;
lead us not into temptation,
keep us, bring us to salvation.

Meter	8.7.8.7.7.7.8.8
Based on	Psalm 145:15, 16; Matthew 6:9–13
Theme	Mealtime/Lord's Prayer
Written	22 November 1972
Translation of	"Sláva bud Tobe, Bože náš," Old Czech Lutheran 16th cent.
Suggested tune	FREU DICH SEHR

It was customary in Old World families and at church gatherings to sing a mealtime prayer, and this particular hymn was a standard one. As "Speise Vater, deine Kinder" became a favorite table prayer in German circles, this one served the same function in Slovak homes and churches. I remember hearing this particular hymn sung at a dinner table in a parsonage in Slovakia within the past decade. The text originated among Old Czech Lutherans in the 16th century and appeared in the *Cithara Sanctorum* of 1636.

God, My Lord, My Strength

God, my Lord, my strength, my place of hiding
And confiding
In all needs by night and day;
Though foes surround me,
And Satan marks his prey,
God shall have his way.

Christ in me, and I am freed for living
And forgiving,
Heart of flesh for lifeless stone;
Now bold to serve him,
Now cheered his love to own,
Nevermore alone.

Up, weak knees and spirit bowed in sorrow!
No tomorrow
Shall arise to beat you down;
God goes before you
And angels all around;
On your head a crown!

Meter	10.4.7.5.6.5
Based on	Psalms 71; 141
Theme	Trust / Cross and Comfort
Written	20 April 1967
Translation of	"Pán Bůh jest má sila," Old Czech Lutheran, 16th cent.
Suggested tune	PÁN BŮH, Prague Gradual, 1576

This translation is a cento and paraphrase of the original six-stanza post-Reformation Old Czech Lutheran hymn as found in the classic Slovak Lutheran hymnal, the *Cithara Sanctorum* of 1636. Taking the thoughts of the original, I restated them in my own style within the metric and melodic parameters of this strong Czech text and tune. The ready adoption of the translation by American congregations testifies to the hymn's adaptability while providing the church with a sturdy affirmation of trust and a melody that conveys the strength of the text.

Greet Now the Swiftly Changing Year

Greet now the swiftly changing year
With joy and penitence sincere.
Rejoice, rejoice, with thanks embrace
Another year of grace.

Remember now the Son of God
And how he shed his infant blood.
Rejoice, rejoice, with thanks embrace
Another year of grace.

For Jesus came to wage sin's war;
This Name of names for us he bore
Rejoice, rejoice, with thanks embrace
Another year of grace.

His love abundant far exceeds
The volume of a whole year's needs.
Rejoice, rejoice, with thanks embrace
Another year of grace.

With such a Lord to lead our way
In hazard or prosperity,
What need we fear in earth or space
In this new year of grace?

"All glory be to God on high,
And peace on earth!" the angels cry.
Rejoice, rejoice, with thanks embrace
Another year of grace.

God, Father, Son, and Spirit, hear:
To all our pleas incline your ear;
Upon our lives rich blessings trace
In this new year of grace.

Meter	LM 8.8.8.8
Based on	Psalm 90; Luke 2:21
Theme	New Year's Day / Name of Jesus
Written	14 January 1968
Translation of	"Rok nový zase k nam prišel," Old Czech Lutheran, 17th cent.
Suggested tune	ROK NOVÝ, Závorka's *Kancionál*, 1602

Perhaps the most traditional New Year's and Name of Jesus hymn in Slovak hymnody is this 16th-century Old Czech Lutheran favorite. My earliest memory of it goes back to my childhood years in East Chicago, Indiana, and the observance of New Year's Eve in our parsonage, when we would gather around my mother at the piano at midnight and sing this ancient hymn. The next morning the walls of the church next door shook to the exuberant singing of it by the congregation. My translation reduces the original 15 stanzas to seven. The first line of the English text has undergone several changes, the first of which reacted to the inclusive language movement which asserted itself shortly after the hymn was translated, beginning "Greet, man, the swiftly..." This was altered to "Now greet ..." and finally, to "Greet now..." which I prefer. It may be found under any of the three opening lines. The traditional tune, here taking its title from the opening words of the original text, *ROK NOVÝ* (New Year), is from Závorka's *Kancionál*, 1602. The tune appears in both isometric and rhythmic forms, the latter being the older and preferred by the latest tune book. As a curiosity that may interest someone other than myself, while recuperating after an operation in the hospital on Christmas Eve, 1983, I heard a recording of a Corelli *Concerto Grosso*, one of whose themes closely resembled this old hymn tune.

Hear Me, O My Precious Love

Hear me, O my precious Love,
When I call upon you;
Strengthen me, O Lord above,
For my trust is on you.
Loudly now my voice is crying,
Mournfully my heart is sighing:
Comfort me, comfort me, comfort me,
Worn and weary, sad and dreary
"Return, O sinner, and love only Me,
With cross and stripe from sin I set you free;
Come repenting!

Take away all sinful fear,
Jesus, my Salvation:
For I long to have you near,
Lord, my Consolation.
Willingly I too would languish,
Follow you in cross and anguish.
Only you, only you, only you
Will I cherish lest I perish.
Ah, dearest Jesus, come, deliver me
From grief and want, I pray, and deign to be
My Sustainer.

Lord, be merciful, I pray,
Pardon my transgression!
Let my soul no longer stray;
Make it your possession.
On the cross your bitter torment
Wrought my dying soul's restorement,
So that I, even I, even I,
By your merit life inherit.
Ah, dearest Jesus, come and bear me up
Above these agonies: remove my cup!
Lord, have mercy!

Meter	Irregular
Based on	2 Corinthians 1:2–7
Theme	Lent/Repentance
Translation of	"O lásko má, uslyš mne," by Jeremiáš Lednický (d. 1685)
Suggested tune	O LÁSKO MÁ, P. Fábry ms. 1698

This Lenten hymn, bearing the Latin subtitle, "Amor meus, audi me," was either written by Jeremiáš Lednický, or was a translation of a Latin hymn or ode by that title. Lednický was the Slovak Lutheran author of 25 hymns, 14 of them original. This typically Pietistic hymn was a Lenten favorite in my father's church, and one I enjoyed accompanying the congregation on the organ during Lenten vespers in my late teens. It was my first attempt at hymn translation at the age of twenty in East Chicago, Indiana, while I was working nights at the Inland Steel Mill, earning tuition for my seminary education.

Heaven's Dawn Is Breaking Brightly

Heaven's dawn is breaking brightly, happy Christmas morn!
Of the blessed Virgin Mary Jesus Christ is born.

> *Chorus*:
> To Him let us sing, praise and honor bring;
> O Thou precious, tender Infant, to Thy name we sing;
> O Thou precious, tender Infant, to Thy name we sing!

Hear the angel song proclaiming: "Peace to all the earth!
Have no fear, I bring you tidings of your Savior's birth!"

> *Chorus*

Meter	13.13.5.5.13.13.
Theme	Christmas
Translated	1957
Translation of	"Svetlo svetu dnes nastalo" (Text by Andrej Hlinka, tune by Josev Chladek, in *Nábožný krestán*, Ruzomberok, Czechoslovakia, 1928)

Here We Kneel at Your Feet

Here we kneel at Your feet,
Father, as we pray,
Bless our vows as we meet,
be with us today!
Come what may good or ill—
In the days ahead,
we can still trust Your will
to be safely led.
We can trust You, our Lord,
for all we receive;
as we build on Your word,
firmly we believe,
and to You we cleave.

Lead us, Lord, on Your way
as through life we go;
in the night, let the ray
of Your goodness glow.
Fix our mind, heart, and eyes
on your grace and love,
every gift a surprise
showered from above.
Let us, please, walk with You,
in Your love abide;
Savior, Friend, Shepherd true,
Best, most faithful Guide,
always at our side!

Translation of	"Pred Ťebou klàkáme" (Milan Šromo)
Tune	"Largo" from Dvorak's 11th Symphony

How Lovely and How Pleasant

How lovely and how pleasant
When people dwell in peace
And love is ever present
To bind them each to each,
And love is ever present
To bind them each to each.

As dew upon the mountain
Refreshes every flower,
So love springs like a fountain
For those who know its power,
So love springs like a fountain
For those who know its power.

Like sweetest oil pervading
This temple where we meet,
So flows a joy unfading
O'er those at Jesus' feet,
So flows a joy unfading
O'er those at Jesus feet.

Meter	7.6.7.6.7.6.
Based on	Psalm 133
Theme	Unity/Harmony
Written	18 March 1966
Translation of	"Jak rozkošne a skvele," author unknown
Suggested tune	WIR HATTEN GEBAUET, German folk tune, 1823
	PLEASANT by Allan Mahnke

This Slovak text is evidently a versification of Psalm 133, but the original has been either lost or misplaced. At any rate, it antedated and indirectly inspired the original hymn I wrote five years later, "How pleasant, Lord, when people live." The tune for this hymn likewise cannot be recalled, though it can be sung nicely to the German folk tune, *WIR HATTEN GEBAUET,* a Christmas melody for "When Christmas morn is dawning."

Let Our Gladness Banish Sadness

Let our gladness banish sadness all throughout creation!
God, whose favor sent our Savior, praise with adoration!
He is born in a stall,
Now he lies, Infant small,
In a manger, heavenly Stranger, Lord of all, Lord of all.

Whom the sages and the ages anxiously awaited,
Angels proudly herald loudly in their songs elated.
Let us, too, in these days,
Thankful hearts gladly raise;
To the tender Infant render all our praise, all our praise.

Child appealing, Light revealing, Jesus Christ, our Pleasure;
God, yet very Son of Mary, Heaven's Gift and Treasure.
Mighty King, gentle Friend,
As our Lord to us bend,
With your blessing us caressing, now descend, now descend.

Meter	14.14.6.6.14.
Based on	Luke 2:1–14
Theme	Christmas/Incarnation
Written	21 November 1957
Translation of	"Čas radosti," Slovak version of "Omnis mundus jucundetur" by unknown author, 17th cent.
Suggested tune	ČAS RADOSTI, 14th cent. Bohemian melody

Not strictly a carol, this Christmas hymn deserves special mention. It is the "Adeste fideles" of Slovak Christians, whether Lutheran or Catholic. It is probably of medieval Latin origin, identified as "Omnis mundus jucundetur," and may go back as far as the 14th century with its Latin text and Bohemian tune. The Slovak version appeared in *Cantus Catholici* in 1655, from which it moved into the later editions of the Lutheran *Cithara Sanctorum*, and from thence into two English versions, as "Come rejoicing, praises voicing" in *The Lutheran Hymnal,* 1941, in a composite translation, and then in the *Lutheran Book of Worship,* 1978, in a conflation incorporating most of my translation. This version appears without alteration in a number of Slovak carol collections and choir settings.

Lo, What a Wonder

Lo, what a wonder fills all the world with joy,
Mary, the Virgin poor, bears a baby Boy,
Son of the living God, Lord of the earth,
Blesses poor Bethlehem with his glad birth.

Softly the Mother rocks Jesus in her arm,
Singing this lullaby of such tender charm:
"Sleep, little Child of mine, peacefully rest,
Of your poor swaddling clothes make you a nest."

Meter	11.11.10.10.
Theme	Christmas
Translated	1957
Translation of	“Veselosť velká sa svetu zjavila” (Text by Andrej Hlinka in *Nábožný krestan,* Ružomberok, Czechoslovakia, 1921; tune origin unknown)

Look! Judah's Lion Wins the Strife

Look! Judah's Lion wins the strife
and conquers death to give us life:
Alleluia!
Come, join in joyful praises!

Like David, so our David, too,
the jeering giant Goliath slew:
Alleluia!
Oh, sing with festive voices!

The fiercest of our foes he foils,
and waves aloft the victor's spoils:
Alleluia!
Now let us shout his praises!

Our Samson storms death's citadel,
and carries off the gates of hell:
Alleluia!
Oh, praise him for his conquest!

The chains of death he broke in two
when he arose to life anew:
Alleluia!
To him all praise be given!

He frees the prisoned and oppressed,
and pardons all whom sin possessed:
Alleluia!
Oh, praise him for his mercy!

In festal spirit, song, and word,
to Christ our risen, reigning Lord:
Alleluia!
all praise and thanks be rendered!

Acclaim the holy Trinity
for this all-glorious victory:
Alleluia!
and now sing gladly, Amen!

Meter	8.8.4.7.
Based on	Revelation 5:5; Hebrews 7:14
Theme	Easter
Translated	1976
Translation of	"Aj, ten silný lev udatný," Old Czech Lutheran, Tobiáš Závorka's *Kancionál,* 1602
Suggested tune	JUDAH'S LION, Adam Skultéty's *Partitúra*, 1798

A rearranged cento of the original of this Old Czech Lutheran Easter hymn appeared in an English translation by John Bajus in *The Lutheran Hymnal*, 1941. This revision and retranslation of that version was made during the preparation of the *Lutheran Book of Worship* in 1976, retaining only lines 1:1 and 7:1,4 of *The Lutheran Hymnal* version. The text was revised 9 March 1992.

This hymn, almost equally with "Now greet the swiftly changing year," shakes the rafters of Slovak Lutheran churches during the Easter festival in the land of their origin. It is rich with Scriptural allusions to the Messiah and his Old Testament prototypes.

Make Songs of Joy

Make songs of joy to Christ our head, Alleluia!
He lives again who once was dead! Alleluia!

Our life was purchased by his loss, Alleluia!
He died our death upon the cross. Alleluia!

O death, where is your deadly sting? Alleluia!
Assumed by our triumphant King! Alleluia!

And where your victory, O grave, Alleluia!
When one like Christ has come to save? Alleluia!

Behold, the tyrants, one and all, Alleluia!
Before our mighty Savior fall! Alleluia!

For this be praised the Son who rose, Alleluia!
The Father and the Holy Ghost! Alleluia!

Meter	8.4.8.4.
Based on	1 Corinthians 15:20–26, 55–57
Theme	Easter
Written	11 March 1976
Translation of	"Zpivejmež všickni vesele," by Juraj Tranovský 1636
Suggested tune	ZPIVEJMEŽ VŠICKNI VESELE, Chorvát *Velká Partitúra, 1936*

Only two Slovak Easter hymns were to be found in *The Lutheran Hymnal* of 1941. The publication of the *Lutheran Book of Worship* (1978) afforded an opportunity to add another translation of a Tranovský hymn dating from 1636, but to a melody of unknown date from the *Velká Partitúra* (Large Tune Book) of Juraj Chorvát (1936). The original 12-stanza text was condensed to six, retaining representative stanzas for use in an era when lengthy hymns are no longer in vogue.

Oh, What Tidings Bright

Oh, what tidings bright come to us tonight!
Oh, what tidings bright come to us tonight!
Light of light to us descending,
God himself our gloom is ending,
Oh, what tidings bright come to us tonight!

Hear we now a voice bidding us rejoice.
Hear we now a voice bidding us rejoice.
He who in the Godhead rested
Now in flesh is manifested,
To redeem us all from the devil's thrall!

Glory pure and bright breaks upon our night.
Glory pure and bright breaks upon our night.
See the fields aglow and blazing
And the hills in light amazing!
Oh, what tidings bright come to us tonight!

Meter	10.10.8.8.10.
Theme	Christmas Eve
Translated	1979
Translation of	"Dobrá novina"

Out to the Hills

Out to the hills, to the forest run,
What is that burning there like the sun?
Joy supernal's there appearing,
None has ever been so cheering.
Run, shepherds, run to the stable mean,
Then come and tell us what you have seen.

"There a young Virgin has borne a Child,
There in a manger he lies so mild,
Our Messiah long awaited,
Born a man, yet uncreated;
Come, let us worship our noble Lord,
Add yet our voice to the angel chord!"

O Son of God, sent from heav'n above,
Grant us poor sinners your gracious love,
That we may extol you ever,
Praise and worship you, dear Savior;
Come, 0 Redeemer, and with us dwell,
Bless us, beloved Immanuel!

Meter	9.9.8.8.9.9.
Theme	Christmas Eve
Translated	1957
Translation of	“Do hory, do lesa, valasi” (Text by Andrej Hlinka)

Rise Up, Bethl'em Shepherds, Rise

Rise up, Bethl'em shepherds, rise!
Lift our eyes up to the skies!
Listen to the word
No one's ear has heard:
"There is born to us a Savior,
God's own Son with heav'nly favor;
Let us go and greet
Him with praises meet!

Gifts we give he will receive
On this happy Christmas Eve
From our hearts of love
Kindled from above.
He will hear the prayers we send him,
Grant them, and to us will bend him,
That we all may share
His own glory there.

Meter	7.7.5.5.8.8.5.5.
Theme	Christmas Eve
Translated	1957
Translation of	"Vstante hore valasi" (Štefan Pyšný, Ms. collection in Archives of the Society of St. Adalbert, Trnava, Czechoslovakia, 1932

Shepherds All, Come

Shepherds all, come, and give ear to our song!
Shepherds all, come, for the Savior is born!
See what this very day we are given:
Our one Redeemer sent down from heaven.
Glory to God!

Shepherds all, come, and abandon your sheep,
Go to the stable, your Savior to seek;
There in a manger lies Christ anointed,
Whom as our Savior God has appointed.
Glory to God!

Now join the shepherds, to Bethlehem go,
That we like them God's redemption may know;
Here is the Word made flesh, bow before him,
He dwells among us, let us adore him.
Come and adore him, the Savior of all.

Meter	10.10.10.10.4.
Theme	Christmas Eve
Translated	1979
Translation of	"Nesiem vám noviny" (Author and composer unknown, from *Suchovný spevņk,* 1882)

Shepherds of Bethlehem

Shepherds of Bethlehem,
Come, see the diadem
Sparkling brightly in the heavens high;
Out of that blinding glow
To all who dwell below
Angels shout their very happy cry:
Lo, a poor maiden bore a pure Baby
And laid him down in a cradle of hay,
And laid him down in a cradle of hay.

Angels declare to us
Tidings most glorious:
Christ the Lord has left his throne above,
Now to our race descends
And to our nature bends,
God and man in one to show his love.
Lo, a poor maiden bore a pure Baby
And laid him down in a cradle of hay,
And laid him down in a cradle of hay.

"O precious Floweret
In your crude bassinet,
Bless and keep our valleys and our fields
That we may honor you
And render service due
With the bounty that our pasture yields."
Lo, a poor maiden bore a pure Baby
And laid him down in a cradle of hay,
And laid him down in a cradle of hay.

Meter	6.6.9.6.6.9.5.5.10.10.
Theme	Christmas Eve
Translated	1957
Translation of	“Povstaňte v rýchlosti” (Pavlin Bajan ms. Collection, Archives of the Society of St. Adalbert, Trnava, Austria-Hungary, 1783)

Slumber, Lovely Baby

Slumber, lovely Baby,
May the rough crib hay be
Soft beneath you, newborn Boy,
Jesus, gift of purest joy
We will rock you soothingly
That your sleep may smoother be.
Jesus, our dear Jesus,
Dream a dream that eases
Your fond mother's pain,
Your fond mother's pain.

Meadow, farm and mountain,
Rippling stream and fountain,
Welcome him with gifts and flow'rs
To this lovely land of ours,
To the song of winging birds
We will add our joyful words,
Join the whole creation
In our adoration,
With our glad refrain,
With our glad refrain.

Woods, now calm your noises,
Still your whispered voices,
Let the Infant have his sleep,
Resting where the straw be deep;
And the roses burning red
Send soft fragrance to his bed.
Quiet, lambs, the Baby
Sleeping here so gravely
Will forever reign,
Will forever reign.

Meter	6.6.7.7.7.7.6.6.5.5.
Theme	Christmas Eve
Translated	1979, by Andrew Roy and Jaroslav Vajda
Translation of	"Búvaj dietà krásne" (Štefan Pyšný, ms. with notes, Vrbov, Czechoslovakia, 1922)

Tell Us, Shepherds, Why So Joyful

Tell us, shepherds, why so joyful, what was it you saw?
What was it that made you tremble, made you run for awe?
"We saw a little Child,
Wondrous and, oh, so mild,
Born in Bethlehem this night."

How is it that no one heard this, none but you alone?
I would have gone with you gladly, had I only known.
"Angels proclaimed the Word,
Theirs was the voice we heard,
That our Savior Christ was born."

Reach to us, O little Jesus, reach your little hand,
In your infant arms enfold the souls of every land
Here make your welcome home,
To all your servants come,
Blest Redeemer whom we love!

Meter	13.13.6.6.7.
Theme	Christmas
Translated	1957
Translation of	"Povedzte nám, pastierovia" (Andrej Ozym *Kancionál,* Archives of the Slovak National Museum, Turc. Sv. Martin, Czechoslovakia, 1808)

Wake to the Wonder

Wake to the wonder appearing above
God has created for us out of love!
Never before has the world been so visited,
Never before has the world been so visited,
Never before have we seen such a sight
Filling the heaven and earth with its light.

Shepherds, be calm, you have nothing to fear;
I bring you tidings of comfort and cheer.
I am a messenger sent from the throne of God,
I am a messenger sent from the throne of God,
I come to you with his very own word:
Go, see in Bethlehem Jesus your Lord!

What you have waited for God to you brings;
Go there and you will find the King of kings:
Jesus, an infant, yet Ruler of rulers he,
Jesus, an infant, yet Ruler of rulers he,
There in a manger on hay in a stall
Lies your Redeemer, the Savior of all!

Meter	10.10.12.12.10.10.
Theme	Christmas Eve
Translated	1979
Translation of	"Vstávajte, pasteri" (Eastern Slovakia carol, (A. Furdanič ms. collection, Archives of the Society of St. Adalbert, Trnava, Czechoslovakia, 1922)

Wake Up, Brother, Listen

Wake up, brother, listen to the wondrous news,
What at midnight startled all our lambs and ewes.
They had just come in from grazing
And lay down when the amazing light appeared,
And a sound from heaven woke them, strange and feared.

Come to Bethl'em, come now, to the blessed site,
We shall see what happened there this very night.
Just to spend a little while there,
And to see the precious Child there, in the hay,
Wrapped in swaddling garments, as the angels say.

Meter	11.11.8.11.11.
Theme	Christmas Eve
Translated	1957
Translation of	“Vstávaj, bratku” (origin unknown)

While Mary Rocks Her Child to Rest

While Mary rocks her child to rest,
Crying and wakeful at her breast,
Soothing him, softly shuts his eyes
And sings to him sweet lullabies:
"O precious, so lovely, O Jesu mine!
O precious, so lovely, O Jesu mine!

"You are my sweetness, made of flesh,
You are my gladness, high and fresh,
Sleep, tender Rose, and warm my heart;
With all my love I gave you birth:
O precious, so lovely, O Jesu mine!
O precious, so lovely, O Jesu mine!

"Of mighty rulers you are King,
All that we need your love will bring,
Here on the straw so weak, so small,
You are the Savior, Lord of all:
O precious, so lovely, O Jesu mine!
O precious, so lovely, O Jesu mine!"

Meter	8.8.8.8.10.10.
Theme	Christmas Eve
Translated	1957
Translation of	“Keď Mária plačucemu” (Origin unknown, in *Cantus Catholici* Trnava, 1655)

Your Heart, O God, Is Grieved

Cantor: O God, Father in heaven, have mercy on us.

Your heart, O God, is grieved, we know,
By every evil, every woe;
Upon your cross-forsaken Son
Our death is laid, our peace is won.

Cantor: O Son of God, Redeemer of the world, have mercy upon us.

Your arms extend, O Christ, to save
From sting of death and grasp of grave;
Your scars before the Father move
His heart to mercy at such love.

Cantor: O God, Holy Spirit, have mercy upon us.

O lavish Giver, come to aid
The children that your word has made.
Now make us grow and help us pray;
Bring joy and comfort, come to stay.

Meter	LM and chant
Based on	Psalm 51
Theme	Kyrie/Repentance
Translated	24 September 1969
Translation of	"Známe to, Pane Bože nás," Juraj Tranovský, 1636
Suggested tune	ZNÁME TO, PANE BOŽE NÁS, Škultéty *Partitúra, 1798*

The Slovak Lutheran hymnal, the *Tranoscius,* contains at least 12 Kyries for liturgical use during the church year. One of the general Kyries is this 9-stanza hymn which I abbreviated to three and translated for *Laudaumus,* the Lutheran World Federation hymnbook of 1970. Usually each section of the Kyrie is addressed to one of the Persons of the Trinity and is prefaced by a chant sung by the worship leader, or cantor. I retained that distinctive element in this abbreviated version.

This type of Kyrie can be substituted for the liturgical responses is Luther's *Deutsche Messe* is used.

Translations: German Hymns, Carols, and Songs

A Dove Flew Down from Heaven

A dove flew down from heaven,
A dove rare and pure,
In angel garb appearing,
To greet a maid demure:
"All grace I bring you,
Tender, lovely maid,
No soul with such adorning
Has ever been arrayed."
Mercy, Lord, have mercy.

"I bring you joyous greetings:
The Lord is with you!
A Child you will be bearing;
You must believe it's true.
So welcome, welcome,
Open wide your heart,
That God upon this visit
His favor may impart.
Mercy, Lord, have mercy.

To this the Virgin bowing,
Responded with awe:
"If this is what He wishes,
His wish shall be my law
Yet more than willing
I surrender me,
If such Love is my Master,
His servant I will be."
Mercy, Lord, have mercy.

And so the Gift was given,
Our Helper in need,
New Life to dwell among us,
Eternal God indeed!
This Jesus Christ-Child,
Son whom Mary bore,
Is come to be our Savior,
To heaven our open Door.
Mercy, Lord, have mercy.

Meter	7.5.7.6.5.5.6.6.6.
Theme	Christmas/Annunciation
Translation	14 October 1970
Translation of	"Es flog ein Taublein weisse," ca. 1600

All Glory, Praise, and Blessing

A11 glory, praise, and blessing
To God the holy Trinity,
For planting and increasing
Our faith in Him who set us free,
On whom our trust is grounded,
Our house built on a rock,
Our life by grace surrounded.
Our Shepherd's precious flock,
Dear children to Him clinging,
Who, welcomed once again,
Join saints and angels singing
Amen, amen, amen!

Meter	7.8.7.8.7.6.7.6.7.6.7.6.
Based on	Psalm 103
Theme	Praise
Written	5 February 1991
Translation of	"Nun lob, mein' seel'," den Herren, St. 5
Suggested tune	NUN LOB, MEIN' SEEL'

A translation of stanza 5 of *NUN LOB, MEIN' SEEL'* as found in *Gemeinde Lieder,* #2, attributed to Konigsberg, 1548.

All Who Crave a Greater Measure

All who crave a greater measure
Of this blessed Christmas pleasure,
Loo-la, loo-la, loo-la,...
Pause and hear the Virgin mother
Sing to sleep our heavenly Brother,
God's and her beloved Son:
"Loo-la, loo-la, loo-la,...
Softly, softly slumber, Jesus, dearest Child."

"Take the brightest flowers of morning,
Garlands for your crib's adorning,
Loo-la, loo-la, loo-la,
Sleep, my Joy, who would not choose you,
Sleep, my Hope, I dare not lose you,
Sleep, my true, my heavenly Bread.
Loo-la, loo-la, loo-la,...
Softly, softly slumber, Savior of the world."

Meter	8.8.8.8.8.8.7.8.8.11.
Theme	Christmas Eve
Translated	4 September 1976
Translation of	“Alle, die ihr Gott zu ehren,” by Paul Gerhardt

Break Forth in Praise to God

Break forth in praise to God,
You cheerful cherubim;
To yours our voices add,
You shining seraphim.
With reverence discreet
Your feet and faces cover;
To taste of joy so sweet
From God, our heav'nly Lover,
Unite our earthly tongues
With your celestial songs:
Holy, holy, holy, Lord God of Sabaoth,
You are the most high God,
Lofty, sublime, and holy,
Lofty, sublime, and holy.

Before your majesty
We join the heav'nly throng
To stand before your throne
And share their endless song.
Eternal Three-in-One,
We view with awe and wonder,
O bright angelic Sun,
O undiminished Splendor,
We glorify, adore,
And praise you evermore:
Holy, holy, holy, Lord God of Sabaoth,
You are the God of might,
To you we sing thrice "Holy!"
To you we sing thrice "Holy!"

The Father now we laud,
The Maker of all things;
The Savior, Son of God,
Most worthy King of kings;
And Holy Spirit, you,
Your children gently feeding,
As you have made us new,
To our salvation leading,
So by the faith you give,
May we in glory live.
Joyful, joyful, joyful, are all who dwell with you,
O blessed Trinity,
You free us from all sorrow,
You free us from all sorrow.

Meter	6.6.6.6.6.7.6.7.6.6. and Refrain
Theme	Trinity/Thanksgiving
Translated	28 October 1979
Translation of	“Auf, auf, du Gottes Lob,” by Wilhelm Osterwald (1820–1887)

This hymn to the Holy Trinity as well as the Hymn of the Day for the 15th Sunday after Pentecost (traditional lectionary) was requested by Concordia Publishing House for its choral setting of the German original.

Translations of J.S. Bach's Christmas Oratorio Chorales

#5. Wie soll ich dich empfangen?

O Lord, how shall I meet you,
the One so long desired?
O Lord, how shall I greet you,
the most to be admired?
O light from heaven, Jesus,
shine on and in me, too,
that I may know what pleases
a gift from God like you.

#12. Brich an, o schönes Morgenlicht

There breaks the lovely Morning Light,
God's new day dawns upon you!
You shepherd folk, aghast with fright,
the angel speaks to calm you.
That promised newborn infant Boy
shall be our comfort and our joy,
the devil's power constraining,
and peace at last attaining.

#17. Schaut hin, dort liegt im finstern Stall

See One born in a stable stall
who wields dominion over all:
the Virgin's Child in cradle rude,
where oxen lately looked for food.

#28. Dies hat er alles uns getan

No greater love was ever known
than God's love for everyone:
for this let Christendom rejoice
with ever grateful heart and voice!
Kyrieleis! (or: Mercy, Lord!)

#33. Ich will dich mit Fleisz bewahren

Christ, my constant inspiration
from my birth
here on earth
to life's consummation!
Knowing you will leave me never,
I will be
joyfully
joined to you forever.

#35. Seid froh dieweil

Be happy then,
be happy then,
that, of all men,
our Savior comes true God and Man, anointed
God's very Son,
that Holy One,
is born in David's town, as God appointed.

#46. Dein Glanz all Finsternis verzehrt

Your brightness, Christ, consumes the night,
the gloomy darkness turns to light,
we find you here beside us.
Shed your clear rays
on all our days,
and to your glory guide us.

#53. Zwar ist solche Herzens-stube

See the human heart where all is
bleak and dark, a gloomy place,
by no means a princely palace.
Ah, but when your gleam of grace
shines within this once-dark dwelling,
everything with light is filling.

#59. Ich steh an deiner Krippen hier

Beside your manger-bed I stand,
dear Jesu, my soul's yearning;
I come with nothing in my hand
but gifts of yours returning.
Take all I have, my soul, my heart,
my mind and spirit, strength and art:
whatever gift may please you.

Dearest Lord Jesus, Why Are You Delaying

Dearest Lord Jesus, why are You delaying?
Come, see what burdens my soul are dismaying;
Come now and take me wherever You will,
Save me, oh, save me; Your promise fulfill!
Dearest Lord Jesus, why are You delaying?
Come, see what burdens my soul are dismaying.

It is enough, Lord, so come and deliver
Body and soul from evil forever
Come now, my fading assurance renew,
All that I am I surrender to You.
Come, see what burdens my soul are dismaying,
Come, as You promised, no longer delaying.

Meter	Irregular
Theme	Cross and Comfort
Translated	26 November 1986
Translation of	“Liebster Herr Jesu, wo bleibst du so lange,” origin unknown

Delicate Child of Royal Line

Delicate Child of royal line,
Now take your rest and slumber.
Sheep in the meadow lately fed
Share in your peace and slumber
        Close your eyes tight,
        Calm is the night,
Slumber, my dear One, slumber.

Brightest of angels trail your train,
Row upon endless number,
Filling the sky with bursting joy,
Trumpets and harps and drummers.
        Close your eyes tight,
        Safe in their light
Slumber, my dear One, slumber.

Meter	8.7.8.7.4.4.7.
Theme	Christmas Eve
Translated	23 October 1972
Translation of	“Kindelein Zart,” Anon.

For Your Mercy I Implore You

For your mercy I implore you,
Father, hear my fearful cry;
As your child I come before you,
Light my pathway lest I die.
Stop the foes who mock and hound me
Save me from their deadly harm;
When your love and might surround me,
I rest safely in your arm.

Meter	8.7.8.7.D.
Theme	Trust
Translated	24 May 1983
Translation of	“Deines Kinds Gebet erhöre”

Hear Me, Help Me, Gracious Savior

Hear me, help me, gracious Savior,
Turn in mercy, I implore;
Should you mark sins, I could never
Stand before you evermore.

Shall my sorrow last forever,
Shall my enemies rejoice?
Weak and helpless, O my Savior,
I await your soothing voice.

Meter	8.7.8.7.
Theme	Cross and Comfort
Translated	10 March 1983
Translation of	“Lass, O Herr, mich Hulfe Finden”

If God Is Absent, All the Cost

If God is absent, all the cost
And pains that build the house are lost;
If God the city does not keep,
The watchful guards as well may sleep.

In vain you rise before the sun,
Still hungry when your work is done;
The bread you fret about is found,
When you awake, upon the ground.

The Lord, whose love for all we share
Makes every child of ours his heir,
And in his strong protective hand
The young he blesses safely stand.

How blest the parents, who to heaven
Devote the children God has given;
No shame or scandal shall they know
As God protects them from the Foe.

To God the Father and the Son
And Holy Spirit on one throne,
Whom saints here and above adore,
Be glory now and evermore.

Meter	LM (8.8.8.8.)
Theme	Home/Family
Translated	7 December 1975
Translation of	"Wo Gott zum Haus nicht gibt sein Gunst," by Johann Kohlross (d. 1558). First stanza: Isaac Watts altered.

In Bethlehem a Wonder

In Bethlehem a wonder
Is born a Child for me;
And when this Gift I ponder,
His own I wish to be.
Ah, yes, ah, yes, his own I wish to be.

O little Child, be to me
More precious than before,
In happy times or gloomy
I wish to love you more.
Ah, yes, ah, yes, I wish to love you more.

True God, I now discover
You in my flesh and blood;
Gladly I bind me over
To you, my highest Good.
Ah, yes, ah, yes, to you, my highest Good.

Meter	7.6.7.6.10.
Theme	Christmas
Translated	1969
Translation of	“Zu Bethlehem Geboren,” Frederick von Spee, *Kolner Psalter,* 1638

Now Shine, Bright Glow of Majesty

Now shine, bright glow of majesty
Your long-prepared epiphany;
Our way lit by your burning,
To you we are returning,
Our journey through this earthly night
Immersed in your baptismal light.
O highest, holy Jesus Christ,
Never will you forsake us;
You are the Sun that feeds our lives;
By your strong hand now take us
And lead us from this gloomy thrall
Into your royal banquet hall,
Where we shall see you All-in-All.

Meter	Irregular
Theme	Epiphany
Translated	14 September 1981
Translation of	“Nun Schein, du Glanz der Herrlichkeit,” Anon. c. 1590

Now to This Babe So Tender

Now to this Babe so tender,
Now to this Babe so tender,
Your heart in love surrender,
In spirit gladly take him
Up in your arms and rock him:
O Jesus, O Jesus so sweet,
O Jesus so sweet.

Bend to the Baby singing,
Bend to the Baby singing,
Your offerings to him bringing,
Come, show how you adore him,
Lift laud and praise before him:
O Jesus, O Jesus so sweet,
O Jesus so sweet.

His hands and feet caressing,
His hands and feet caressing,
His heart, too, greet in blessing,
In humble awe come near him,
As God and Word revere him:
O Jesus, O Jesus so sweet,
O Jesus so sweet.

Now spend your life in serving,
Now spend your life in serving
This Gift beyond deserving,
Until with angels sharing
You wear the crown he's wearing.
O Jesus, O Jesus so sweet,
O Jesus so sweet.

Meter	7.7.7.7.7.8.5.
Theme	Christmas Eve
Translated	23 October 1972
Translation of	“Lasst Uns das Kindlein Wiegen,” Anon., 1604

O Father, Send the Spirit Down

O Father, send the Spirit down,
The Gift of gifts we most would own,
Upon your dear Son's prompting.
We pray, as we were taught by him,
Our cup of joy fill to the brim,
And never leave us wanting.

No one in all the world can claim
This noble Gift by force or fame
We have no power to gain it.
Here nothing counts but love and grace,
And God's acceptance of the price:
Christ's life and cross obtain it.

Meter	8.8.7.8.8.7.
Theme	Pentecost/Holy Spirit
Translated	23 September 1975
Translation of	"Gott Vater, sende deinen Geist," stanzas 1 and 2 of a 12-stanza hymn by Paul Gerhardt (1656)

O Joyous Christmas Night

O joyous Christmas Night,
None in all time so cheering,
Wherein the heav'nly Sun,
Our Christ makes his appearing!
Bright gleam of Jacob's Star,
Sweet, happy, hopeful Ray,
Come, pierce the whole wide world
With light this beauteous Day!

All Christians now rejoice,
Fresh hope your terrors stilling,
For God has kept his word,
His promises fulfilling;
True to his loving pledge
He sends his bodied Word
For us to see and hold,
Our gracious God's Reward.

The world is blest today
With this most holy Savior,
A gift of such vast worth
We stammer at his favor;
Our praises will not make
Him richer than He is,
But he enriches us
With his eternal bliss.

Meter	6.7.6.7.6.6.6.6.
Theme	Christmas Eve
Translated	3 February 1980
Translation of	"Erfreute Weinachtsnacht," Anon.

Since You Are Risen from the Dead

Since you are risen from the dead,
the grave shall not confine me,
the path you opened I shall tread,
no chains of fear to bind me;
for where you are I shall arrive,
and all the way rejoicing.

Meter	8.7.8.7.8.8.7.
Based on	John 14:19
Theme	Resurrection/Easter
Translated	26 August 1988
Translation of	“Weil du vom Tod’ erstanden ist”
Suggested tune	DENN DU WIRST MEINE SEELE

Sleep, My Little One

Sleep, my little one, Sleep, my little Son,
Sings the Virgin Mother pure;
Sleep, my lofty Lord, Sleep my precious Ward,
So sings Joseph at the door.

Refrain
Sing, all creation, this marvelous night
The first sweet song to greet your King;
Fill all the stable and heaven with light,
And join with angel choirs to sing.

Sleep, my hope, my heart's renewal,
Sleep, my life's most treasured Prize,
Sleep, my Flower, Sleep, my Jewel,
Softly, softly, close your eyes.
Refrain

Meter	Irregular
Based on	The Christmas Story
Theme	Christmas Eve
Written	15 January 1988
Translation of	"Schlaf, mein Kindelein," 1697
Suggested tune	traditional Alsatian carol

Sleep Softly, Softly, Beautiful Jesus

Sleep softly, softly, beautiful Jesus,
Sleep softly, darling Child,
You close your eyes, the whole world sleeps,
All night the heavenly Father keeps,
Keeps watch for us, for us,
Keeps watch for us, for us.

See Mary and Joseph standing nearby
While still the cattle lie,
Soon will the shepherds running come
To see the wonder of Bethlehem,
To marvel and adore,
To marvel and adore.

Meter	10.6.8.8.6.6.
Theme	Christmas Eve
Translated	23 October 1972
Translation of	“O Schlafe, Lieblicher Jesu,” Anon.

Sleep Well, Dear Heavenly Boy

Sleep well, dear heavenly Boy, sleep well,
In slumber take your rest.
Soft angel wings, Immanuel,
Will fan you in your nest;
And we poor shepherds, kneeling here,
Sing you our lullaby sincere:
    Slumber, slumber,
    Rest in peaceful slumber.

Around you Mary folds her care
To watch the nighttime through,
And Joseph dares not stir the air
Lest he awaken you;
The little sheep in barn and stall
Before the Infant silent fall,
    Slumber, slumber,
    Rest in peaceful slumber.

The rage of those you've come to save
Will take your life one day,
And lay you in an early grave—
So rest you while you may.
Poor Child of heaven, your eyelids close
And spend this night in sweet repose.
    Slumber, slumber,
    Rest in peaceful slumber.

Meter	8.6.8.6.8.8.4.6.
Theme	Christmas Eve
Translated	25 January 1971
Translation of	“Schlaf wohl, du Himmelsknabe du,” Anon., ca. 1850

The Rescue We Were Waiting For

The rescue we were waiting for
Has come most undeservedly,
While we were groping on the floor
Of deep despair, what did we see?
The hand of Jesus, God's own Son,
Came reaching down to us alone:
No one but he could save us.

Chained by the law and its demands
And crippled by the curse of sin,
All offerings smeared by guilty hands
The walls of hopelessness closed in,
While in the mirror all I saw
Was weakling, rebel, fatal flaw—
And found no one to save me.

The law, I found, was not the way
To life and health, to joy and peace;
I'd piled up debts I could not pay,
From death there was no sure release.
And then, when in the deepest throes
Of gloom, I heard the hammer blows
Constructing my salvation.

The gift I had no right to claim,
A life to compensate my loss,
By grace from God the Father came:
My Substitute upon my cross.
My pardon there was read to me,
Beneath that God-forsaken tree—
And I am free forever!

Secure within his warm embrace,
Join in the Savior's freedom song:
Show Christ to every downcast face,
Shout Christ to all the dying throng!
Sing loving Father, gracious Son,
Sing living Spirit, freedom won,
For now and through all ages!

Meter	8.8.8.8.8.8.7.
Theme	Justification
Paraphrased	26 September 1975
Paraphrase of	"Es ist das Heil," by Paul Speratus, 1523
Suggested tune	NUN FREUT EUCH
	ES IST DAS HEIL

So many chorales are versified dogma, stating incontrovertible truths in square solid verse not intended to be judged as poetry, thus resulting in a boring exercise for many worshipers, especially those for whom the chorale is strange. I had wondered how certain rugged chorales could be rewritten in contemporary, more poetic language and illustrated with more imagery. This paraphrase of "Es ist das Heil" attempts to do that, and, to the extent that it succeeds, may inspire other experiments that would retain the strength and certitude of the chorale and garb it in fresh clothing and personalize the worshiper's response to the faith once delivered to the saints. I can imagine such confessional (not penitential) renditions utilizing the pictures and logic of a C. S. Lewis or a Helmut Thielecke to convey the orthodox doctrines in the fresh idiom of today's theologians.

This particular cento (the original had 14 stanzas) and paraphrase has been widely used by individual congregations, but it is not yet known in most Lutheran churches where the 10-stanza translation of the original would be most familiar.

A slight variation in the meter was made in the first and third lines of each stanza, providing a syllable for each note of the line-ending slur, thus propelling the hymn from the very beginning.

Three Angels Are Singing

Three angels are singing the best song of all:
it echoes throughout the heavenly hall.

The song they are singing, so pure, so clear:
the love of God that all may hear.

Go, search for the love most glorious:
you'll find it hanging on a cross.

See what distress and feel what pain,
when Christ the Son of God is slain.

He saves us from the death he died
for us when he was crucified.

Now let us all sing that all may know
the God of love who loved us so.

Meter	Irregular
Based on	Medieval carol
Theme	Lent
Written	11 April 1990
Translation of	"Es sungen drei Engel"
Tune	ES SUNGEN DREI ENGEL

Upon the suggestion of several musicians, and inspired by Paul Manz's improvisation on the tune "In dulci jubilo," a seven-stanza cento of the longer original provided the basis of this "translation" which attempts to capture the mood and thrust of the original German Lenten carol. The prominent emphasis on Mary in the original was omitted to focus on the Savior as the subject of the angels' song. I restated stanza five positively, and added a sixth stanza to tie it to the first, suggesting our participation in the angels' song.

The tune accommodates the lengthening and shortening of lines in each stanza, so typical of many ballads and folk songs.

Up, O Shepherds

Up, O shepherds, up from sleep,
Break your slumber's fastening.
For a time forsake your sheep,
To the manger hastening.
Sing now: "What a blessed night,
Bringing us salvation's light,
For to us from heaven's throne
Comes the Father's only Son!"

Shepherds, just go bravely in,
There's no cause for terror.
Comfort, grace, and peace within—
Never were they nearer.
At this cradle, come to view
How the Savior welcomes you.
See his heart with love afire:
Do not spurn this Babe's desire.

Precious little Child divine,
Yet the Lord's anointed:
Though we be so few and plain,
Don't be disappointed.
Please receive our homage true,
Son of God, we worship you.
Brighter shine these stars and moon
Than the sun at height of noon.

Meter	7.6.7.6.7.7.7.7.
Theme	Christmas Eve
Translated	25 January 1971, rev. 26 October 1986
Translation of	“Auf, ihr Hirten,” Tyrolean carol

Wake, Shepherds, Awake

Wake, shepherds, awake,
Your sadness forsake.
Bright angels are swinging
From heaven and singing:
    "Your joy is now near,
    The Savior is here!"

Come, shepherds, in haste
To Someone so chaste:
With flutes fill his heart full
Of songs gay and artful;
    Come, find in a stall
    The Savior of all.

They came and they heard
The wonderful word,
Then told one another
Of Jesus, their Brother,
    And everyone found
    A King to be crowned.

They greeted with joy
This heavenly Boy
In wonder amazing,
In carols and praising.
    Their pipes echo still
    At night on the hill.

Meter	5.5.6.6.5.5.
Theme	Christmas Eve
Translated	23 October 1972
Translation of	“Ihr Hirten, erwacht,” Rhine carol, ca. 1840

What Love, Lord Jesus, That You Go

What love, Lord Jesus, that you go
So willingly to offer
Yourself for me, a sinner who
Has caused what you must suffer.
Let me at least, my Great High Priest,
Walk in your footsteps weeping;
My tears shall flow with cries of woe,
Watch o'er your sorrows keeping.

'Tis I, Lord Jesus, I confess,
Who should have borne sin's wages
And lost the peace of heavenly bliss
Through everlasting ages.
Instead I hear you volunteer;
My punishment you carry.
Your death and blood lead me to God,
Where I by grace may tarry.

Lord Jesus, for such love divine
What can I find to render?
There is no treasure I call mine
That I would not surrender:
Myself alone, and all I own,
In love to serve before you;
And then at last, when time is past,
In heaven I shall adore you.

Meter	8.7.8.7.4.4.7.4.4.7
Based on	John 19:16, 17
Theme	Lent
Written	20 July 1987
Translation of	"So gehst du nun, mein Jesu hin"
Suggested tune	SO GEHST DU NUN

The English translation of "So gehst du nun, mein Jesu, hin" by Kaspar F. Nachtenhofer (1651) was made for *The Lutheran Hymnal* (1941) by W. G. Polack. Upon a request from MorningStar Music Publishers, this text was updated and paraphrased for a choral setting of stanzas 1, 3, and 5.

World, for All Your Gain and Pleasure

World, for all your gain and pleasure,
Your horizons gleaming bright,
I desire the lasting treasure
As I face the coming night.
Death, I know, must end this strife,
Life will once give way to Life;
All the best is yet to be,
Peace and joy eternally.

When I know such life awaits me,
I can live more freely here;
Christ, my guide and hope, supports me,
Fills my days on earth with cheer.
Here I see his work begun,
In his rising victory won.
But the best is yet to be:
Life with him eternally.

Meter	8.7.8.7.7.7.7.7.
Theme	Heaven/Hope
Translated	1 September 1971
Translation of	"Welt, ade, ich bin dein müde," by Abraham Teller (1649) st.1 and Johann Georg Albinus (1624–79) st.2.

Translations: Hungarian Hymns, Carols, and Songs

Blessed Be the Precious Baby

Blessed be the precious Baby,
newborn Prince in Bethl'em's stable!
Welcome we the Gift God gave us;
who but he was born to save us?

See the Morning Star arising!
Who can sleep through such surprising?
Hear the happy breezes bringing
news the angel choirs are singing.

Celebrate this Evening holy,
everyone, both great and lowly:
gift from heaven meant to please us,
birthday of our Savior, Jesus!

Meter	LM (8.8.8.8.) Trochaic
Theme	Christmas Eve
Translated	23 March 1983
Translation of	"Adlott legy kisdedecske"
Suggested tune	ZEPDOL, Zoltain Kodaly (1882–1967)

This and the following two Hungarian hymns were selected for inclusion in the Lutheran World Federation hymn book, *Laudamus*, for its 1984 meeting in Budapest, Hungary. I was asked to versify the literal English translation.

From the Shadow of My Pain

From the shadow of my pain,
from the shadow of my pain,
unto you, my God, I cry:
hear my fervent prayer,
let me not despair,
nor be swallowed by my sorrows
In this prison where I sigh.

No one seeks to do me harm,
no one seeks to do me harm,
but my enemy is me
and your judgment dread
breaking on my head.
There's no hiding from your chiding;
save my soul from jeopardy

Lord, I beg you, crush my pride,
Lord, I beg you, crush my pride,
give me true repentance, please!
Something in me cries:
let me realize
how I hurt you and desert you!
What will bring me to my knees!

I am wracked by endless sobs,
I am wracked by endless sobs,
yet my weeping brings no tears.
Morning, noon, and night,
Satan lies in wait,
and resisting his persisting,
I am slain by my own fears.

Let your holy will be done,
Let your holy will be done;
I surrender to your rod
if someone may gain
from my grief and pain.
Ah, but rather, like a father,
save me still, my gracious God!

Meter	7.7.7.5.5.8.7.
Theme:	Christian Life/Repentance
Translated	23 March 1983
Translation of	"Kinok arnyekaibol," Weores Sandor (b. 1913)
Suggested tune	by Sulyoh Imre (b. 1912)

Who's That Sitting on the Ground?

Who's that sitting on the ground,
center of a motley crowd?
Did you see him looking at us,
hear his gentle words?

Says a gruff man with a frown:
"Go away, you little ones!
Children cannot understand him;
he is Gods own Son!"

Ah, but we do understand,
and we love that kindly man.
Can't we offer little praises
if a songbird can?

Listen to the Master say:
"I will not turn you away;
more than birds, you make me happy
when I hear you pray."

Meter	7.7.8.5.
Theme	Children
Translated	23 March 1983
Translation of	“Pazzitdombon uldogel,” Szedo Denes (b. 1922)
Suggested tune	by Zotain Kodaly (1882–1967)
	CHILDREN LOVE HIM by Tom Leesberg-Lange

Translations: Hispanic Hymns, Carols, and Songs

Breath of the Living God

Soplo de Dios viviente

Breath of the living God on the waters in the beginning moving,
Breath of the living God, you fill all creation with fruitful life.

Chorus:
Come now and live within us, and with your gifts enrich us:
Breath of the living God, O most holy Spirit of the Lord!

Breath of the living God, you conceived the Son, Jesus, to be like us
Breath of the living God, so you recreate all who live in him.
Chorus

Breath of the living God, you bring us to life in baptismal water,
Breath of the living God, we new creatures live by your living breath.
Chorus

Meter	6.11.6.10. and chorus
Words	Osvaldo Catena
Music	Popular Norwegian melody, arr. by Lorraine Florindez (1926)

Come, Shepherds, Come

Venid, pastores

Come, shepherds, hurry, to Bethlehem run,
to the wonder the prophets foretold!
I will not leave, till I've worshipped the Son
of the King of the heavenly fold.

Come, shepherds, come, leave your flocks in the field
and go see what the angels announced;
Go with great joy there to welcome the Gift
God has promised the world and to us:

Chorus
Follow the Bethlehem Star
to the world's brightest Dawn,
And you will come to the door
where the Savior is born.

Meter	10.9.10.9. and refrain
Theme	Christmas Eve
Text	Puerto Rican carol

On a Lonely Field

En la noche los pastores

On a lonely field at midnight,
Shepherds kept their flocks near Bethlehem,
When a choir of angels suddenly
Filled the sky with light and singing:
"Glory be to God! Christ is born today!"

Refrain:
Go, adore the Baby Lying in a manger There in Bethlehem!

In the East appears a Daystar,
Wise men follow it to Bethlehem,
There they find the Child and worship Him,
Honor Him with gifts and praises;
So let us today Royal homage pay.

Refrain

Christians do the same each Christmas,
Worshiping the Child of Bethlehem,
Filled with joy and thanks and reverence,
Greet the Gift of God with singing.
Tell the world again: Love and Peace are yours!

Refrain

Sweetest Song of This Bright Season

Dulces cantos entonemos

Sweetest song of this bright season
Is the one glad hearts compose:
Jesus is the joy and reason
For the peace his birth bestows;
So, all children sing and say:
Peace and joy! It's Christmas Day!

Hear the holy angels singing
"Glory be to God on high!"
To the world their song is bringing
Joy and peace that will not die.
So, all children sing and say:
Peace and joy! It's Christmas Day!

To that holy Child be giving
All our lives though weak and small,
Then with Jesus in us living,
Tell and show his love to all:
So, all children sing and say:
Peace and joy! It's Christmas Day!

Meter	8.7.8.7.7.7.
Words	Hector Hoppe, 1954
Music	Carl Gottlieb Hering

The King the Wise Men Found

Los magos que llegaron

Chorus:
The king the wise men found in Bethlehem
Was the King they came to worship—the Messiah.
We now make that same glad journey
As we worship You with them.

From a foreign land afar we come to see You,
In our deep dark night You send a Star to guide us.
Promised Morning Star, announce the new day's dawning;
Glowing in our hearts, Your light will never fail us.
Chorus

To the holy Child who came to earth from heaven
We present the gift of myrrh, a sign of sadness.
Long-awaited Star, announce the new day's dawning;
Burning in our hearts, Your light will never fail us.
Chorus

To the King of kings we worship as an Infant
We present the gift of gold fit for a monarch.
Glory be to God and to God's most Beloved!
Glory be on high for peace and love on earth!
Chorus

Text	M. Fernandez Juneos
Tune	Puerto Rican Christmas carol

Translations: Latin Hymns, Carols, and Songs

Hail the Savior's Very Body

Hail the Savior's very Body
From the Virgin Mary's womb,
There upon the cross suspended
Bears for us the bitter doom,
From whose side flows blood and water,
Sinners' holy remedy:
May that Body be our comfort
In our final agony.

Meter	8.7.8.7.D.
Based on	Luke 22:20; John 19:34 and parallels
Theme	Eucharist
Written	30 August 1988
Suggested tune	AVE VERUM CORPUS

This text is a new translation of the traditional “Ave verum corpus” text ascribed to Innocent VI (d. 1362) to a setting by Camille Saint-Saëns (1835–1921).

Translations: Czech Hymns, Carols, and Songs

Christ, the Model of the Meek

Christ, the model of the meek,
though with the Godhead one,
God the Father's most beloved
and sole-begotten Son,
set aside his majesty
to take the sinner's place.
Who would go so far as this
to show one's love and grace?

While a helpless infant still,
he had to flee his foes,
and, a man, rejected by
the people whom God chose;
Yet he came to seek and serve
the wayward and the lost,
faithful to his Father's will
and heedless of the cost.

Second Adam that he was,
he took the first one's stead;
by his tears and bloody sweat,
he earned his children's bread.
Like a shepherd good and true,
he seeks the straying lamb,
feeds the flock and keeps it safe,
and gives his life for them.

When the time had fully come
in God's eternal plan,
lo, a virgin maid gave birth
to Christ, the Son of Man;
in the starkest manger bed
the King of glory lay,
come to make his home among
the poorest of the day.

Target of the Devil's rage,
and by his own disowned,
cursed by strangers and condemned,
abandoned by his friends,
King of all, he could not find
a place to rest his head;
on that royal head he wore
a crown of thorns instead.

For the joy you came to give
you meekly went to die,
teaching us to bear our cross
to know your kind of joy.
Give us faith to follow you
through cross to faith's reward,
loving as you showed us how,
our humble Servant Lord.

Meter	7.6.7.6.D.
Based On	Philippians 2:5–11
Theme	Humility/Pre-Lent
Written	17 July 1989
Translation of	"Kristus, priklad pokory" by Lucas of Prague (1460–1528)
Suggested tune	KRISTUS, PRIKLAD POKORY, *Bohemian Brethren Hymnal,* 1501, as found in Michael Weisse's *Ein New Geseng Buchlen,* 1531, and in Jan Roh's (Horn's) *Piesne Duchownie Ewangelitske,* 1541

One of several Bohemian Brethren hymns translated from their Czech originals for possible inclusion in the new Moravian Hymnal.

Lucas of Prague, a prominent figure in the pre-Reformation Bohemian Brethren movement, was born c. 1460, receiving his B.A. from the University of Prague in 1481. The next year he joined the Unitas Fratrum, in 1490 became a member of their Select Council, and in 1500 was consecrated Bishop of the Unity. He contributed 11 hymns to the *Bohemian Hymn Book,* 1501, among them this text which has been widely used ever since in Slavic hymnals of all denominations, including the *Cantus Catholici* of 1655 by way of the Slovak Lutheran *Cithara Sanctorum* (*Tranoscius*) of 1636. 106 other hymns by Lucas appear in the 1561 edition of the Bohemian Brethren hymnal. Lucas compiled the first (1501) Bohemian Brethren hymnal of 89 hymns, which was followed by the 1505 hymnal containing some 400 hymns. Lucas died December 11, 1528.

The tune comes from an unknown composer and was probably used with the text in 1501, although copies of that hymnal have not been found. The tune does appear in Michael Weisse's German Brethren hymnal of 1531, and in John Horn's (Roh's) 1541 Czech hymnal.

The six-stanza English translation (and paraphrase) is based closely on the eight-stanza original

Faithful Christians, One and All

Faithful Christians, one and all,
join in jubilation:
pause in wonder to recall
Jesus' incarnation.
Praise the peerless grace of God
for his promise to us,
that, fulfilled in his dear Son,
prompts our alleluias.

What the Trinity once sealed
deep in secret meeting
was by Gabriel revealed
in angelic greeting:
"Lowly maid from Galilee,
blest above all others,
God has chosen you to be
the Messiah's mother."

There the Son of God would dwell
all divine, all human,
from our hearts our fears dispel
and with joy illumine!
Who could ever doubt such love,
serving, dying for us?
Who would not with hosts above
join in Mary's chorus?

Magnify the Lord with me,
every generation,
for the year of jubilee
dawns for every nation.
Christ the Prince of Peace is here,
do not dare to miss him;
welcome this God's Gift most dear
and, adoring, kiss him.

Meter	7.6.7.6.D
Based on	Luke 1:26–38, 46–55
Theme	The Annunciation/Christmas
Translated	23 August 1989
Translation of	"Vsichni verni krestane," by Martin Michalec, 1541
Suggested tune	GAUDEAMUS PARITER

This translation of the Bohemian hymn by Martin Michalec was made for a new edition of the Hymnal for the Moravian Church in America. The original 9-stanza Christmas hymn was reduced to four stanzas. The original was taken from the 1979 edition of the Evangelical Bohemian Brethren hymnal and the 1971 edition of the Slovak Lutheran hymnal, the *Cithara Sanctorum*. The hymn first appeared in the 1541 Bohemian Brethren hymnal, compiled by Jan Roh (Johann Horn), the composer of the well-known tune *GAUDEAMUS PARITER.*

God Almighty, Lord Most Holy

Cantor: Kyrie, eleison

God almighty, Lord most holy,
worthy to be worshiped solely,
loving as you only are:
mercy, Lord, mercy, please!

Lord, we beg you, show your mercy
to the weak and undeserving;
nowhere else can we find hope:
mercy, Lord, mercy, please!

To the sinners truly grieving
you turn willingly forgiving,
good and gracious that you are:
mercy, Lord, mercy, please!

Cantor: Christe, eleison

Christ, true Son of the Father,
born of Mary virgin Mother,
only you can
truly have mercy on us.

By your living and teaching,
by your mighty works and preaching,
only you can
truly have mercy on us.

For your suffering and dying,
make us grateful hear our crying:
only you can
truly have mercy on us.

Cantor: Kyrie, eleison

Holy Spirit, consolation,
gift of grace for our salvation,
do your saving work in us:
mercy, Lord, mercy, please!

May we always love you dearly
and desire you most sincerely,
praising you with heart and life:
mercy, Lord, mercy please!

Lord most patient, most forbearing,
  Lord most loving, Lord most caring,
  bring us safely home at last:
    mercy, Lord, mercy, please!

Meter	Irregular
Based on	Psalm 32:5, 1 John 1:8,9, etc.
Theme	Kyrie/Repentance
Written	22 July 1989
Translation of	"Hospodine, všemohouci," Bohemian Brethren, 16th cent.
Suggested tune	HOSPODINE

One of several Bohemian Brethren hymns translated from the original Czech for possible inclusion in the new Moravian Hymnal.

Kyries were a standard element in the liturgy of the pre-Reformation and Reformation churches. The *Cithara Sanctorum* of George Tranovsky, 1636 has nine of them, at least one for each major season of the church year and several general Kyries, of which this is probably the most used, ranking in popularity with the vernacular versions of the Christmas "Kyrie, fons bonitatis" and Luther's "Kyrie, Gott Vater in Ewigkeit."

In my translation of another general Slovak/Czech Kyrie, "Your heart, O God, is grieved," the nine-stanza original was abbreviated to three stanzas, whereas in this Kyrie I wanted to preserve the nine-stanza form to allow for lengthier meditation on the confession of sins and to preserve the flavor of the original custom.

Though of Bohemian Brethren origin, this text (and tune) is not found in the 1979 edition of the Czech Brethren Hymnal currently in use in Bohemia. It has been preserved for posterity by the numerous editions of the Slovak Lutheran hymnal of George Tranovsky (1636), who brought it into the classic hymnal he compiled and which is still used to this day by Slovak Lutherans.

The tune appears without the cantor's chant in the Partitura, 1956 (in use on the Continent), whereas it appears with the chant in the American accompaniment book, Kucharik's *Duchovna Cithara* of 1933. The present setting of the melody is from a manuscript accompaniment book from 1750. The meter is irregular as are most Kyries, which pose no problems with European texts which accommodate a floating accent.

How Shall We Thank You, Christ, Our Lord?

How shall we thank you, Christ, our Lord,
for holy life and blood outpoured?
Who else assumed our debt and death,
who else deserves our trust and faith?

Your dying cleansed the world of sin,
and all who die with you are clean,
washed in your blood, we lose our stains,
and with your cross you break our chains.

Your willing death upon the cross
has earned God's priceless gift for us:
the Spirit by whose power we kill
our pride, and do our Father's will.

The life you lived you lived that we
might live that life eternally,
your eager Spirit shows us how
we can enjoy it even now.

How shall we praise you, Christ, our Lord,
for holy life and blood outpoured?
Who else assumed our debt and death,
who else deserves our trust and faith?

Meter	LM
Based on	2 Corinthians 5:21; 1 Peter 1:18,19, etc
Theme	Lent/Good Friday
Written	13 November 1989
Translation of	"Kriste, jenž jsi smrt podstoupil," 1541
Suggested tune	BEATUS VIR

Another of several Bohemian Brethren hymns translated from the Czech original for possible inclusion in the new Moravian Hymnal.

This 7-stanza original hymn by Brother Jan Augusta (1500–72) was shortened to 4 stanzas with a repetition of the first stanza concluding the Lenten hymn.

The melody is known in American hymnals as *BEATUS VIR,* a title given to the old Czech melody by the compilers of The Lutheran Church—Missouri Synod *Worship Supplement* (1969) and which appeared in the *Lutheran Book of Worship* (1978) at No. 419. The original Slavic text associated with this tune was a paraphrase of Psalm 1 by Jan Blahoslav (1523–71), hence the naming of the tune *BEATUS VIR.*

Let Us Sing With Heart and Voice

Let us sing with heart and voice
praise to our Creator,
who, to make the world rejoice
sent its Liberator
From a virgin came a child,
every prophecy fulfilled,
born to be our Savior;
for a world by sin defiled
died as God his Father willed,
earning us His favor.

Who had ever heard such news,
that the Lord of angels
and the King of heaven would choose
such a way to save us?
Yet by such a birth as this
Christ would gain and seal the bliss
of the hopeless creature.
Even angels, wondering long,
make this theme their Christmas song:
God in human nature!

What amazing love and grace,
peace beyond all knowing,
that the Lord of time and space
lies where cows are lowing!
Shall the angels only sing
praises to the newborn King
sleeping in the manger?
Greet the Shepherd come to keep
all the precious lambs and sheep
safe from mortal danger.

Meter	7.6.7.6.7.7.6.7.7.6.
Based on	Luke 2:1–20
Theme	Christmas/Incarnation
Written	20 July 1989
Translation of	“Velebme vždy s veselim”
Suggested tune	DIES EST LAETITIAE

One of several Bohemian Brethren hymns translated from the Czech original for possible inclusion in the new Moravian Hymnal.

The original Bohemian five-stanza Christmas hymn by Jan Taborsky (lit.John the Taborite), a former Roman Catholic priest by the name of Jan Vilimek, who became a member of the Bohemian Brethren Unity’s Select Council. Taborsky contributed this and five other hymns to the first Brethren hymnal published by Lucas of Prague in 1501. Taborsky, whose birth date is unknown, died April 28, 1495 in Leitomish, Bohemia.

The translation is a cento of the strongly theological yet poetic text by the pre-Reformation writer, and was wedded to the tune DIES EST LAETITIAE, whose origin is shrouded in debate. It is traced by some to a 15th century German tune. Bohemian scholars place its composition in the 14th century finding the tune in a Bohemian collection of tunes in the Vysebrod manuscript of 1410. Its melodic lines would suggest a Slavic origin.

The Taborsky text is not a translation of the medieval Latin “Dies est laetitiae,” which has been translated into many languages since its origin has been dated as early as the 11th century.

Now Go to Sleep

"Now go to sleep," the mother coos,
"Rest, my dear Son."
The whole night through she gently soothes
That precious One.
"Slumber, most gracious Child of heav'n,
True God and Lord,
My fondest wish:
May all you love
Be your reward."

"Hush, slumber now all through the night
Softly, my Dove.
Warm be your bed, my soul's Delight,
My Pearl, my Love;
Your honor and your glory fill
All heav'n and earth,
Angelic choirs and myriad stars
Sing at your birth."

"The Child's asleep. The angels' song
Is silent now.
You nations, come and kneel with me,
In worship bow,
With open arms and hearts receive
God's very Son;
Salvation, joy, and peace he brings
To everyone."

Meter	8.4.8.4.D.
Based on	The Christmas Narrative
Theme	A lullaby by Mary to the Christ-Child
Translated	19 October 1992
Translation of	"Chtic aby spal," a Czech Christmas carol (1647) by Adam Vaclav Michna (c. 1600–70)
Tune	Also probably by Adam Michna

On October 1, Petr Kepka, a recent Czech immigrant in Burlington, Vermont, sent me a collection of 48 Czech original and translated carols, and asked me to translate a third of them into English. The carol at the head of his list was "Chtic aby spal" (lit. "Wanting him to sleep"), a charming rendition of which I had first come upon in a recording by Opus in Czecho-Slovakia (Stereo #9112 1765), recorded in 1981 and released in 1986 under the title *Christmas Carols, Musica Bohemica*. I was fascinated by the carol on the recording and wanted to translate it at once, but did not have the words until I received the text and tune from Mr. Kepka six years after I purchased the record in Slovakia.

I reduced the original four stanzas to three, omitting the flowery bucolic third stanza, while retaining the other three stanzas with their strong theological content, and attempting to render them in an almost literal transcription in contemporary English idiom.

Out of the Forest a Cuckoo Flew

Out of the forest a cuckoo flew, cuckoo!
Down to the manger her Lord to view, cuckoo!
And there she honors him as she sings
Her praises to the King of kings.
Cuckoo, cuckoo, cuckoo!

There sits a dove on a little tree, curroo!
Adding his song to the harmony, curroo!
He wants to show, this happiest morn,
His thankful heart that Jesus is born.
Curroo, curroo, curroo!

Meter	11.11.9.9.(8).6.
Theme	Christmas
Translated	1965
Translation of	"Zezulka z lesa vylitla" (Czech carol of unknown origin)

This Glorious Easter Festival

This glorious Easter festival,
let everyone with joy recall
how Jesus died and rose for all.

Reviled by those he came to save,
he died amid the most depraved,
and rested in a borrowed grave.

But now, arisen from the tomb,
he frees the prisoners of doom,
rekindles hope and scatters gloom.

The Spirit gives the corpse new breath,
new life emerges from thin death,
the Body rises with the Head.

Now all creation join in praise,
the fields and flowers in beauty blaze
to celebrate this Day of days.

Remember barren Golgotha,
see in full regalia!
With angels sing: Alleluia!

Meter	8.8.8.
Based on	Colossians 1:12–23a; 1 Peter 1:3–9, and Easter Lessons
Theme	Easter/Resurrection/Hope/New Life
Written	24 July 1989
Translation of	"Slávne Kristovo vzkrišeni"
Tune	SLÁVNE KRISTOVO VZKRIŠENI

This is another of several Bohemian Brethren hymns translated from the original Czech for possible inclusion in the new Moravian Hymnal.

This anonymous text by a Bohemian Brethren author appeared in the 1505 Czech hymnal in 11 stanzas. This translation/parapharase is a 6-stanza cento of the original, attempting to render the thoughts of the original in contemporary language with allusions incorporated from parallel references to the Easter event from the Epistles.

The tune is found in the Czech *Evangelicky zpevnik,* 1979 (No. 336) and in Joseph Kucharik's *Duchovona cithara,* 1933, with slight variation. The melody, by an unknown Bohemian composer, dates back to the Bohemian Brethren Czech hymnal of 1505.

Translations: Portuguese Hymns, Carols, and Songs

As Out of the Stem the Branch Grows

Refrain:
As out of the stem the branch grows,
and out of the branch the bloom,
So was the Savior born of Mary,
so did our salvation come.

By the Spirit's holy wisdom,
Mary spoke the will of God,
So do all who by that Spirit
spread that holy will abroad.
Refrain

God does not judge by appearance,
nor by measures we apply;
What the world considers worthless
God will raise and glorify.
Refrain

Violent ones, His word will crush you,
greedy ones, His breath is fire!
But the ones who follow Wisdom
shall receive their heart's desire.
Refrain

In that day, in that day surely,
what has never been will be:
Wolf and lamb and ox and lion,
side by side in harmony.
Refrain

In that day, in that day surely,
God will stretch His mighty hand,
And the world will watch in wonder
as we claim our promised Land.
Refrain

Bring Your people out of bondage,
make a path through our Red Sea;
By your love and by Your promise,
Lord, have mercy set us free!
Refrain

Meter	8.7.8.7. and Refrain
Based on	Luke 1:46–55
Theme	The Magnificat /Liberation
Written	18 March 1988
Translation of	"Da cepa brotou a rama," Portugese text by Reginaldo Veloso
Suggested tune	DA CEPA BROTOU A RAMA by Redinaldo Veloso

This is one of two Brazilian/Portuguese songs by Reginaldo Veloso for which an English translation was requested by Gerhard Cartford. The text highlights the liberation motif in Mary's Song, praying for its fulfillment with God's people in bondage.

Hymn of the Night

If the darkest night surrounds me,
And I walk the brink of unseen, lurking dangers,
I will have no fear, for Light, your Light, is with me.

If the raging storm engulfs me,
Jesus will be sleeping calmly in my lifeboat;
I will have no fear, for Peace, your Peace, is with me.

If the desert overwhelms me,
If I faint and think I'll die for lack of water,
I will have no fear, for Wells, your Wells, are near me.

If the unbelieving scorn me,
And your enemies and mine connive to kill me,
I will have no fear, for Life, your Life, is in me.

If my friends should all forsake me,
Leave me orphaned, poor and homeless, lost and lonely,
I will have no fear, for, Father, you are with me.

If the darkest night surrounds me,
And I walk the brink of unseen, lurking dangers,
I will have no fear, for Light, your Light, is with me.

Meter	8.12.12.
Theme	Psalm 139:7–12
Written	22 January 1989
Translation of	"Huno da Noite," Brazilian hymn, author unknown

Subject Index

Adoration

Advent

Aging

Anniversary

Annunciation

Ascension

Assurance

Baptism

Called by the Spirit

Care

Charity

Children

Christ

Christian Education

Christian Life

Christianization of the Slavs

Christmas

Church

Church Anniversary

Church Growth

Church Militant

Close of Worship

Commemoration

Commitment

Communion of Saints

Community

Concern

Confirmation

Conflict

Cross and Comfort

Day of Judgment

Death

Dedication

Dedication of a Church

Devotion

Discipleship

Dismissal

Divine Mercy

Doxology

Easter

Enlightenment

Epiphany

Eternal life

Eternal values

Evangelism

Faith

Family

Fatherhood of God

Fathers

Father's Day

Following Christ

Forgiveness

Friendship

Fullness of love, joy, and peace

Funeral

God's love in Christ

Good Shepherd

Gospel

Gratitude

Guidance

Health and Healing

Heaven

Higher learning

Holy Spirit

Holy Week

Home

Hope

House of Worship

Humility

Hunger

Husbands

Incarnation

Installation

Institutional Anniversary

Invitation

Joy

Justification

Kingdom of God

Lent

Lesser Festivals

Liturgical

Lord's Supper

Love Divine

Marriage

Mealtime

Ministry

Mission

Morning Prayer

Mortgage burning

Mother's Day

Music

Nation

New Creation

New Year

Peace

Penitence

Pentecost

Post-Communion

Promise

Protection

Purpose

Rededication

Redemption

Regeneration

Renewal

Repentance

Rest

Restoration

Resurrection

Retirement

Reverence for God's Name

Sanctuary

Seminary Training

Service

Slovak Lutheran Church

Social Concern

Song of the Saints

Spiritual Liberty

Stewardship

Talents

Teaching

Thanksgiving

The Church in Mission

The Word

Training

Transfiguration

Trinity

Trust

Union with Christ

Unity

Vision

Vocation

Wedding

Wedding Anniversary

Wholeness

Witness

Women's Mission

Worship and Praise

Youth

Metrical Index

SM and Refrain

SMD

CM

LM (8.8.8.8.)

13.13.13.13.13.13.

14.14.6.6.14.

14.14.8.8.6.5.

Irregular

Refrain and 8.8.8.5.

Sonnet

Index of Scripture Texts

Tune Index

Index of First Lines

A

B

F

G

H

I

J

L

M

N

S

T

U

W

Y

Z